# THE THIRD DAY AT GETTYSBURG & BEYOND

# MILITARY CAMPAIGNS OF THE CIVIL WAR

# The Third Day at
# GETTYSBURG
## & Beyond

### EDITED BY GARY W. GALLAGHER

*The University of North Carolina Press*

*Chapel Hill & London*

© 1994 The University of North Carolina Press

All rights reserved

Manufactured in the United States of America

The paper in this book meets the guidelines for permanence
and durability of the Committee on Production Guidelines for
Book Longevity of the Council on Library Resources.

Library of Congress Cataloging-in-Publication Data
The Third day at Gettysburg and beyond / edited by
Gary W. Gallagher.

p.   cm. — (Military campaigns of the Civil War)

Includes bibliographical references and index.

ISBN 0-8078-2155-1 (cloth : alk. paper).

1. Gettysburg (Pa.), Battle of, 1863.   I. Gallagher, Gary W.

II. Series.

E475.53.T56   1994

973.7′349—dc20      94-752

CIP

98   97   96   95   94      5   4   3   2   1

# CONTENTS

*A. Wilson Greene*

**FROM GETTYSBURG TO FALLING WATERS**

Meade's Pursuit of Lee

161

# INTRODUCTION

This collection of essays addresses topics broadly related to the third day at
Gettysburg. It inaugurates the Military Campaigns of the Civil War series,
which will bring modern scholarship to bear on controversial issues and
leaders, explore previously ignored dimensions of various campaigns and
battles, and combine interpretation and fresh research in ways designed to
benefit both professional historians and interested lay readers. In ranging
over a spectrum of subjects, these six essays illuminate some of the ways
in which campaigns influenced the civilian sphere and how expectations
from home in turn affected men in the armies. Such connections often
remain obscure in the literature on the Civil War. Writers interested in
campaigns too often have treated their subjects as if the armies fought in
antiseptic isolation from political or social forces; similarly, those interested in the societies behind the lines frequently have managed to explore
the war years without mentioning the vast armed struggles waged by
Union and Confederate armies. The result has been a bifurcated view
of the war that can distort or obscure as much as it reveals. Volumes in
the Military Campaigns of the Civil War series, while usually emphasizing leadership, tactics, and strategy, will seek always to place operations
within the wider context of the war.

The third day at Gettysburg presents a number of interesting points
of departure. As the final violent spasm of Lee's raid into Pennsylvania,
fighting on July 3 set the stage for Confederate retreat and subsequent
attempts to make sense of what had happened over the preceding month.
The first essay looks at how men within the Army of Northern Virginia
and Confederate civilians viewed the campaign in July and August 1863.
Did they see Gettysburg as a major turning point for Lee and his army?
Did they pair it with the surrender of John C. Pemberton's forces at Vicksburg as comparable disasters boding ill for the future of the Confederacy?
Questioning the dominant interpretation of Gettysburg as a debacle that
spread gloom across the South, this essay suggests a far more muted
contemporary Confederate reaction to the campaign in Pennsylvania.

The relationship between R. E. Lee and James Longstreet has engaged the attention of several generations of students interested in Gettysburg. Longstreet stood at the center of the great postwar debate among former Confederates searching for explanations of southern defeat. The principal villain for Jubal A. Early and other Lost Cause writers, Longstreet defended himself so ineptly that his stock, already low across the South by the 1870s, dropped to a point where many blamed him for the debacle at Gettysburg and by extension the failure of the Confederacy. William Garrett Piston examines Lee's and Longstreet's respective plans for the third day's battle, emphasizing the meager available sources and the consequent difficulty of reaching firm conclusions. His reading of the evidence spares neither Lee nor Longstreet—though readers comfortable with views inspired by the Lost Cause school of authors, which remain widely held more than a century after their first appearance, likely will find Piston's essay unsettling.

Longstreet's assault against the center of the Union line formed the centerpiece of the third day's battle at Gettysburg. Easily the most famous infantry attack in American history, it has come to symbolize doomed courage in the face of overwhelming odds. Carol Reardon demonstrates that Pickett's Charge provoked acrimony in the Confederacy almost immediately, and that during the ensuing decades ex-Confederates waged a literary war to control public perceptions of the military moment hailed as the "high water mark of the Confederacy." Passionate debates about which Confederate units went farthest, retreated first, suffered the heaviest losses, and either supported or failed to support other units filled articles and books that in time formed a subliterature on Gettysburg. In charting the ebb and flow of claims and counterclaims among Virginians and those from other southern states, Reardon traces the process by which layers of myth and distortion adhered to a skeleton of truth about an assault that remains imperfectly understood.

The strikingly similar careers of two of George E. Pickett's brigadiers are the subject of Robert K. Krick's biographical essay. The war produced few more arresting images than that of Brig. Gen. Lewis Addison Armistead, his hat at sword point, struggling across the stone wall on Cemetery Ridge before receiving a mortal wound within Union lines. Brig. Gen. Richard Brooke Garnett's last moments were scarcely less dramatic—a mounted figure in open view of thousands of Union soldiers looking for targets, he toppled from his horse with a mortal wound just a few dozen paces short of the northern lines. Recounted endlessly over the years (and in Armistead's case portrayed by dozens of artists), the final moments of these two Virginia soldiers loom prominently in the catalog of memorable vignettes from Gettysburg. Yet the literature contains virtually nothing of substance on either man apart from their roles on July 3, 1863. Krick's essay, based on a rigorous search through materials in the National Archives and elsewhere, offers the first substantial treatment of Armistead's and Garnett's larger military careers. In the course of tracing the professional lives of his subjects, Krick lays to rest some durable myths about the men, reveals a good deal about service in the antebellum United States Army, and underscores the potential for reconstructing at least the public dimension of individuals who left scant literary remains.

The Federal soldiers who turned back Pickett's Charge never have received the attention accorded their Confederate opponents. Robert L. Bee focuses on one of those defenders, Sgt. Benjamin Hirst of the 14th Connecticut, who left revealing letters relating to the third day at Gettysburg. Although instructive as documents containing details about the activities of the 14th Connecticut, the letters hold greater promise as evidence about a northern soldier's attitudes toward the war, his relationship with comrades, and the importance of ties to his family and neighbors back in Connecticut. Informed by recent scholarship on common soldiers, Bee's analysis of Hirst's letters reveals how antebellum attitudes, prior experiences during the war, and a desire to satisfy expectations of relatives and friends affected both Hirst's behavior on July 3 at Gettysburg and his subsequent written accounts of the battle.

A. Wilson Greene closes the volume with an examination of George Gordon Meade during the eleven days following the repulse of Longstreet's assault. Should Meade have launched a counterattack on July 3? Did his timidity permit Lee to reach the Potomac unmolested? And why did he fail to strike at the Army of Northern Virginia as it lay pinned against that flooded river for several days? Most writers have been hard on Meade. Indeed, some have suggested that he frittered away an opportunity to inflict serious, perhaps even mortal, damage to Lee's army. Greene suggests that Abraham Lincoln's manifest unhappiness with the general's pursuit of Lee has colored virtually all later assessments. Drawing on testimony from the principal Federal officers, as well as a range of other sources, Greene concludes that Meade's opportunities often have been exaggerated and his blunders magnified. The Union commander might have accomplished more, concedes Greene, but overall he managed the Army of the Potomac well in the wake of Gettysburg.

These six essays illustrate the rich opportunities for inquiry relating to Civil War military campaigns. Even a subject so intensively studied as Gettysburg affords a range of potential approaches. By defining a campaign to include both important antecedents and immediate and long-term consequences, historians can enrich understanding of events too often dismissed as interesting only to narrow specialists. The military literature on the Civil War, though admittedly immense, stands ripe for investigators wishing to examine old questions from different perspectives, raise new questions, and exploit previously untapped sources.

The contributors to this volume cooperated readily at every stage of the process. They met initial deadlines, responded with uniform good humor when I picked innumerable nits, and otherwise made this project a great pleasure to carry out. The many tales of friendships lost during joint ventures seemed remote indeed as I worked with Bob Bee, Will Greene, Bob Krick, Bill Piston, and Carol Reardon. George Skoch, whose maps enhance four of the essays, proved to be an equally pleasant collaborator. The many persons who helped the contributors are acknowledged at the end of individual essays. At the University of North Carolina Press, Kate Douglas Torrey provided encouragement and sound counsel, Ron Maner proved a tolerant and expert editor, and Stephanie Wenzel, whose keen copyeditor's eye has helped me in the past, once again did a superior job with the manuscript. Finally, I wish to express thanks to the Research and Graduate Studies Office of the College of the Liberal Arts at Penn State, which provided generous support for the preparation of maps and the index.

# THE THIRD DAY AT GETTYSBURG & BEYOND

*The Impact*

*of Gettysburg on the*

*Army of Northern Virginia*

*and the Confederate*

*Home Front*

## LEE'S ARMY HAS NOT LOST

## ANY OF ITS PRESTIGE

*Gary W. Gallagher*

A canvass of Confederate sentiment in the summer of 1863 suggests that many southerners did not view the battle of Gettysburg as a catastrophic defeat. R. E. Lee's soldiers typically saw it as a temporary setback with few long-term consequences for their army. Although conceding the conflict's heavy toll in casualties, they considered neither their withdrawal from the battlefield nor the retreat from Pennsylvania as evidence that the Federals had won a decisive victory. On the home front, civilians generally drew a sharp distinction between Gettysburg and Vicksburg. The latter represented an unequivocal disaster in which the Confederacy lost an entire army, huge quantities of arms, and reliable access to the states of the Trans-Mississippi. Gettysburg presented a far more ambiguous result, and few observers believed that it anticipated eventual failure in the Eastern Theater. In a season marked by the loss of Vicksburg and Port Hudson, the opening of major Union naval operations against Charleston, and Braxton Bragg's inept maneuvering during the Tullahoma campaign, Lee's operations in Pennsylvania did not stand out as especially harmful to the Confederate cause.[1]

Yet Gettysburg and Vicksburg usually appear in the literature on the Civil War as twin calamities that marked a major turning point in the conflict. Emory Thomas struck a common note in his perceptive history of the Confederacy by observing that Gettysburg and Vicksburg, together with unsuccessful diplomatic initiatives in Europe, triggered among white southerners a "severe loss of confidence in themselves." Similarly, James M. McPherson noted in his influential history of the Civil War and Reconstruction that the "losses at Gettysburg and Vicksburg shook the Confederacy to its foundations."[2] Both Thomas and McPherson cited Josiah Gorgas to illustrate their point. "Events have succeeded one another with disastrous rapidity," wrote the Confederate chief of ordnance on July 28, 1863. "One brief month ago we were apparently at the point of success. Lee was in Pennsylvania, threatening Harrisburgh, and even Philadelphia. Vicksburgh seemed to laugh all Grant's efforts to scorn, & the Northern papers had reports of his raising the siege." Thirty days later, Lee had retreated from Pennsylvania, Vicksburg and Port Hudson had fallen, and irreplaceable men and matériel had been lost. "Yesterday we rode on the pinnacle of success—today absolute ruin seems to be our portion," stated an apparently shaken Gorgas. "The Confederacy totters to its destruction." Quoting Gorgas as a man "who best bespoke the mood" in the South, Thomas concluded that "evidence of Southern vincibility was very real in the summer of 1863."[3]

Before I make the case that Gettysburg did not thrust most Confederates into depression, it is important to acknowledge that various witnesses did portray it and Vicksburg as comparably devastating reverses, questioned Lee's generalship, or believed the campaign weakened the morale and reduced the physical prowess of the Army of Northern Virginia. Representative of the latter group was John B. Jones, the famous "rebel war clerk," whose diary for July 9 read, "The fall of Vicksburg, alone, does not make this the darkest day of the war, as it is undoubtedly. The news from Lee's army is appalling." After prophesying on July 10 that if Lee returned to Virginia, "a great revulsion of feeling" would sweep the Confederacy, Jones recorded on July 17 that "Gen. Lee has recrossed the Potomac! Thus the armies of the Confederate States are recoiling at all points, and a settled gloom is apparent on many weak faces." Robert Garlick Hill Kean of the Bureau of War reacted almost identically. "This week just ended has been one of unexampled disaster since the war began," he wrote on July 12. In addition to Vicksburg and Bragg's withdrawal, "it turns out that the battle of Gettysburg was a virtual if not an actual defeat."[4]

Similarly gloomy opinions existed within the Army of Northern Virginia. "Our cause is, undoubtedly, at serious disadvantage just now," remarked William Nelson Pendleton, Lee's chief of artillery, on July 18. "The loss of Vicksburg is in itself not very injurious; but Grant's army being set free to co-operate with Rosecrans is a serious evil. Our failure at Gettysburg and these events on the Mississippi will give us a vast deal of trouble." On the same day Pendleton wrote, one of Lee's soldiers despaired about the fall of Vicksburg and Federal threats along the coast of North Carolina. Sarcastically alluding to Lee's withdrawal across the Potomac as "what we call retreat under cover of night," this North Carolinian hoped the war would soon end. "The men are saying they will stop it next spring if nobody else can," he warned. "You understand of coarse that I think they intend fighting no longer. They are looking for those men who can whip 10 Yankees to show up. If they don't we will be whipped."[5]

Lee's performance elicited criticism from a variety of individuals. Robert G. H. Kean confided to his diary on July 26 that "Gettysburg has shaken my faith in Lee as a general." Calling the battle "worse in execution than in plan," Kean thought it "the worst disaster which has ever befallen our arms." Maj. Eugene Blackford of the 5th Alabama announced bitterly that his "blind confidence in Gen. Lee is utterly gone. . . . To hurl his Army against an enemy entrenched on a mountain top, it exceeds my belief." In another harsh appraisal, Brig. Gen. Wade Hampton labeled the campaign a "complete failure" and deplored Lee's assaults against a position that "was the strongest I ever saw." Some soldiers cloaked criticisms in more gentle language, as when Alexander McNeil of Joseph B. Kershaw's brigade stated that "our wise Gen. Lee made a great mistake in making the attack."[6]

The staggering carnage at Gettysburg may have motivated thousands of men to slip away from their units on July 4. "The day after the last battle at Gettysburg," Lee informed Jefferson Davis on July 29, "on sending back the train with the wounded, it was reported that about 5,000 well men started back at night to overtake it." This message followed by two days one in which Lee told Davis of "many thousand men improperly absent from this army" and asked for a presidential proclamation of amnesty to lure them back. Lee himself issued an appeal to stragglers and deserters on July 26.[7] It is impossible to determine precise motivations for men who left the ranks (the need to attend to harvests may explain many of the absences), but the timing and scale of the problem in July and August imply a relationship between Gettysburg and the desertions.[8]

The impact of Gettysburg on the peace movement in North Carolina is more easily identified. William Woods Holden, editor of the Raleigh *North Carolina Standard* and the state's leading proponent of a negotiated end to the conflict, had decided by mid-June 1863 that "the people of both sections are tired of war and desire peace." One of the editor's biographers notes that the "twin Confederate disasters at Gettysburg and Vicksburg," together with considerable local support for an earlier proposal to end the war, "convinced Holden that he should strike a bolder blow for peace." Throughout the summer and fall, Holden and his compatriots vociferously pressed their cause in North Carolina.[9]

Although the foregoing evidence suggests Gettysburg sent destructive tremors through Lee's army and across the South, a substantial body of testimony contradicts the idea that most Confederates classified Gettysburg as a debacle equivalent to Vicksburg, lost confidence in Lee, or believed that his army incurred irretrievable damage during the campaign. Inside the Army of Northern Virginia, soldiers stressed their tactical victory on the first day, the supreme gallantry of their assaults against powerful Federal positions, and the inability of the enemy to drive them from the field or administer a killing blow during the retreat. The following assessment relies almost exclusively on writings from the period July–August 1863 in seeking to convey a sense of how Confederates at the time chose to conceive of the campaign. It draws on the letters and diaries of more than 140 individuals and a number of newspapers, a pool that includes soldiers from various states in Lee's army, their comrades in service outside the Army of Northern Virginia, and civilians in states across the Confederacy. Although conclusions based on a sample this small must be tentative, these witnesses leave no doubt that Confederate reaction to Gettysburg covered a wider spectrum than is commonly supposed.

Many newspapers initially cast Lee's raid in a positive light. Notable among these was the proadministration Richmond (Daily) *Dispatch*, which asserted on July 13 that the "Battle of Gettysburg was, on our part, a triumphant success—an overwhelming victory." That same day, the Lynchburg *Virginian* suggested Lee's maneuvering in Pennsylvania had disrupted Union plans to advance against Richmond from the south. Moreover, the Army of Northern Virginia had fought "one of the bloodiest battles of the war, and inflicted upon the enemy injuries which, in all probability, exceed anything he has yet suffered in a pitched battle. Their own admissions respecting their appalling loss in officers, prove this." Pronouncing the Federals already "severely chastized," the *Virginian* predicted Lee's command would inflict further damage before recrossing the Potomac. Various newspaper accounts trumpeted, among other things, up to 40,000 Union prisoners, the Army of the Potomac in retreat toward Baltimore, and the deaths of prominent northern officers.[10]

Much of the southern press remained loath to label Lee's raid a failure analogous to Vicksburg even after his army returned to Virginia. The *Dispatch* spoke on July 18 of "both good and evil" results and was "disposed to think that the good more than balances the evil." Lee had not accomplished all that he wished, but his expedition had provided relief to war-ravaged northern Virginia, gathered enormous quantities of supplies, and above all "taught the Yankees that they, as well as we, are open to invasion." After mentioning the retreat from Pennsylvania, the fall of Vicksburg, and other reverses during the first two weeks of July, the Charleston *Daily Courier* "pass[ed] by the retrograde movement of Gen. Lee with the single observation that we feel no uneasiness concerning that great Captain and his invincible army." Three days later the *Daily Courier* disparaged the North's initial burst of joy over "the capture of Vicksburg, and the falling back of Lee." Further reflection had tempered northern celebration because it became clear that the Army of the Potomac lost the first phase of Gettysburg and held its ground thereafter only through "frightful sacrifice." Lee retired "from the field in perfect order and slowly . . . while his antagonist remained on his heights, appalled by the desperate valor of the Confederates."[11]

All accounts were not so favorable. The Charleston *Mercury*, which habitually found little to praise in the Davis government's management of the war, on July 30 declared it "impossible for an invasion to have been more foolish and disastrous"—a stance strikingly at odds with the paper's earlier calls for a Confederate offensive. Few editors opted to join the *Mercury* in painting the campaign in predominantly dark hues, though many printed reporter William Alexander's piece on the battle that questioned Lee's decision to follow the successes of July 1 with additional assaults the next day.[12]

Reports in newspapers and the Federal failure to deliver a crushing stroke against Lee's army led many civilians to see Gettysburg as less ruinous than Vicksburg. Writing on July 9, 1863, South Carolinian Emma Holmes termed Vicksburg "a terrible blow to our cause" that would "prolong the war indefinitely." But when early notices of a triumph in Pennsylvania gave way to descriptions of Lee's retreat, Holmes observed calmly, "It certainly does not appear to be the great victory at first announced, though a very great battle." "Lee has recrossed the Potomac, in admirable order, and the army in splendid trim and spirits without loss," she noted on July 17 in her last entry devoted to the Pennsylvania campaign: "His retreat from Gettysburg was strategic, to draw Meade's army from the high hills behind which they took refuge." Floride Clemson, a granddaughter of John C. Calhoun living in Maryland, did not "think the times ever looked so dark" as they did on July 17—Vicksburg and Port Hudson had fallen, and rumor said the Yankees had taken Charleston as well. As for Lee, he was "not conquered, but weakened." A physician serving with the military in Richmond pronounced both Vicksburg and Gettysburg "serious blows" but immediately clarified his relative assessment of the two: "The latter was not a defeat—an accident only prevented it from being the ruin of the Yankees." Although the "accident" went unidentified in this letter, the surgeon manifestly considered Vicksburg a more harmful reverse.[13]

Catherine Edmondston of North Carolina, whose voluminous diary is a grand storehouse of information about the war behind the lines, learned of Pemberton's capitulation from a "Dispatch which freezes the marrow in our bones." "I have no heart to write," she stated the next day. "Vicksburg has fallen! It is all true." Like Emma Holmes, Edmondston also experienced a rapid change of emotions regarding Lee's fate—"Glorious news" of a stunning victory arrived on July 9; just two days later came the first reports of a withdrawal. Certain by July 17 that Lee was back in Virginia "in safety & unmolested," she praised God but acknowledged "sore disappointment." By July 25, she could report, with open disdain for the Federals, that "Gen Lee's army said to be in fine condition—in Va Meade crossing the Potomac in 'pursuit,' the North much exasperated against him for 'allowing Lee to escape.'"[14]

The old fire-eater Edmund Ruffin also distinguished between Gettysburg and Vicksburg. Events along the Mississippi constituted "a disaster primarily because it will free Grant's army to go elsewhere." Upset that first reports of a smashing success in Pennsylvania proved groundless, Ruffin nevertheless treated Lee's campaign as anything but a tragedy. The Confederates had driven the enemy back during the battle of Gettysburg and then, carrying an immense quantity of captured stores, executed a leisurely march back to the Potomac, where they held a line along the river for more than a week without disturbance. "All this does not indicate that Gen. Lee had suffered a defeat at Gettysburg, or that Meade had any idea that he had gained a victory, or was strong enough to assume an aggressive position," insisted Ruffin. Had Meade really won a victory on July 1–3, he would have "followed upon the rear of Lee's very slowly retreating army." [15]

Even more revealing was Governor Joseph E. Brown's public statement to the people of Georgia on July 17. Brown urged his constituents not to despair over the "late serious disasters to our arms, at Vicksburg and Port Hudson, together with Gen. Bragg's retreat with his army to our very borders." Nowhere did the governor mention Lee or Gettysburg, though thousands of Georgians served in the Army of Northern Virginia. It seems reasonable to infer that Brown placed the Pennsylvania campaign, which involved a retreat from enemy territory rather than from Confederate ground, in an entirely different category than operations along the Mississippi and in southeastern Tennessee. [16]

So also did Jefferson Davis. Unfailingly supportive of Lee in the weeks after Gettysburg, the president conveyed to his most trusted field commander profound disappointment with developments in the Western Theater. "I have felt more than ever before the want of your advice during the recent period of disaster," wrote Davis in late July. "You know how one army of the enemy has triumphed by attacking three of ours in detail, at Vicksburg, Port Hudson and Jackson." Less than a week had passed when Davis, clearly concerned about his home state, again raised the subject of troubles in the West: "I need your counsel but must strive to meet the requirements of the hour without distracting your attention at a time when it should be concentrated on the field before you." Lee previously had told Davis of his "regret for the fall of Vicksburg" and now responded that "reverses, even defeats" were inevitable and should be used to summon greater commitment from the people. If its citizenry's determination proved equal to the challenge, the Confederacy would triumph. Pleased with Lee's reply, Davis remarked "that after the first depression consequent upon our disasters in the West" it appeared "our people will exhibit that fortitude . . . needful to secure ultimate success." [17]

Numerous diaries and letters of Confederates outside Virginia described Lee as unbeaten and unbeatable in early 1864—a telling indication that they did not consider Gettysburg a serious defeat. In July 1863, before details about the Pennsylvania campaign reached her in the Trans-Mississippi, Kate Stone hoped "Lee the Invincible" would offset dire news from Vicksburg. Ten months and the retreat from Gettysburg wrought no change in her attitude toward Lee. "A great battle is rumored in Virginia," she wrote in May 1864, "Grant's first fight in his 'On to Richmond.' He is opposed by the Invincible Lee, and so we are satisfied we won the victory." That same May, Tennessean Belle Edmondson commented on the war in the East: "They say we have had a glorious victory in Virginia, but a dearly bought one—loss heavy on both sides—the Confederates Victorious as always under our brave Gen. Lee." An officer serving in Louisiana revealed kindred sentiments on May 27, 1864, in reacting to conflicting rumors of clashes between Lee and Grant. "I believe nothing one way or the other, until further word is received," stated Felix Pierre Poché. "But I continue to have complete faith in General Lee, who has never been known to suffer defeat, and who probably never will." [18]

Within Lee's army, soldiers such as Reuben A. Pierson of the 9th Louisiana analyzed Vicksburg and Gettysburg in very different ways. "I had nearly despaired of hearing from home," he wrote his father on July 19, 1863, from near Bunker Hill, "as we had already received the news of the fall of the Queen City Vicksburg." The surrender of Pemberton's army jolted Pierson out of a sense of growing optimism: "Before receiving the news of the sad misfortune I began to imagine that the dawn of peace had already commenced arising but now a dark pall is thrown over the scene and the lowering clouds of new troubles seem to be enveloping the bright rays of a few short weeks ago." Yet he remained confident of victory—due in large part to the prowess of the Army of Northern Virginia, which he saw as undiminished by the recent campaign. "We have just returned from an extensive tour into Pennsylvania," he reported almost casually. Thousands of prisoners, thousands of cattle and horses, and other valuable material had been taken from the enemy. Desperate fighting at Gettysburg yielded heavy losses and no clear winner—though Pierson estimated Union casualties at 30,000–50,000, far greater than the Confederate total. The Confederate army lay safely in Virginia "in fine health and spirits and if the yankees advance upon us we will give them a dread of the hardy boys of Gen. Lee's command." [19]

Trust in Lee remained high in the Army of Northern Virginia. Five weeks after Gettysburg, Eli Pinson Landers of William T. Wofford's brigade asked his mother to give "the Vicksburg boys" his respects. "I know it is bad to fight under officers without confidence," he stated. "I wish they had such officers as we have got. . . . General Lee has the confidence of our whole army." Another Georgian, "once more in Dixie, safe and sound" on

July 18, affirmed his readiness "for anything that may turn up, either to move forward, or backward, run or fight, or anything else Robert E. Lee wants me to do." Sgt. William Beverley Pettit of the Fluvanna Artillery scolded his wife on July 26 for being "too severe on General Lee and President Davis. They are without their peers, now upon this globe." Col. James Drayton Nance, who commanded a brigade in Lafayette McLaws's division, conceded serious troubles in the West but spoke glowingly of the situation in Virginia: "Our army is in good condition, and is constantly improving and increasing. There is more reason to expect now a victory at the next onset between Gen. Lee and Meade than there has been on other occasions."[20]

A pair of foreign observers highlighted the strong bond between Lee and his men in the immediate aftermath of the battle. On the afternoon of July 3, Lt. Col. Arthur James Lyon Fremantle, a colorful British officer temporarily attached to James Longstreet's headquarters, rode among Confederate soldiers along Seminary Ridge in the wake of the Pickett-Pettigrew assault. Fremantle marveled at the spirit of a group of gunners whom he engaged in conversation. Lee rode by as they spoke, prompting a flurry of comments: "When they observed General Lee they said, 'We've not lost confidence in the old man: this day's work won't do him no harm. "Uncle Robert" will get us into Washington yet; you bet he will!' &c." Capt. Justus Scheibert of the Prussian army found the army's spirit "so extraordinary that the weary troops received the old general with enthusiastic cheers, despite the retreat and deluded hopes. Sincere calls, such as 'Old Lee is still alive! Now all is well!' etc., expressed the true sentiments of the men." Nothing the Prussian had seen in the Confederacy "touched and moved me more than the faithfulness of these thoroughly drenched, muddy, and ragged warriors to their noble leader in the disappointment of defeat."[21]

Knowledge that they had not been driven from the field enabled Lee's soldiers to treat Gettysburg as no more than a bloody disappointment. Many of them emphasized the dramatic Confederate triumph on July 1, rationalizing the costly repulses on the second and third days as inevitable because of the enemy's strong positions. "The first day our arms met with complete success," William Aiken Kelly of the 1st South Carolina observed soon after the battle, "every point which we attacked was carried, and the loss of the enemy far exceeded ours." The next two days "were not so successful"—though Kelly would "not say we were defeated by the enemy." The Federals held ground of "the strongest kind" and enjoyed superior numbers. "Had they left their protection, I think we would have defeated them," he concluded. "As it is, I consider that we were victorious on the first day, and that the other two were drawn battles, for on the 4th, the time we fell back, it is reported that the enemy did the same."[22]

Reuben Pierson similarly spoke of whipping the Federals badly on July 1 and driving them from their outer works before failing "to carry the heights on which their batteries were planted." Like Kelly, he also mentioned a Union predilection for safe ground: "They know we are superior in valor to their men and therefore always seek some advantages of position." Pierson placed casualties during the campaign in perspective as well, conceding the loss of "many noble and gallant men" but suggesting that "we should have lost equally as many in a battle of Virginia and besides we would not have procured a single lot of supplies."[23]

A lieutenant in the 11th North Carolina of J. Johnston Pettigrew's brigade echoed Pierson in placing Gettysburg in a broader military context. Although characterizing the battle as a very bloody encounter that extracted an "awful cost" from his regiment, William B. Taylor saw Gettysburg as just part of a larger season of campaigning: "I suppose that there will be one more battle this summer or fall," he mused on July 29, 1863, from Culpeper, "and if we do have a fight here we will give them one of the worst thrashings they ever got." Taylor inferred that the desultory Federal pursuit following July 3 indicated the Army of the Potomac lacked the fortitude to defeat Lee's army.[24]

The absence of aggressive Federal tactics either at Gettysburg or thereafter elicited extensive comment from Lee's soldiers. Charles Minor Blackford conceded a technical defeat because the southern assaults "failed to carry the enemy's lines." But he quickly stressed that "we held our own, slept on the battle-field and remained there for twenty-four hours without molestation, showing that we had so punished the enemy that they were incapable of an advance." A private in the Amherst Artillery wrote in his diary on July 4, "The Yanks have not come down from the hills east of Gettysburg and have shown no desire to attack us at any time during the day." In several later entries, this gunner alluded to the complete absence of offensive moves from the enemy. Looking back over the previous five weeks on August 15, 1863, Edgeworth Bird, a quartermaster in Henry L. Benning's brigade, remarked that the "Battle of Gettysburg so disabled Meade, that he is unable to resume the offensive." The Federals fought well when shielded by "rock walls built on the mountain side and tops,"

Bird had stated previously, but their "army retreated at the same time our fellows fell back and did not attempt to follow up."[25]

The natural strength of the Union line impressed almost all the Confederates. Brig. Gen. Stephen Dodson Ramseur, whose aggressiveness in battle matched that of anyone in the army, stated that "the enemy occupied a Gibralter of a position." Colonel Nance averred that his men understood they were not more successful only because "the position, against which they were thrown, was well nigh *impregnable*." A Georgian who wrote from a Union hospital after the battle concurred with Nance, relating that an appreciation of the enemy's advantage in ground and supplies rendered the repulse "not attall discouraging to our army." Edgeworth Bird told his wife how the Confederates "found the enemy posted in a terribly secure position," adding that the attempt to drive Federals from "the heights and mountains at Gettysburg was certainly very unfortunate." Characteristic of the way in which soldiers accepted the disappointments of the campaign yet denied losing the battle, Bird stated that Lee "had met no defeat, but certainly failed in his plans at Gettysburg, and at great loss." A surgeon in A. P. Hill's corps put the case succinctly: "We drove the Yankees three miles from the battlefield to a long range of hills, from which it was impossible to dislodge them."[26]

There was no loss of honor in failing to capture such positions. Dutifully reporting to his fiancée that "our glorious army was repulsed at Gettysburg," Dodson Ramseur admired how "our gallant troops stormed and restormed" the enemy lines, "sometimes successfully but finally we were compelled to withdraw from the unequal contest." Edgeworth Bird lauded the infantrymen who "performed heroic deeds, and died heroic deaths" in doomed efforts to dislodge the entrenched Federals. As the attackers "rushed up into the very jaws of death," noted an appreciative artillerist, "our men performed deeds of daring and heroism which covered them with glory." Col. David Wyatt Aiken of the 7th South Carolina wasted few words in illustrating the same point: Pickett's soldiers "made several brilliant charges, but failed in driving the enemy from their walls."[27]

No one captured the sense of honorable failure better than Fremantle, who addressed the subject on July 14, four days after he had left the Army of Northern Virginia and entered Union lines. Hearing talk among northerners of the "total demoralization" of the rebels, Fremantle ventured the opinion that "Lee's army has not lost any of its prestige at the battle of

Gettysburg, in which it most gallantly stormed strong intrenchments defended by the whole army of the Potomac, which never ventured outside its works, or approached in force within half a mile of the Confederate artillery."[28]

Lee's official report of the campaign also touched on this subject. After describing the commanding ground held by the Federals, Lee lavished praise on the soldiers who tried to seize it. "The conduct of the troops was all that I could desire or expect," wrote the appreciative general, "and they deserve success so far as it can be deserved by heroic valor and fortitude." Their ultimate failure at Gettysburg in no way diminished his "admiration of their noble qualities" or his "confidence in their ability to cope successfully with the enemy."[29] Such words undoubtedly bolstered his men's feelings of worthy striving against impossible obstacles and helped cushion the disappointment of repulse.

If the Federals had been denied their wonderful defensive position, agreed many Confederates, the battle would have gone differently. "I think we were too confident," admitted Virginia artillerist William Watts Parker. "We had forgotten the power of the spade and the immense advantages which position may give." Parker claimed that not a single man wanted to retreat across the Potomac—they sought only an opportunity "to whip the Yankees any day on a *fair field*." Brig. Gen. Clement A. Evans adopted an almost smug tone in a July 8 postmortem on the battle: "At some points the Yankees fought pretty stubborn but where ever we had a fair field we whipped & slaughtered them in great numbers." In a follow-up analysis two days later, the Georgian termed the enemy "uneasy—not confident of their ability to whip us." Events of July 1 indicated "how easily we can whip them on fair ground." Employing essentially the same language, an artillerist in Richard S. Ewell's corps stated that it was evident the Yankees would not leave their high ground to "advance upon us, where we might whip them, for there we would be on equal grounds." As judicious a man as E. Porter Alexander, who had directed the First Corps artillery in the heaviest fighting on July 2–3, remarked that he thought Lee would seek another battle—"and we are all anxious for it, thinking that we had not a fair showing at Gettysburg."[30]

Another thread running through Confederate accounts was that want of supplies rather than the Federal army dictated Lee's decision to retreat. General Evans's diary for July 9 singled out the lack of regular rations as the army's "greatest difficulty." Were food not a problem, "the Campaign in Maryland and Pennsylvania could be prolonged indefinitely but this difficulty will force us back to Virginia sooner than all the Yankee army ever could." The day after the battle, a captain in Harry T. Hays's Louisiana brigade recorded that "Gen. Lee at this time gave the Federal General a fine opportunity of attacking him, but it was declined." Because Lee had ammunition for just two days and "was far distant from his depots of supply," he "was obliged to put himself on the defensive." Another Louisiana soldier remarked that at Gettysburg each "party seemed to hazard all upon the issue and we should have gained the day but for a want of cannon ammunition." A North Carolinian sketched a stalemate on the battlefield followed by withdrawal precipitated by logistical needs. After the Federals threw out skirmishers on July 4 and "pretended as if they intended to advance upon us," the two armies, both *badly* crippled, retired in different directions." "If we had only remained 'till next day we could have claimed the victory," believed this officer. "But our supplies were exhausted, and a retrograde movement absolutely necessary." [31]

With typical astuteness, Porter Alexander examined the recent campaign in a letter to his father shortly after returning to Virginia. As Lee's former chief of ordnance and the premier Confederate artillerist, he was especially sensitive to the problem of procuring ammunition at great distances from secure bases of supply. Three days of severe fighting at Gettysburg had left the army "almost entirely out of ammunition," a circumstance that seemed inevitable in campaigns of this type. "I do not think we can ever successfully invade," thought Alexander, "the ammunition question alone being enough to prevent it." No amount of courage and tactical gain could overcome this deficiency because "our army is not large enough to stand the casualties even of a victory in the enemy's country." [32]

A comment from FitzGerald Ross suggests the focus on supplies may have been quite general in the ten days after the battle. An Englishman serving as an officer in the Austrian Hussars, Ross accompanied Lee's army into Pennsylvania and mingled with a number of generals and their staffs. He noted the reaction when word of Lee's decision to recross the Potomac filtered through the army as it lay near Hagerstown: "Many were disappointed at this decision, as it had been the general opinion that the army was only waiting for fresh supplies to recommence offensive operations." It is not clear whether Ross noticed this phenomenon just among the officers with whom he spent most of his time or if it existed within the ranks as well. [33]

Whatever the answer to that question, Brig. Gen. Ambrose R. Wright and "Jeb" Stuart exemplified those about whom Ross wrote. "What our next movement will be I cannot tell," Wright stated while near Hagerstown on July 7, "but I think that as soon as we get our ammunition supplied, we shall march in the direction of Washington." Wright hoped that recent heavy rains had not disrupted the flow of supplies to the degree that withdrawal into Virginia would be Lee's only option. As for Stuart, he thought the Confederates had "the better of the fight at Gettysburg," retiring only because of their inability to hold the ground they captured and a lack of sufficient ammunition. Lee's maneuvering the Federals out of Virginia represented the "grandest piece of strategy ever heard of"; 10,000 reinforcements and *"plenty of ammunition"* after Gettysburg would have permitted the army to achieve decisive results. After a period to recuperate and gather strength, Stuart predicted a return to Pennsylvania— "it is the only path to peace."[34]

A sense that the northern populace had gotten off too easily also provoked some unhappiness about recrossing the Potomac. "I had rather have stayed [north of the river] if wee could have been successful," wrote Capt. S. G. Pryor of the 12th Georgia on July 16. "I hated the idea of falling back again. I wanted them to feel the war more, have it at their homes; the people where the army has been know something about it." LeRoy S. Edwards of the 12th Virginia, writing on July 7, expressed strong reservations about returning to the Confederacy. He preferred that "the people of this country should feel more in their homes of war and thereby more fully appreciate the condition of Virginia, and note our unwavering undying determination to prosecute to the last, the end we had in view when we first marched to arms."[35]

Less strident but still willing to carry the war northward again was William L. Barrier of the 1st North Carolina Cavalry. Guessing that Lee meant "to make Pennsylvania feel the effects of war before he recrosses the Potomac," Barrier empathized with the "badly frightened" Pennsylvania Dutch who "take their little bundles under their arms and leave their homes to the ravages of the army." "It looks hard to see so fine a country overrun by an army," wrote Barrier, "but I guess it is fair."[36]

These frequent allusions to maintaining their position after July 3, the enemy's impressive advantage in ground and timidity in the open field, and the critical shortage of ammunition and other supplies help to explain a widespread conviction among Lee's soldiers that the Federals had not demonstrated superiority on the field at Gettysburg. That conviction led in turn to a defiant affirmation of the Army of Northern Virginia's spirit. Four days after the battle, while the Confederates faced a doubtful future north of the Potomac, Ambrose Wright wrote that the army had reached Hagerstown "in good condition, (except a scarcity of artillery ammunition) and in fine spirits." Just after crossing to the southern side of the Potomac, a member of the 24th Georgia exuded confidence in predicting it would take Meade a long time to drive the Confederates out of their new lines: "We have given him one whipping since we have been over here and if he fools with us we will give it to him again." On July 16, Charles Minor Blackford described a relaxed and confident air at Bunker Hill, where the soldiers were "washing and dressing up again and repairing the ravages of the campaign upon their scanty wardrobe." "They are in fine spirits," concluded Blackford, "and not the least depressed by the results of the invasion." As both "crippled up" armies rested in early August, Surgeon Welch anticipated no imminent Union movement. The army was "in splendid health and spirits," and the "Yankees dread us too much" to initiate any action. Maj. Gen. Lafayette McLaws, whose division had suffered very heavy casualties on July 2, similarly detected the army's "old spirit" in mid-August as it awaited Meade's next move in northern Virginia.[37]

Some men tied their comments to reports of wavering morale behind the lines. "There is a terrible band of veterans here yet," Edgeworth Bird assured his wife on July 19. In light of events in Mississippi, Tennessee, and at Charleston, he proudly held up the Army of Northern Virginia as "the great hope of the South." Comments by soldiers returning from furloughs in August left Bird "astonished at the state of public feeling in Georgia." "They say Georgia is now almost whipped, and she has hardly ever had an armed heel on her soil," he wrote from the stern perspective of one who had seen war-ravaged Virginia. "The army here thinks it can whip its weight in wild cats and has no mistrusts or apprehension," he stated pointedly. "I hope there is no truth in these reports." Captain Pryor worried that civilians in Georgia had become despondent and willing to give up the cause, assuring his wife that people on the home front "kneed not fear: the old veterans of Lee's army isent whiped, never has been, and I think [it] will be a long time before they are whiped." Capt. Green Berry Samuels, a Virginian in George H. Steuart's brigade, also implored his wife not to feel discouraged: "We still have a grand army to battle for us . . . and by God's grace we will soon strike the enemy such a blow, that his hopes of subjugation will be as far off as before the fall of Vicksburg." Two weeks later Samuels ventured the hope that the army, which was "in fine health," would punish the Yankees "for the horrid barbarities inflicted upon the helpless citizens within their lines."[38]

Back in Richmond, Josiah Gorgas evidently heard such positive reports from Lee's army. His diary entries in August and early September reflect greater optimism than the oft-quoted passage of late July. All seemed quiet on Lee's front, he recorded on the twenty-fourth, "and his army appears to be nearly in its original good condition." Gorgas estimated shortly thereafter that 600 men a day were swelling Lee's ranks. By September 6, the ordnance chief alluded to the army's "excellent condition" and speculated that Lee was considering taking the offensive and perhaps marching into Maryland.[39]

An appreciable minority of soldiers went beyond protestations of good morale to paint a positive picture of the entire campaign. Their criteria for determining success included damage to northern civilians, capture of animals and supplies, and Union losses at Gettysburg. A quartet of Georgians touched on each of these topics. "We had a nice time of it in Pennsylvania," observed Lt. Joseph Hilton of the 26th Georgia, "and have inflicted serious injury upon the corpulent Dutch farmers of that loyal state." Sidney J. Richardson of the 21st Georgia concentrated on four-legged acquisitions: "We have taken a great many wagon horses, and beef cattle over here, it is one of the greatest raids this army ever made." The army had to fight in Pennsylvania, but Richardson believed there would have been combat in any case. On July 8, a soldier in Wofford's brigade alluded to hard marching and fighting since his last letter home: "We gave them another good whipping. . . . The enemy admit a loss of 25,000 men."[40]

Clement Evans deplored the fact that the campaign "accomplished a good deal but still the army & the Public are both disappointed." Expectations were too high. For the Army of Northern Virginia to capture Washington, destroy the Army of the Potomac, and end the war in six weeks, as some evidently hoped, "was a physical impossibility." Such unreasonable goals cast a shadow over the army's solid gains. The Confederates took a thousand wagons, perhaps 2,000 horses, many provisions, and "taught the Pennsylvanians what war is & left in their state a great battle field to contemplate, with a large town full of their thousands of wounded." More than that, Evans believed that the Confederates "can make the Yankee army behave very respectfully in Virginia for the balance of the Summer."[41]

What of R. E. Lee? He knew better than anyone else the objectives of the campaign, the tactical story at Gettysburg, and the extent of Confederate casualties. A series of letters written within a month of the battle, primarily to Jefferson Davis and Mrs. Lee, underscore the fact that he did not consider the campaign a major disappointment with ominous implications for his army and the Confederacy. On the contrary, as Lee described it, the foray into Pennsylvania accomplished much of what he had set out to do.

It is important to keep in mind Lee's goals before discussing his response to the campaign.[42] He favored a movement into the North for strategic and logistical reasons. A continued stance along the Rappahannock River invited Joseph Hooker's Army of the Potomac to "force this army back within the entrenchments" of Richmond or to pin it down while Federals on the Peninsula approached the Confederate capital from the southeast. If Lee marched northward with a reinforced Army of Northern Virginia, however, he could pull Hooker after him, siphon Union troops "from the Southern coasts and give some respite in that quarter," and perhaps find an opening to strike an effective blow. On June 25, from opposite Williamsport, Maryland, he summarized for Jefferson Davis the minimum he hoped to achieve: "I think I can throw Genl Hooker's army across the Potomac and draw troops from the south, embarrassing their plan of campaign in a measure, if I can do nothing more and have to return."[43] In terms of logistics, a raid into Pennsylvania promised the dual benefits of providing a respite for the farmers of north-central Virginia and the Shenandoah Valley and affording Lee's army access to badly needed food and fodder in the North.[44]

Lee first informed President Davis of the failed assaults at Gettysburg in a message dated July 4, conjecturing that "the enemy suffered severely" while acknowledging "our own loss has not been light." Three days later, with the army at Hagerstown, a second letter to Davis isolated the strong Union defensive position and logistical difficulties as the principal reasons for the retreat. Lee also wrote to his wife, Mary, on July 7, assuring her that "our noble men are cheerful & confident." He expanded on the topic of morale (and mentioned again Meade's "much shattered" force) on the eighth. "Though reduced in numbers by the hardships & battles through which it has passed since leaving the Rappahannock," he stated to Davis regarding his army, "its condition is good and its confidence unimpaired." Lee was "not in the least discouraged," and his faith "in the fortitude of this army" remained unshaken. Reiterating on the tenth and eleventh that the army was in "good condition," Lee mentioned that ammunition had

**GEN. ROBERT E. LEE**
Francis Trevelyan Miller, ed.,
*The Photographic History of the
Civil War*, 10 vols. (New York:
Review of Reviews, 1911),
10:61

been replenished but that food was becoming a problem because of the swollen Potomac.[45]

On July 12, Lee wrote to both Davis and Mary. In obvious reference to inaccurate newspaper coverage, he told Mary that "our success at Gettysburg was not as great as reported." The army had "failed to drive the enemy from his position" and had withdrawn to the Potomac. He reported all quiet to Davis, adding that if the waters of the Potomac had not risen, everything "would have been accomplished that could have been reasonably expected"—the Army of the Potomac pushed north of the river, Federal troops drawn from the Virginia and Carolina coasts, and a summer offensive by the enemy thwarted. His next letter to Mary placed the raid in a quite favorable context: the army had returned "rather sooner than I had originally contemplated, but having accomplished what I purposed on leaving the Rappahannock, viz., relieving the Valley of the presence of the enemy & drawing his army north of the Potomac."[46]

About this time Lee met with Maj. John Seddon, brother of the Confederate secretary of war, who later related the details of the conversation to Henry Heth.[47] Though not direct evidence, these comments correspond closely with Lee's written statements in July 1863 and bear specifically on how he viewed Gettysburg. As Heth quoted Seddon, the general argued that the heavy loss at Gettysburg did not exceed what "it would have been from the series of battles I would have been compelled to fight had I remained in Virginia." According to Seddon's account of the meeting, Lee rose from his chair after making this comment, gestured forcefully, and said, "Sir, we did whip them at Gettysburg, and it will be seen for the next six months that *that army* will be as quiet as a sucking dove."[48]

Once back in the lower Shenandoah Valley, Lee reported to Davis that his men needed shoes and clothing but enjoyed "good health and spirits." He soon shifted the army to Culpeper, whence he wrote Mary that his men had "laboured hard, endured much & behaved nobly." Echoing Clement Evans, he asserted, with implicit self-criticism, that the army "ought not to have been expected to have performed impossibilities or to have fulfilled the anticipations of the thoughtless & unreasonable." More explicitly self-critical was a letter in which he confessed to cousin Margaret Stuart that the "army did all it could. I fear I required of it impossibilities." His movement across the Potomac had pulled the Federals north of the river, he informed Stuart, where they might have stayed "if we only could have been strong enough." The army had behaved "nobly and cheerfully, and though it did not win a victory it conquered a success." With no hint that he believed his soldiers less than equal to the task, he observed: "We must now prepare for harder blows and harder work."[49]

When Jefferson Davis expressed concern on July 21 about the absence of information on casualties, Lee promised an official tally as soon as he received one. "As far as I can judge," he went on to say, "the killed, wounded, and missing from the time we left the Rappahannock until our return will not fall short of twenty thousand." The number of wounded and missing would be especially large. Many of the former had to be left in Pennsylvania; the missing included thousands of stragglers (some of whom had begun to return to the army) in addition to prisoners and the "wounded unfit to be transported." As to the Federals, information derived from local citizens and Union prisoners indicated an Army of the Potomac "much reduced in numbers" that seemed "content to remain quiescent."[50]

Lee gave Davis his fullest assessment of Gettysburg in a letter of July 31. The president had sent a censorious clipping from the Charleston *Mercury*, which Lee labeled ill-informed and contradictory. "No blame can be attached to the army for its failure to accomplish what was projected by me," wrote Lee, "nor should it be censured for the unreasonable expectations of the public." Taking full responsibility, Lee admitted to Davis, as he had to Margaret Stuart, that he probably "expected too much" of his men's "prowess & valour." But in his opinion the army achieved "a general success, though it did not win a victory." He had thought victory within reach while on the field and still believed that "if all things could have worked together it would have been accomplished." Had he known the final assaults on July 3 would fail, he would have followed another course—though what "the ultimate result would have been is not so clear to me." The army's loss had been "very heavy"; however, so had that of the enemy, whose impaired condition made possible Lee's safe retreat.[51]

Lee's comments shared basic themes with those of many of his officers and men. The Confederates had faced a well-positioned foe at Gettysburg, fought gallantly but without ultimate success, and lost heavily while inflicting such reciprocal damage the Federals shunned any counteroffensive. Withdrawn in part because of problems of supply, the army retained its high morale during the retreat and after it recrossed the Potomac. Lee's suggestion that the raid accomplished most of its objectives was a more positive reading than all save a handful of his men gave the campaign, but he knew better than they the capture of Washington or the destruction of the Army of the Potomac never had been goals. The Federals seemed content to sit quietly as the summer passed; Richmond faced no immediate threat; and the army had procured animals and food while north of the Potomac. Thus Lee could speak of a "general success" despite a costly reverse in the campaign's showcase battle.[52]

While there is no reason to dismiss Lee's postcampaign analysis as dishonest, some might question his lenient criteria for judging success. On three points at least he could have admitted greater disappointment. First, he originally hoped to stay north until late summer or early fall to partake of northern bounty and keep the enemy off guard.[53] Second, he almost certainly had not envisioned retiring to the Rappahannock River line so quickly after he returned to Virginia (whenever that might have been). Finally, despite his many allusions to Union casualties, the enormity of Confederate losses must have chastened him more than he betrayed.

Indeed, a hint of hidden disappointment surfaced in early August when persistent criticism in newspapers such as the Charleston *Mercury* provoked Lee to tender his resignation. "I have seen and heard of expression of discontent in the public journals at the result of the expedition," wrote

the general to Jefferson Davis. "I do not know how far this feeling extends in the army. My brother officers have been too kind to report it, and so far the troops have been too generous to exhibit it." But Lee acknowledged that some of his soldiers likely harbored doubts about him, and no matter how able an officer might be, "if he loses the confidence of his troops disaster must sooner or later ensue." For this reason, and because of his uncertain health, Lee requested that Davis "take measures to supply my place." The president wasted no time in assuring his "dear friend" that there was no one "more fit to command" and that isolated carping could not "detract from the achievements which will make you and your army the subject of history and object of the world's admiration for generations to come." With that comforting reassurance in hand, Lee dropped the subject.[54] A fair interpretation of this coda to the campaign might be that while Lee did not believe he had been defeated in Pennsylvania, he harbored a sense of lost opportunity that left him easily wounded by criticism.

If Lee emerged from Pennsylvania poised but with some ambivalence about the campaign, his mood conformed to that of most of his soldiers and their kinfolk at home. There was reason not to despair over the campaign. After all, the Federals in Virginia *were* almost "as quiet as a sucking dove" for the rest of 1863 and well into the spring of 1864. The army's cocky assurance that every battle would be a victory regardless of the odds received a jolt at Gettysburg, but the vast majority of Lee's soldiers remained in the ranks and looked to him with undiminished confidence. Although casualties had been hideous, the Army of Northern Virginia (as well as other Confederate armies) had absorbed brutal losses on other fields and recovered rather quickly. From a civilian perspective, the negative results of the Pennsylvania campaign seemed largely transitory when contrasted with the loss of Vicksburg and other dire news in June and July 1863. Confederates across the South persisted in viewing Lee as an invincible commander whose army increasingly sustained the hopes of the entire nation. For them, as for most of the men in the Army of Northern Virginia, Gettysburg was not a harbinger of eventual ruin.

### ACKNOWLEDGMENTS

The author acknowledges the kind assistance of Joseph T. Glatthaar and George C. Rable, who took time from very hectic schedules to read this essay, and of William A. Blair, Keith Bohannon, and Peter S. Carmichael, all of whom brought to his attention important material turned up during their own research.

### NOTES

1. It is worthwhile to note that Gettysburg did not loom as large in 1863 as it does today. A number of factors explain why it eventually captured the popular imagination as *the* decisive turning point of the Civil War—among them Lincoln's decision to explore the meaning of the war in his remarks at Gettysburg in November 1863, the immense volume of Lost Cause writings that focused on Gettysburg in search of the key to Confederate defeat, the sheer scale of the battle, and the fact that it represented the deepest penetration into northern territory of any southern army. But in attempting to gauge the immediate impact of Gettysburg on the Confederacy, it is important to bear in mind that Lincoln's speech lay months ahead, Lost Cause warriors would not emerge as a major force for a decade, and no one knew that Gettysburg would be the bloodiest engagement of the conflict and the geographical high-water mark of Confederate arms. In sum,

the battle now perceived as the most famous military event in American history did not overshadow all other campaigns at the time.

2. Emory M. Thomas, *The Confederate Nation, 1861–1865* (New York: Harper & Row, 1979), 243–44; James M. McPherson, *Ordeal by Fire: The Civil War and Reconstruction* (New York: McGraw-Hill, 1992), 332.

3. Josiah Gorgas, *The Civil War Diary of General Josiah Gorgas*, ed. Frank E. Vandiver (University: University of Alabama Press, 1947), 55; Thomas, *Confederate Nation*, 244. For McPherson's use of Gorgas's diary, see *Ordeal by Fire*, 332, as well as his *Battle Cry of Freedom: The Civil War Era* (New York: Oxford University Press, 1988), 665.

4. J. B. Jones, *A Rebel War Clerk's Diary at the Confederate States Capital*, 2 vols. (1866; reprint, Alexandria, Va.: Time-Life Books, 1982), 1: 374, 381; Robert Garlick Hill Kean, *Inside the Confederate Government: The Diary of Robert Garlick Hill Kean*, ed. Edward Younger (New York: Oxford University Press, 1957), 79.

5. Susan P. Lee, *Memoirs of William Nelson Pendleton, D.D.* (1893; reprint, Harrisonburg, Va.: Sprinkle Publications, 1991), 297; B. R. Kinney to W. H. Badgett, July 18, 1863, typescript in Research Collections, Fredericksburg and Spotsylvania National Military Park, Fredericksburg, Va.

6. Kean, *Inside the Confederate Government*, 84; Blackford's letter of July 18, 1863, to an unnamed recipient quoted in L. Minor Blackford, *Mine Eyes Have Seen the Glory* (Cambridge, Mass.: Harvard University Press, 1954), 220–21; Wade Hampton to Joseph E. Johnston, July 30, 1863, quoted in Herman Hattaway and Archer Jones, *How the North Won: A Military History of the Civil War* (Urbana: University of Illinois Press, 1983), 414; Alexander McNeil to his wife, July 8, 1863, Alexander McNeil Letters, Kershaw's Brigade File, Gettysburg National Military Park Library, Gettysburg, Pa. Uneasiness about Lee's aggressive tactics surfaced during the battle itself. Capt. Joseph Graham, whose Charlotte Artillery supported James Johnston Pettigrew's infantry on July 3, described how the prospect of direct assaults against formidable Federal positions recalled raw images of past failures. Pettigrew's infantry "moved right through my Battery," wrote Graham in late July 1863, "and I feared then I could see a want of resolution in our men. And I heard many say, 'that is worse than Malvern Hill,' and 'I don't hardly think that position can be carried,' etc., etc., enough to make me apprehensive about the result" (Joseph Graham to William Alexander Graham, July 30, 1863, quoted in William Alexander Graham, *The Papers of William Alexander Graham*, vol. 5 [1857–63], ed. Max R. Williams and J. G. de Roulhac Hamilton [Raleigh: North Carolina Office of Archives and History, 1973], 514).

7. U.S. War Department, *The War of the Rebellion: A Compilation of the Official*

*Records of the Union and Confederate Armies*, 127 vols., index, and atlas (Washington, D.C.: GPO, 1880–1901), 27(3):1048, 1041, 1040 (hereafter cited as *OR*; all references are to series 1). On the problem of desertion after Gettysburg, see Douglas Southall Freeman, *Lee's Lieutenants: A Study in Command*, 3 vols. (New York: Charles Scribner's Sons, 1942–44), 3:217–19, which offers a good brief discussion, and Richard Reid, "A Test Case of the 'Crying Evil': Desertion among North Carolina Troops during the Civil War," *North Carolina Historical Review* 58 (July 1981), which challenges the conventional view that North Carolinians deserted in especially large numbers because of the antiwar activities of William Woods Holden in their home state.

8. Regiments that had lost key officers, incurred especially heavy losses at Gettysburg, or lacked good leadership in general faced special problems of morale. One such unit was the 23rd North Carolina of Alfred Iverson's brigade. Subjected to needless butchery through Iverson's criminal sloth on July 1, the 23rd limped through July with declining morale and thinned ranks. "Our soiders are very near give up all hope of ever whiping the Yanks," wrote one member on July 17. Another remarked that the regiment needed "recruits here verry bad. There is but 7 in our Company. Times are verry disheartening here at present." This man was nonetheless sad to learn of a call for more conscripts from North Carolina: "I dont think their is any their to spair." J. F. Coghill to Pappy, Ma, and Mit, July 17, 1863, J. F. Coghill Papers, Southern Historical Collection, Wilson Library, University of North Carolina, Chapel Hill (hereafter cited as SHC); W. J. O. McDaniel to Mrs. Torrence, July 20, 1863, quoted in Haskell Monroe, ed., "'The Road to Gettysburg'—The Diary and Letters of Leonidas Torrence of the Gaston Guards," *North Carolina Historical Review* 36 (October 1959): 516. The 23rd lost 282 of its 316 men at Gettysburg, a percentage of 89.2 that ranked second only to the 8th Virginia's 92.2 percent casualties. See John W. Busey and David G. Martin, *Regimental Strengths and Losses at Gettysburg* (Hightstown, N.J.: Longstreet House, 1986), 298.

9. William C. Harris, *William Woods Holden: Firebrand of North Carolina Politics* (Baton Rouge: Louisiana State University Press, 1987), 131–32. For a good brief discussion of the peace movement in North Carolina, see chap. 18 of W. Buck Yearns and John G. Barrett, eds., *North Carolina Civil War Documentary* (Chapel Hill: University of North Carolina Press, 1980).

10. Richmond (Daily) *Dispatch*, July 13, 1863; Lynchburg *Virginian*, July 13, 1863. See the Richmond (Daily) *Dispatch*, July 8, 1863, for a comparison of Gettysburg to Hannibal's victory of annihilation over the Romans at Cannae. The best brief account of southern newspaper coverage of the battle is in J. Cutler Andrews,

*The South Reports the Civil War* (Princeton, N.J.: Princeton University Press, 1970), 302–19.

11. Richmond (Daily) *Dispatch*, July 18, 1863; Charleston *Daily Courier*, July 14, 17, 1863.

12. The *Mercury* is quoted in Freeman, *Lee's Lieutenants*, 3:168; a brief discussion of the impact of Alexander's account is in Andrews, *South Reports the Civil War*, 316–17. Some civilians felt betrayed by what they saw as dishonest press accounts. Upon learning of Lee's repulse, for example, Virginian William M. Blackford railed against newspapers that had reported "a grand and crowning victory" (Blackford, *Mine Eyes*, 222).

13. Emma Holmes, *The Diary of Miss Emma Holmes, 1861–1866*, ed. John F. Marszalek (Baton Rouge: Louisiana State University Press, 1979), 281–83; Floride Clemson, *A Rebel Came Home: The Diary and Letters of Floride Clemson, 1863–1866*, ed. Ernest J. Lander, Jr., and Charles M. McGee, Jr. (rev. ed., Columbia: University of South Carolina Press, 1989), 37; William Alexander Thom to Pembroke Thom, August 31, 1863, quoted in Catherine Thom Bartlett, ed., *"My Dear Brother": A Confederate Chronicle* (Richmond, Va.: Dietz Press, 1952), 106. In *Civil Wars: Women and the Crisis of Southern Nationalism* (Urbana: University of Illinois Press, 1989), 211, George C. Rable emphasizes the importance of newspapers in molding women's perceptions of Lee's campaign: Gettysburg should have completed a "process of demoralization" triggered by high casualties and the absence of prospects for peace, "but curiously it did not. In many parts of the Confederacy, wildly inaccurate accounts led women to believe for a month or more that Lee had soundly whipped the Federals and was marching on Philadelphia or Baltimore or Washington."

14. Catherine Ann Devereux Edmondston, *"Journal of a Secesh Lady": The Diary of Catherine Ann Devereux Edmondston, 1860–1866*, ed. Beth Gilbert Crabtree and James W. Patton (Raleigh: North Carolina Division of Archives and History, 1979), 425–27, 434, 440.

15. Edmund Ruffin, *The Diary of Edmund Ruffin*, ed. William Kauffman Scarborough, 3 vols. (Baton Rouge: Louisiana State University Press, 1972–89), 3:54, 68–69.

16. "To the People of Georgia," Macon (Ga.) *Journal and Messenger*, July 22, 1863.

17. Jefferson Davis to R. E. Lee, July 28, August 2, 11, 1863, Lee to Davis, July 16, August 8, 1863, in Dunbar Rowland, ed., *Jefferson Davis Constitutionalist: His Life and Letters*, 10 vols. (Jackson: Mississippi Department of Archives and History, 1923), 5:579, 584–85, 588–89. In his postwar memoir, Davis observed

of Lee's raid into Pennsylvania that the "wisdom of the strategy was justified by the result" (Jefferson Davis, *The Rise and Fall of the Confederate Government*, 2 vols. [1881; reprint, New York: Thomas Yoseloff, 1958], 2:447).

18. Kate Stone, *Brokenburn: The Journal of Kate Stone, 1861–1868*, ed. John Q. Anderson (Baton Rouge: Louisiana State University Press, 1955), 230, 284; Belle Edmondson, *A Lost Heroine of the Confederacy: The Diaries and Letters of Belle Edmondson*, ed. William and Loretta Galbraith (Jackson: University Press of Mississippi, 1990), 126; Felix Pierre Poché, *A Louisiana Confederate: Diary of Felix Pierre Poché*, ed. Edwin C. Bearss (Natchitoches: Louisiana Studies Institute of Northwestern State University of Louisiana, 1972), 126.

19. R. A. Pierson to W. H. Pierson (his father), July 19, 1863, Pierson Family Papers, Tulane University, New Orleans, La.

20. Elizabeth Whitley Roberson, *Weep Not for Me Dear Mother* (Washington, N.C.: Venture Press, 1991), 112; Lt. Joseph Hilton to his cousin, July 18, 1863, Hilton Family Papers, MS #387, Georgia Historical Society, Savannah, Ga.; Charles W. Turner, ed., *Civil War Letters of Arabella Speairs and William Beverley Pettit of Fluvanna County, Virginia: March 1862–March 1865*, 2 vols. (Roanoke: Virginia Lithography & Graphics, 1988–89), 1:140; James Drayton Nance to Mr. Brantly, August 16, 1863, James Drayton Nance Papers, South Caroliniana Library, University of South Carolina, Columbia, S.C.

21. Arthur J. L. Fremantle, *Three Months in the Southern States: April–June, 1863* (1863; reprint, Lincoln: University of Nebraska Press, 1991), 270–71; Justus Scheibert, *Seven Months in the Rebel States during the North American War, 1863*, ed. William Stanley Hoole (1868; reprint, Tuscaloosa, Ala.: Confederate Publishing, 1958), 119.

22. "From Our Army," a letter from William Aiken Kelly printed in the Charleston *Daily Courier*, July 22, 1863.

23. R. A. Pierson to M. C. Pierson (his sister), August 11, 1863, R. A. Pierson to [?], [ca. July 10, 1863], Pierson Family Papers. The undated letter, which is a fragment, was written from Hagerstown, Maryland: "Our army has fallen back to Hagerstown, Md. six miles from the Potomac and we are now resting from the fatigue of our long trip."

24. William B. Taylor to his mother, July 29, 1863, quoted in Greg Mast, "Six Lieutenants: Vignettes of North Carolinians in America's Greatest Battle," *Military Images* 13 (July–August 1991): 12–13.

25. Charles Minor Blackford to his wife, July 7, 1863, in Susan Leigh Blackford et al., comp. and eds., *Letters from Lee's Army, or Memoirs of Life in and Out of the Army in Virginia During the War Between the States* (New York: Charles Scribner's Sons, 1947), 189–90; Henry Robinson Berkeley, *Four Years in the Con-*

*federate Horse Artillery: The Diary of Private Henry Robinson Berkeley*, ed. William H. Runge (Chapel Hill: University of North Carolina Press for the Virginia Historical Society, 1961), 52–54; Edgeworth Bird to Sallie Bird, August 15, July 7, 9, 1863, in John Rozier, ed., *The Granite Farm Letters: The Civil War Correspondence of Edgeworth & Sallie Bird* (Athens: University of Georgia Press, 1988), 135, 115, 118.

26. Stephen Dodson Ramseur to Ellen Richmond, July 8, 1863, Stephen Dodson Ramseur Papers, SHC; James Drayton Nance to Mr. Brantly, August 16, 1863, Nance Papers; William B. Sturtevant to Jimmy, July 27, 1863, Metal Case 3, S 785, Museum of the Confederacy, Richmond, Va.; Edgeworth Bird to Sallie Bird, July 7, 12, 1863, in Rozier, *Granite Farm Letters*, 115, 122; Spencer Glasgow Welch to his wife, July 17, 1863, in Spencer Glasgow Welch, *A Confederate Surgeon's Letters to His Wife* (1911; reprint, Marietta, Ga.: Continental Book Co., 1954), 59.

27. Stephen Dodson Ramseur to Ellen Richmond, July 19, 8, 1863, Ramseur Papers, SHC; Edgeworth Bird to Sallie Bird, July 7, 1863, quoted in Rozier, *Granite Farm Letters*, 115; William Beverley Pettit to his wife, July 8, 1863, quoted in Turner, *Letters of Spears and Pettit*, 1:132; David Wyatt Aiken to his wife, July 11, 1863, quoted in Annette Tapert, ed., *The Brothers' War: Civil War Letters to Their Loved Ones from the Blue and Gray* (New York: Times Books, 1988), 162–63.

28. Fremantle, *Three Months*, 297.

29. *OR* 27(2):309. Lee's report was dated July 31, 1863.

30. William Watts Parker to the Richmond *Sentinel*, July 10, 1863 (printed in the *Sentinel* on July 27, 1863), quoted in Robert K. Krick, *Parker's Virginia Battery, C.S.A.* (rev. ed., Wilmington, N.C.: Broadfoot, 1989), 190–91; Clement A. Evans to his wife, July 8, 10, 1863, quoted in Robert Grier Stephens, Jr., *Intrepid Warrior: Clement Anselm Evans, Confederate General from Georgia. Life, Letters, and Diaries of the War Years* (Dayton, Ohio: Morningside, 1992), 231, 235; William Beverley Pettit to his wife, July 8, 1863, in Turner, *Letters of Spears and Pettit*, 1:133; Edward Porter Alexander to his father, undated letter (written after July 13 while the army was encamped near Winchester), quoted in Marion Alexander Boggs, ed., *The Alexander Letters, 1787–1900* (1910; reprint, Athens: University of Georgia Press, 1980), 251–52. For a discussion of attitudes among soldiers about the acceptability of fighting behind defensive works, see Gerald F. Linderman's *Embattled Courage: The Experience of Combat in the American Civil War* (New York: Free Press, 1987).

31. Stephens, *Intrepid Warrior*, 232; William J. Seymour, *The Civil War Memoirs of Captain William J. Seymour: Reminiscences of a Louisiana Tiger*, ed. Terry L. Jones (Baton Rouge: Louisiana State University Press, 1991), 79; R. A. Pierson

to M. C. Pierson, August 11, 1863, Pierson Family Papers; Joseph Graham to William Alexander Graham, July 30, 1863, in Graham, *Papers of Graham*, 5 : 514.

32. E. Porter Alexander to his father, undated letter (written after July 13 while the army was encamped near Winchester), quoted in Boggs, *Alexander Letters*, 251–52.

33. FitzGerald Ross, *Cities and Camps of the Confederacy*, ed. Richard B. Harwell (Urbana: University of Illinois Press, 1958), 80. Ross's account of the Gettysburg campaign and its aftermath first appeared in *Blackwood's Edinburgh Magazine* in 1864 and 1865. For a discussion of Ross and the publication history of his travel memoir of the Confederacy, see Harwell's introduction to *Cities and Camps of the Confederacy*.

34. Ambrose R. Wright letter of July 7, 1863, printed in the Augusta (Ga.) *Daily Constitutionalist*, July 23, 1863; James E. B. Stuart to his wife, July 10, 13, 1863, quoted in James E. B. Stuart, *The Letters of Major General James E. B. Stuart*, ed. Adele H. Mitchell (n.p.: Stuart-Mosby Historical Society, 1990), 327–28.

35. S. G. Pryor to Penelope, July 16, 1863, quoted in Charles R. Adams, Jr., ed., *A Post of Honor: The Pryor Letters, 1861–63. Letters from Capt. S. G. Pryor, Twelfth Georgia Regiment and His Wife, Penelope Tyson Pryor* (Fort Valley, Ga.: Garret, 1989), 377–78: LeRoy S. Edwards to his father, July 7, 1863, quoted in LeRoy S. Edwards, *Letters of LeRoy S. Edwards Written During the War between the States*, ed. Joan K. Walton and Terry A. Walton (n.p., [1985]), letter no. 31.

36. William Lafayette Barrier to his father, July 14, 1863, quoted in Beverly Barrier Troxler and Billy Dawn Barrier Auciello, eds., *Dear Father: Confederate Letters Never Before Published* (n.p.: Privately published by the editors, 1989), 112–13.

37. Ambrose R. Wright letter of July 8, 1863, in Augusta (Ga.) *Daily Constitutionalist*; Allen C. Jordan to his parents, July 15, 1863, quoted in *Georgia Historical Quarterly* 59 (Spring 1975): 136; Charles Minor Blackford to his wife, July 16, 1863, quoted in Blackford et al., *Letters from Lee's Army*, 193; Spencer Glasgow Welch to his wife, August 10, 1863, quoted in Welch, *Confederate Surgeon's Letters*, 73–74; Lafayette McLaws to his wife, August 14, 1863, Lafayette McLaws Papers, SHC.

38. Edgeworth Bird to Sallie Bird, July 19, August 28, 1863, quoted in Rozier, *Granite Farm Letters*, 125, 145; S. G. Pryor to Penelope Tyson Pryor, August 6, 1863, quoted in Adams, *Pryor Letters*, 385; Green Berry Samuels to his wife, August 7, 21, 1863, quoted in Carrie Esther Spencer et al., comps., *A Civil War Marriage in Virginia: Reminiscences and Letters* (Boyce, Va.: Carr, 1956), 190.

39. Gorgas, *Diary*, 59–61.

40. Joseph Hilton to his cousin, July 18, 1863, Hilton Family Papers; Sidney J. Richardson to his parents, July 8, 1863, Civil War Miscellany, Personal Papers,

Georgia Archives; John A. Barry to his father, July 8, 1863, J. A. Barry Letter, MS #3015, SHC.

41. Clement A. Evans to his wife, July 15, 1863, quoted in Stephens, *Intrepid Warrior*, 249.

42. Only Lee's statements prior to the battle are included here. For his retrospective discussions of why he moved north, see his official report in *OR* 27(2): 312–26 (also printed in R. E. Lee, *The Wartime Papers of R. E. Lee*, ed. Clifford Dowdey and Louis H. Manarin [Boston: Little, Brown, 1961], 569–85), and transcription of conversation between R. E. Lee and William Allan, April 15, 1868, pp. 13–14, William Allan Papers, SHC.

43. R. E. Lee to Jefferson Davis, May 10, 30, June 25, 1863, and Lee to James A. Seddon, May 10, 30, June 8, 1863, in Lee, *Wartime Papers*, 482–83, 496, 498, 505.

44. An indication of Lee's attention to logistics may be found in a letter of June 23 to Jefferson Davis, wherein he reported that Pennsylvania already had yielded enough food to supply Richard Ewell's corps for the next week, while 1,700 barrels of flour lay stockpiled in Maryland for the remainder of the army. See Lee, *Wartime Papers*, 530.

45. R. E. Lee to Jefferson Davis, July 4, 7, 8, 10, 11, 1863, and Lee to Mary Lee, July 7, 1863, in ibid., 538–45. Lee's letter to Davis of July 7 went astray, and the general sent a copy to the president on the sixteenth.

46. R. E. Lee to Mary Lee, July 12, 15, 1863, and Lee to Jefferson Davis, July 12, 1863, in ibid., 547–48, 551–52.

47. Lee and Seddon probably spoke on July 15 or 16. On the sixteenth, Lee informed Secretary Seddon that he had "received the communication sent me by your brother. He will inform you of the arrival of the army at this point. It is a little foot sore, & is much in need of shoes for men & horses" (ibid., 553).

48. Henry Heth, "Letter from Major-General Henry Heth, of A. P. Hill's Corps, A.N.V.," in *Southern Historical Society Papers*, 52 vols. and 2-vol. index, ed. J. William Jones and others (1876–1959; reprint, Wilmington, N.C.: Broadfoot, 1990–92), 5:54–55.

49. R. E. Lee to Jefferson Davis, July 16, 1863; Lee to Mary Lee, July 26, 1863; Lee to Margaret Stuart, July 26, 1863, in Lee, *Wartime Papers*, 552, 560–61.

50. Jefferson Davis to R. E. Lee, July 21, 1863, in Rowland, *Jefferson Davis*, 5:573; Lee to Davis, July 29, 1863, in Lee, *Wartime Papers*, 563–64.

51. R. E. Lee to Jefferson Davis, July 31, 1863, in Lee, *Wartime Papers*, 564–65.

52. It is worth remembering that ten months passed between Gettysburg and the next true Union offensive in Virginia, which began under U. S. Grant's direction in early May 1864.

53. Lee remarked in 1868 that he went into Pennsylvania intending "to move

about, to manoeuver & alarm the enemy, threaten their cities, hit any blows he might be able to do without risking a general battle, & then towards Fall return & recover nearer his base" (transcription of conversation between R. E. Lee and William Allan, April 15, 1868, p. 14, Allan Papers, SHC).

54. R. E. Lee to Jefferson Davis, August 8, 1863, in Lee, *Wartime Papers*, 589–90; Davis to Lee, August 11, 1863, in Rowland, *Jefferson Davis*, 5:588–90. For Lee's brief response to Davis's letter, dated August 22, see Lee, *Wartime Letters*, 593. Lee kept his plans for resignation to himself. After the war, Charles Venable of his staff told Jubal A. Early that no copy of the general's letter to Davis "was ever seen in camp—and I suppose Gen Lee destroyed Mr. Davis's letter to him." Lee's staff learned of their chief's action only when they saw Davis's reply (aides typically opened all official letters for Lee except those from Davis; the latter were opened whenever Lee was away). Once they saw the "drift of the opening sentences" they put the letter aside with Lee's private correspondence to await his return. See Charles A. Venable to Jubal A. Early, January 23, 1876, Jubal A. Early Papers, Library of Congress, Washington, D.C.

*Longstreet,*

*Lee, and Confederate*

*Attack Plans for July 3*

*at Gettysburg*

## CROSS PURPOSES

*William Garrett Piston*

Shortly after dawn on July 3, 1863, Robert E. Lee rode across the Pennsylvania countryside to the far right flank of his army, where the men of the divisions of Lafayette McLaws and John Bell Hood clung to ground they had won in desperate combat the day before. As Lee reined in Traveller to speak with James Longstreet, commander of the First Corps, the distant echo of artillery fire indicated that far to the north Richard Ewell's Second Corps was already engaged against Federal positions on Cemetery Hill and Culp's Hill. Since encountering the Army of the Potomac on July 1, the Confederates had driven their enemies into defensive positions just south of Gettysburg. Ewell and Longstreet had pounded the Federal flanks with some success on July 2, and Lee believed that a renewed, simultaneous attack by their men on July 3 would carry the day, particularly as George Pickett's fresh division had arrived to reinforce Longstreet.

Lee was therefore greatly surprised to learn that instead of attacking to his front as instructed the previous night, Longstreet had, just moments before, ordered a time-consuming flanking maneuver designed to take his men around the Round Tops in an attempt to strike the rear of the Federal army. Lee immediately canceled this but agreed, after a substantial discussion with Longstreet, to leave McLaws's and Hood's divisions in place.

**LT. GEN. JAMES LONGSTREET**
Francis Trevelyan Miller, ed.,
*The Photographic History of the
Civil War*, 10 vols. (New York:
Review of Reviews, 1911),
10:245

Pickett's Virginians, reinforced by troops from A. P. Hill's Third Corps, would instead assault the center of the Federal line along Cemetery Ridge.

This is the generally accepted version of events that set the stage for the immortal, if misnamed, "Pickett's Charge," codified in what remains the best single-volume work on the battle, Edwin B. Coddington's *The Gettysburg Campaign*. In addition to official after-action reports, Coddington relied heavily on the works of southern historian Douglas Southall Freeman. Much of Freeman's extensive analysis of Gettysburg, contained in his famous multivolume works *R. E. Lee* and *Lee's Lieutenants*, is based in turn on the memoirs of Lee's staff officers, whose writings have therefore largely shaped present-day understandings of the battle.[1]

Pickett's Charge, or Longstreet's assault, as it might more properly be called, is so enshrined in legend that relatively little attention has been given to the fact that Lee did not originally intend to attack in such a fashion. It is certainly ironic that during the long, complex postwar debate over the responsibility for the Confederate defeat at Gettysburg, Jubal Early and other members of the Lee cult fabricated fictitious errors on Longstreet's part rather than focus on an area where his conduct is open to legitimate criticism.

An examination of the interaction between Lee and Longstreet concerning the attack on July 3 is significant for several reasons. By confronting the historian with the necessity of reaching conclusions on the basis of scant information, it demonstrates the limits of attempting to analyze and comprehend the past. It also raises questions about the consequences of Lee's style of command, about Longstreet's view of his prerogatives as Lee's subordinate, and about Longstreet's role in the Confederate failure in Pennsylvania.

Historians encounter a wealth of primary source material describing the actions of Lee and Longstreet at Gettysburg, but explanations for these actions are confined to the two men's official correspondence and battle reports. These are without question the sketchiest and least satisfactory of any connected with a major campaign of the war, which makes it unfortunate that neither Lee nor Longstreet left private wartime correspondence that sheds light on their activities on the night of July 2 and the morning of July 3. While Lee collected materials for his memoirs, he died without putting pen to paper. His version of events is therefore limited to three documents available in printed form in the well-known *Official Records* published by the federal government between 1880 and 1902.[2] Longstreet's postwar writings on the subject raise as many questions as they answer.

While still near Gettysburg on July 4, Lee sent a hasty, one-page letter to President Davis. His succinct description of the second and third days of battle made no mention of his changing plans on the morning of July 3 due to any misunderstanding with Longstreet. "On the 2nd July, Longstreet's corps, with the exception of one division, having arrived, we attempted to dislodge the enemy," wrote Lee of the second day, "and, though we gained some ground, we were unable to get possession of his position." "The next day," continued Lee in equally terse fashion, "the third division of General Longstreet having come up, a more extensive attack was made. The works on the enemy's extreme right and left were taken, but his numbers were so great and his position so commanding, that our troops were compelled to relinquish their advantage and retire."[3] This is so cursory that it scarcely sounds like the battle of Gettysburg at all; in terms of "works taken," it is positively misleading.

Lee provided substantially more detail in an outline of operations he submitted to Adj. Gen. Samuel Cooper on July 31. This went beyond narrative to include something of the reasoning behind his operations:

> After a severe struggle [on July 2], Longstreet succeeded in getting possession of and holding the desired ground. Ewell also carried

some of the strong positions which he assailed, and the result was such as to lead to the belief that he would ultimately be able to dislodge the enemy. The battle ceased at dark.

These partial successes determined me to continue the assault next day. Pickett, with three of his brigades, joined Longstreet the following morning, and our batteries were moved forward to the positions gained by him the day before. The general plan of attack was unchanged, excepting that one division and two brigades of Hill's corps were ordered to support Longstreet. . . . The morning was occupied in necessary preparations, and the battle recommenced in the afternoon of the 3d, and raged with great violence until sunset.[4]

Lee again failed to mention a confrontation with Longstreet or a cancellation of his original plans because Longstreet had initiated a flanking maneuver. Instead, he stated that Longstreet spent the morning in "necessary preparations." The letter also implied erroneously that Longstreet's entire corps attacked on July 3 when in fact McLaws and Hood had remained stationary.

Lee did not submit his official report on Gettysburg until January 1864. While historians have generated hundreds of books and articles about the battle, Lee's account of the entire campaign takes up only six printed pages. Like all of Lee's reports, it actually was composed by Charles Marshall, his military secretary. Because Lee's supervision was so intense, however, one rightly can consider the report to be in his words. Marshall recalled after the war that Lee "weighed every sentence I wrote, frequently making minute verbal alterations, and questioned me closely as to the evidence on which I based all the statements which he did not know to be correct." "In short," concluded Marshall, "he spared no pains to make his official reports as truthful as possible."[5]

Of his decision to renew the battle on July 3, Lee noted (through Marshall):

The result of this day's operations [July 2] induced the belief that, with proper concert of action, and with the increased support that the positions gained on the right would enable the artillery to render the assaulting columns, we should ultimately succeed, and it was accordingly determined to continue the attack. The general plan was unchanged. Longstreet, re-enforced by Pickett's three brigades, which arrived near the battle-field during the afternoon of the 2d, was ordered to attack the next morning, and General Ewell was directed to assail the enemy's right at the same time. . . . General Longstreet's dispositions were not completed as early as was expected, but before notice could be sent to General Ewell [his troops had become engaged]. . . . General Longstreet was delayed by a force occupying the high, rocky hills on the enemy's extreme left, from which his troops could be attacked in reverse as they advanced. His operations had been embarrassed the day previous by the same cause, and he now deemed it necessary to defend his flank and rear with the divisions of Hood and McLaws. He was, therefore, re-enforced by Heth's division and two brigades of Pender's, to the command of which Major-General Trimble was assigned.[6]

From these three documents, one can reconstruct what may be designated Lee's First Plan for July 3—as distinct from Lee's Second Plan, which resulted in Pickett's Charge. The First Plan called for Longstreet to attack on the morning of July 3 in conjunction with Ewell, although the time at which Longstreet received orders to do so is not specified in any of Lee's reports. The general battle plan adopted on July 2 "was unchanged." As on the previous day, therefore, Longstreet was to attack by advancing roughly parallel to the Emmitsburg Road—ignoring the Round Tops— in order to strike the Federals at the southern end of Cemetery Ridge. Lee expected Pickett's division to participate but apparently left the details of its employment to Longstreet.[7]

Why did Lee alter his First Plan? Federal troops on the Round Tops delayed Longstreet's dispositions. Precisely how or why this occurred is not clear, but it spoiled Lee's intention of striking both flanks of the Army of the Potomac simultaneously. With a revision of plans necessary, Lee heeded Longstreet's assertion that McLaws and Hood should remain in place to protect his flank during any attack on Cemetery Ridge. Consequently, in devising his Second Plan, Lee changed both the composition and location of the attack. Pickett, together with troops from the Third Corps, would assault the center of Cemetery Ridge frontally rather than attacking its southern end at an angle as McLaws and Hood would have done. Lee, it should be remembered, made no mention in anything he wrote of canceling at the last minute a flanking movement ordered by Longstreet.

Longstreet's report of the battle, submitted on July 27, 1863, and for-

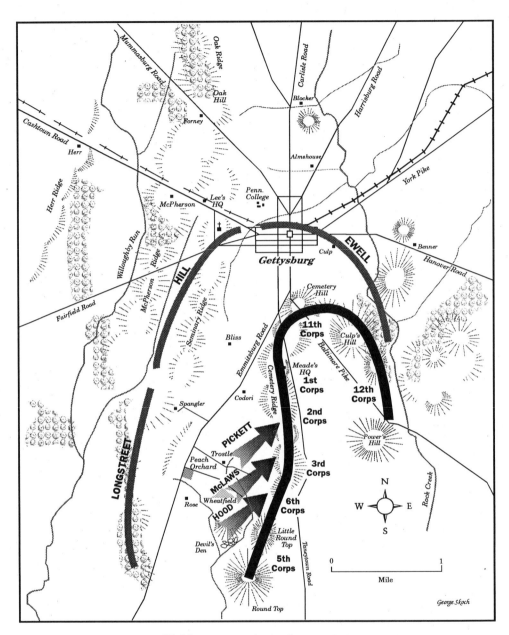

**LEE'S FIRST PLAN.** Had Longstreet advanced as Lee desired, the divisions of Hood and McLaws would have been exposed to devastating flanking fire from Federal troops on the Round Tops and in the valley of Plum Run.

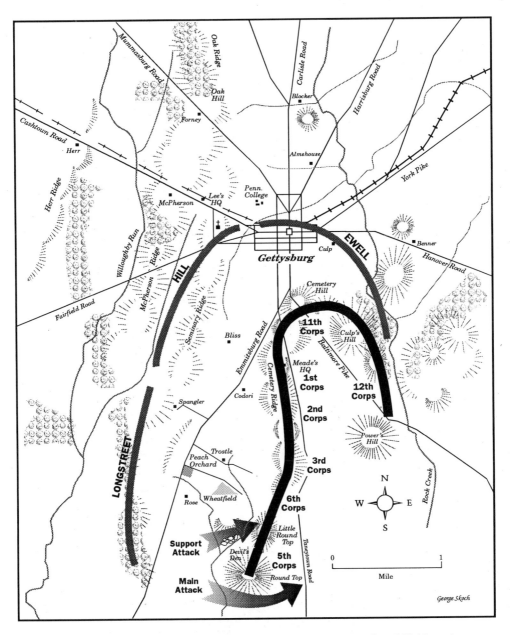

**LONGSTREET'S PLAN.** It is not clear whether Longstreet wanted to shift his entire corps east of the Round Tops, or whether a portion of it would have attacked over the same ground as on the previous day.

warded to Davis as part of Lee's much later report, indicates that the situation was considerably more complex than suggested above. After describing the fighting on July 2, Longstreet wrote of July 3:

> On the following morning our arrangements were made for renewing the attack by my right, with a view to pass around the hill occupied by the enemy on his left [Little Round Top], and to gain it by flank and reverse attack. This would have been a slow process, probably, but I think not very difficult. A few moments after my orders for the execution of this plan were given, the commanding general joined me, and ordered a column of attack to be formed of Pickett's, Heth's, and part of Pender's divisions, the assault to be made directly at the enemy's main position, the Cemetery Hill.[8]

Longstreet himself is therefore the only primary, or wartime, source concerning the flanking movement. But was it unauthorized? Were Longstreet's orders for the flank attack actually the cause of the delay that ruined Lee's plans for Ewell and Longstreet to attack simultaneously, as Coddington, Freeman, and many other historians have claimed? The latter issue is particularly important, as Lee adopted his Second Plan (Pickett's Charge) only after losing hope of launching simultaneous attacks on the flanks of the Federal army.

The question of Longstreet's authorization for the flank maneuver is not as simple as it appears. No one knows precisely what orders Longstreet received, when he received them, whether they were verbal or written, or whether their wording left him any legitimate grounds to exercise discretion. After the fighting on July 2, Longstreet reported to Lee by courier rather than in person. This was an unusual deviation from Longstreet's standard practice. As there was no physical reason why he could not have met with Lee, his decision not to do so remains mysterious. Not even Longstreet's harshest critics, however, have suggested he had an ulterior motive or purposely avoided Lee. In any case, the two commanders did not meet again until shortly after daybreak the following morning.[9] Although Longstreet's official report summarizes the instructions he received from Lee for the second day of the battle, it does not mention any orders from Lee concerning operations for the third day.[10] Perhaps Lee sent orders but Longstreet never received them; that certainly would explain the discrepancy in their reports.

Subordinate infantry and artillery commanders of the First Corps submitted brief and incomplete reports on Gettysburg that shed little light on the issue of Longstreet's intentions for the night of July 2 or for the morning of July 3. Because of his wounds, Hood never prepared a report. Deaths and injuries also prevented many of the officers under Hood and McLaws from reporting. Those who did, focused almost exclusively on their hard fighting of July 2, dismissing the next day with a few sentences. Similarly, Pickett's surviving subordinates concentrated on July 3 in their reports, providing relatively few details about their activities prior to the charge. Lee rejected Pickett's report, apparently because of its overly critical tone. It has since disappeared, thereby frustrating generations of Gettysburg scholars.[11]

The reports of Longstreet's subordinates do indicate that he shifted some troops during the night of July 2. The chaos of the day's battle necessitated this reorganization, which could have been a prelude to attack, defense, or maneuver. None of Longstreet's commanders mentioned receipt of orders for July 3, either for a direct attack or for a flanking maneuver, but absence of such instructions can neither prove nor disprove that Longstreet received specific orders from Lee.[12]

Following the war, Longstreet produced three versions of his actions on the night of July 2 and the morning of July 3. The first, "Lee in Pennsylvania," appeared initially as an article in the Philadelphia *Weekly Times* and subsequently as part of the well-known anthology *The Annals of the War*, published in 1879. Here Longstreet went beyond the flank attack plans described in his battle report, claiming that on the morning of July 3 he suggested to Lee that they make a strategic shift "around the right of Meade's army" to "maneuver him into attacking us."[13] Longstreet also contributed articles to *Century Magazine*'s immensely popular War Series, reprinted between 1887 and 1888 as *Battles and Leaders of the Civil War*. In "Lee's Right Wing at Gettysburg," Longstreet wrote: "I stated to General Lee that I had been examining the ground over to the right, and was much inclined to think the best thing was to move to the Federal left."

*From Manassas to Appomattox*, Longstreet's memoirs published in 1896, echoed his 1863 battle report, stating that on the basis of reports by scouts, he was preparing to "strike the enemy's left, and push it down towards his centre" when Lee arrived and canceled this flanking maneuver. Longstreet made no mention of proposing a strategic maneuver to force Meade into attacking. But in direct refutation of Lee's battle report, which he quoted, Longstreet boldly affirmed what his own report had always implied. Lee, he wrote, "did not give or send me orders for the morning of the third day."[14]

One must seriously question the validity of Longstreet's testimony—first, because many soldiers have presented their hindsight as foresight when writing their recollections and, second, because Longstreet endured almost a quarter-century of attacks on his military record by Jubal Early and other former comrades-in-arms who sought to blame him for the Confederate defeat at Gettysburg and, by extension, for the loss of the war. Longstreet wrote with a spirit of self-justification that unquestionably affected the content and character of his accounts.[15]

The First Corps commander may never have proposed to Lee on the morning of July 3 a strategic move intended to induce the Federals to take the offensive, but it is documented that he thought in such terms while the campaign was under way. Longstreet mentioned the suitability of such a strategy to Brig. Gen. William Barksdale, who before his death on July 2 discussed Longstreet's remarks with Brig. Gen. Benjamin G. Humphreys.[16]

It is much more difficult to judge Longstreet's statement that he received no orders from Lee concerning an attack on the morning of July 3. Although no known primary sources support his claim, one might be tempted, considering the chaotic conditions on any battlefield, to assume that Longstreet's memory was correct and that Lee's orders somehow went astray.[17] However, recently published evidence suggests very strongly that Longstreet indeed did receive specific orders concerning the time, location, and manner of an attack for July 3. It is found in the differing accounts of the battle written by Col. Edward Porter Alexander, who commanded the reserve artillery battalion of the First Corps. Alexander was one of Longstreet's most trusted subordinates. At Gettysburg, as on other fields of battle, the corps commander gave Alexander almost complete tactical control over the placement of the First Corps artillery because he lacked confidence in James B. Walton, his nominal chief of artillery.

Alexander's battle report stated that he prepared to attack on July 3, without mentioning a precise location. The wording does not preclude the possibility that he anticipated supporting Longstreet's flanking maneuver: "Sleeping on the field that night [July 2], and replacing ammunition, at dawn I again placed the whole battalion in position for an attack upon the enemy's new line."[18]

Writing in the popular *Southern Historical Society Papers* in 1877, Alexander noted that sometime before dawn he received orders "to post the artillery for an assault upon the enemy's position"; only later did he learn that this "was to be led by Pickett's division and directed on Cemetery

**COL. EDWARD PORTER ALEXANDER**
Francis Trevelyan Miller, ed.,
*The Photographic History of the Civil War*, 10 vols. (New York: Review of Reviews, 1911), 5:61

Hill."[19] The fact that Cemetery Hill was only later designated the target suggests Alexander's predawn instructions could have been one part of a larger plan by Longstreet that included a flanking maneuver, and that Alexander was redirected after Lee canceled Longstreet's plan.

Although Alexander's recollections of the war, published in 1907 as *Military Memoirs of a Confederate*, indicated that he expected to attack early on July 3, they also support Longstreet's claim that he received no specific orders from Lee:

> Longstreet received no orders during the night, and the troops required for his attack could not be gotten into their positions before noon. . . . During the night the Washington artillery was brought up and disposed with the rest of Longstreet's guns about the Peach

Orchard, with the intention of resuming the battle in the morning. During the night Longstreet had sent scouts in search of a way by which he might turn the enemy's left and believed he had found one with some promise of success. Soon after sunrise, while Longstreet awaited the arrival of Pickett's division with Dearings' battalion of artillery, intending then to extend his right, Lee joined him and proposed an assault upon the enemy's left centre by Longstreet's divisions.

Longstreet demurred, and, as had occurred on the day before, some time was spent in discussion and examination. Although the opposing lines were in full view and easy range of each other, neither seemed anxious to begin an action.[20]

This account is clearly in line with Longstreet's battle report and memoirs, which Alexander cites in his text, and implies criticism of both Lee and Longstreet for failing to make decisions before the morning of July 3.

In an earlier manuscript version of his memoirs not published until many decades later as *Fighting for the Confederacy*, however, Alexander told a different story concerning the night of July 2:

During the evening I found my way to General Longstreet's bivouac, a little ways in the rear, to ask the news from other quarters & orders for the morning. From elsewhere the news was indefinite, but I was told that we would renew the attack early in the morning. That Pickett's division would arrive and would assault the enemy's line. My impression is the exact point for it was not designated, but I was told it would be to our left of the Peach Orchard. And I was told too to select a place for the Washington Artillery which would come to me at dawn.[21]

The reason for the differences in Alexander's book-length accounts may be simple. Alexander began composing the version now known as *Fighting for the Confederacy* in 1897 while residing temporarily in Nicaragua, where he lacked access to printed sources such as Longstreet's memoirs, published the year before. Apparently relying entirely on memory, Alexander wrote that Pickett was to attack Cemetery Ridge early on July 3. But when Alexander returned to the United States and revised his recollections, he deferred to Longstreet's version and wrote that Pickett was meant to extend Longstreet's right flank rather than his left.[22] It is highly unlikely that Alexander changed his account to cover up or excuse errors on Longstreet's part, for in both *Fighting for the Confederacy* and *Military Memoirs* Alexander's critical analysis of the Confederate war effort spared neither Lee, Longstreet, nor any other former comrade whose actions he believed deserving of criticism. Alexander presumably accepted Longstreet's version of what was intended for July 3 because the latter's position as a corps commander should have provided a fuller understanding of the circumstances.

But what if Alexander's memory was correct? Did Longstreet deliberately modify orders from Lee concerning the time and location for the July 3 attack? One can only speculate, but given Lee's loose command style, such an interpretation is at least plausible. Indeed, Longstreet may have considered such a modification routine.

Lee usually granted his subordinates considerable latitude. Some took advantage of this freedom, while others were perplexed by it, as examples from the Gettysburg campaign itself demonstrate. J. E. B. Stuart discovered enough loopholes in the rather specific instructions he received from both Lee and Longstreet to justify, in his opinion, a ride that took him around much of the Federal army.[23] Ewell, commanding at the corps level for the first time, was uncertain how to interpret orders received from Lee on July 1 to avoid a general engagement yet seize Cemetery Hill "if he found it practicable."[24] One can fault the manner in which Stuart and Ewell exercised discretion, but not their right to do so given the wording of their orders. Nor did Lee alter his command style on the basis of Stuart's or Ewell's performance. Throughout his career, Lee rarely interfered with his subordinates once combat began, nor did he expect a constant flow of reports from them. During the combat on the afternoon of July 2, for instance, Lee sent only one order, although only he had the ability to coordinate attacks by his corps commanders. This prompted Arthur J. L. Fremantle, a British soldier visiting the Confederate army, to observe in his diary, "It is evidently his system to arrange the plan thoroughly with the three corps commanders, and then leave to them the duty of modifying and carrying it out to the best of their abilities."[25] A remark Lee made to Prussian officer Justus Scheibert, another visitor during the Gettysburg campaign, confirmed Fremantle's observation: "'I think and work with all my powers to bring my troops to the right place at the right time,' Lee explained, then 'I leave the matter up to God and the subordinate officers.' To interfere at this stage 'does more harm than good.'"[26]

If Lee's command style resulted in orders to Stuart and Ewell that left room for legitimate (if tragic from a Confederate perspective) interpretation, might not this also have been true of any orders Longstreet received on the night of July 2? Might not Alexander have heard Lee's instructions, which a courier could have conveyed verbally, being discussed by Longstreet's staff officers that night without hearing portions of the orders that left Longstreet room to exercise judgment? Tactical adjustments were in fact routine, and Lee had never faulted Longstreet for exercising his best judgment to defeat the enemy. From their earliest association, Lee referred to Longstreet as the staff of his right hand.[27] In his report of the battle of Second Manassas, Lee wrote favorably of the fact that Longstreet anticipated his wishes and ordered an attack on his own initiative. Following the battle of Fredericksburg, Lee praised Longstreet's "quick perception" that allowed him to "discover the projected assaults" of the enemy and the "ready skill" he used "to devise the best means to resist them." He also expressed his indebtedness to Longstreet for "valuable counsel, both as regards the general operations of the army and the execution of the particular measures adopted."[28]

This does not mean that Lee never interfered with Longstreet's tactical arrangements. On the morning of July 2, he ordered McLaws to align his attack perpendicular to the Emmitsburg Road, directly overruling Longstreet's orders to McLaws for a slightly different angle.[29] But this is a rare example. As historian Jay Luvaas notes in a recent study of Lee's generalship, "Lee's theory of command and his conduct at Gettysburg suggest that he felt more comfortable at the operational than the tactical level."[30] When one considers the weight of testimony regarding Lee's absolute trust and confidence in Longstreet,[31] it is not unreasonable to speculate that when instructed to attack on July 3, Longstreet felt free to maneuver around Little Round Top rather than assault Cemetery Ridge. Longstreet himself implied this in a letter he wrote concerning Gettysburg to Lafayette McLaws in 1873. Regarding Lee's command style, he noted that while his chief would indicate what he wanted to accomplish, Lee never "on any occasion order[ed] me to attack, naming the hour, or designating the mode of attack. I believe he invariably left these things to Jackson and myself."[32]

Despite this, there is no foundation for Longstreet's claim that Lee sent no instructions. In light of Alexander's recollections, one may conclude that in some fashion Lee conveyed in rather explicit detail what he wanted the First Corps to accomplish on the morning of July 3. Longstreet's postwar denial of receiving orders represents either false memory or a self-serving splitting of hairs over the difference between verbal and written communications.

Nevertheless, Longstreet's flanking maneuver may be considered "authorized," at least in the sense that Longstreet probably considered modification of Lee's instructions routine, given their command relationship, and justified, given the tactical obstacles his troops faced. If in retrospect such an assumption by Longstreet retarded rather than advanced the chances for Confederate victory, responsibility must rest in some small part on Lee for encouraging such independent action on the part of his subordinates. Moreover, one must avoid the double standard implicit in criticizing Ewell for his failure to take initiative and responsibility on the afternoon of July 1 while faulting Longstreet for showing initiative during the night of July 2 and the morning of July 3.

Did Longstreet's initiative actually spoil Lee's First Plan, thereby "causing" the fatal Pickett's Charge? What were Lee's options after he canceled Longstreet's orders for a flanking maneuver? Lee was, after all, not compelled to accept Longstreet's judgment that the Federal positions on the Round Tops would endanger an assault upon Cemetery Ridge by McLaws, Hood, and Pickett. As Longstreet had yet to move a single unit to his right, Lee could have ordered him to attack immediately from the positions his troops then held. That would have constituted attacking very nearly simultaneously with Ewell.[33]

Was Lee truly compelled to scrap his First Plan? Consideration of this issue reveals Longstreet's great failing in connection with the third day at Gettysburg. Although Pickett reached the battlefield late on July 2, his men arrived on the right flank no earlier than 9:00 A.M. the next day, almost four hours after daylight. The personnel within Pickett's command recorded various times of arrival, but 9:00 A.M. represents the earliest reasonable estimate. It may have been even later. Incredibly, Longstreet failed during the night to order the division into a position where it would be ready at dawn to support either an attack on Cemetery Ridge, a movement around Little Round Top to attack the Federal rear, or, for that matter, a strategic maneuver to force Meade to do the costly attacking. This oversight remains inexplicable. Remarkably, Jubal Early and the Lee cult never focused on this issue, and modern historians of Gettysburg give it scant attention.[34] Yet Longstreet's failure to have Pickett on hand by dawn, or at least very early morning, provides the only logical explanation for Lee's decision to abandon his First Plan. Had Pickett been available for immediate support, from any direction, Lee could have ordered McLaws and Hood to attack from their present positions in order to give Ewell's assault at least a chance of success.

As neither Longstreet nor Lee mentioned the lateness of Pickett's arrival, and Pickett's own report has not survived, the reason for this critical oversight remains unknown. Longstreet may have assumed that Pickett would receive orders directly from Lee; but Pickett was Longstreet's responsibility, and no explanation can absolve him entirely of culpability for this error.

Given the vast attention accorded the battle of Gettysburg, it is sobering to realize that information on key issues such as Confederate direction of the battle on the night of July 2 and the morning of July 3 is limited to a few pages of sketchy and conflicting evidence. Historians consequently make broad assumptions concerning the Confederate commander and his principal subordinate. Clearly, however, Longstreet and Lee were at cross purposes. Writers of the Freeman school assume, without a shred of primary evidence, that this conflict was an outgrowth of the diabolical Longstreet's attempt to force his will on the Christlike Robert E. Lee. It is more logical to assume that it grew out of human error, tragic oversights, the fog of war, and Lee's command style, which routinely delegated important decisions to subordinates. Far from absolving Longstreet entirely from criticism, this interpretation (and all analysis of Gettysburg, one must remember, is interpretative) holds Longstreet responsible for a shocking mishandling of Pickett's division.

Even so, Longstreet's actions on the morning of July 3 hardly caused the Confederate defeat at Gettysburg, nor was Lee's cancellation of his flanking maneuver the key to Confederate failure. In his excellent analysis of the battle, Coddington concludes that Longstreet's flank attack around the Round Tops would have failed.[35] This is speculation, but it is intelligent speculation. Moreover, the fact remains that Lee's First Plan was a monumentally bad one, almost as certainly doomed to failure as Pickett's Charge, which replaced it. In ordering Longstreet to use all three of his divisions to attack Cemetery Ridge, leaving the Round Tops on his right flank, Lee displayed his continued ignorance of the strength and position of the Federal army. Longstreet may have contributed to that ignorance when he chose not to report to Lee in person on the night of July 2. In any case, it is no wonder that once Lee arrived on the scene and had a clearer appreciation for the strength of the Federal positions, he heeded Longstreet's advice to leave McLaws and Hood in place where they could cover the flank.[36] But instead of attacking the northern end of Cemetery Ridge, where the angle of the Federal lines would have minimized their defensive firepower, particularly that of their artillery, Lee sent the flower of his army directly into a shooting gallery at the Federal center.[37]

Reflecting on Gettysburg in 1901, Porter Alexander wrote a friend: "Never, never, never did Gen. Lee himself bollox [sic] a fight as he did this."[38] Responsibility for the Confederate failure in Pennsylvania rests on Lee's shoulders, not those of James Longstreet, but Longstreet's errors certainly contributed to that failure. Why, then, did Jubal Early and his followers not exploit these significant shortcomings on Longstreet's part during their long campaign to blame him for the Confederate defeat at Gettysburg? Apparently nothing but chance prevented their doing so.

The history of the Lee cult has been well-documented by Thomas Lawrence Connelly and other historians.[39] It will suffice to note here that there existed within it a core group whose actions reflected much more than a fanatical devotion to Lee's memory. They formed a distinct anti-Longstreet faction and worked together over a long period of time to destroy Longstreet's military reputation. The inner circle consisted of Early and five of Lee's staff officers—William Nelson Pendleton, A. L. Long, Charles Venable, Walter H. Taylor, and Charles Marshall. A brief review of their complex postwar controversy with Longstreet underscores the fact that while they had a common target, their motives differed. Although Early coordinated their efforts, much of what occurred took place within a pattern of action and reaction. Thus by happenstance rather than plan, the events of July 2 became so controversial that the question of Lee's original plans for the morning of July 3 simply received little attention.

In 1872, two years after Lee's death, Early delivered an address at Washington and Lee University in which he claimed that Lee had intended for Longstreet to attack at dawn on July 2 at Gettysburg. Longstreet's failure to do so, Early claimed, cost Lee the battle and the South its independence. In a similar address the following year, Pendleton, Lee's former chief of artillery, repeated the same charges, accusing Longstreet of willfully betraying the Confederate cause. These accusations were entirely false. As a divisional commander at Gettysburg, Early was hardly privy to Lee's strategy, and his assertions were barefaced lies. Pendleton's own battle report actually proved that Lee was still formulating his strategy on the morning of July 2, but truth obviously did not stand in Pendleton's way. His veneration of Lee and detestation of Longstreet bordered on mental instability.

When the Civil War ended, Early and Pendleton were generally viewed as failures. In Early's case, such judgment was partially—perhaps largely—unfair, but public opinion can be fickle. With a creditable record as a brigade and division commander, Early became heir to Stonewall Jackson's command in 1864 and boldly led his troops to the outskirts of Washington, D.C. But he was solidly defeated by Philip Sheridan's army at Third Winchester, Fisher's Hill, and Cedar Creek. Numerical inferiority explained much of Early's misfortune, yet he was more harshly condemned by the southern press than any other officer since the early campaigns of the war. Moreover, historian Jeffry Wert identifies a consensus in Early's Army of the Valley after Cedar Creek "that their commander's actions doomed the army."[40]

Pendleton was not well known outside the Army of Northern Virginia. Thoroughly dedicated, he was nevertheless unequal to his role as director

**BRIG. GEN. WILLIAM NELSON PENDLETON**
Robert Underwood Johnson and Clarence Clough Buel, eds., *Battles and Leaders of the Civil War*, 4 vols. (New York: Century, 1887), 3:329

of Lee's long arm. One Confederate officer remarked, "Pendleton is Lee's weakness. [He] is like the elephant, we have him & we don't know what on earth to do with him, and it costs a devil of a sight to feed him." Lee never replaced Pendleton, but his role degenerated into that of a figurehead.[41]

Following their speeches at Washington and Lee, Early and Pendleton became increasingly involved in the affairs of Confederate veterans. They apparently sought to win in peacetime, as defenders of Lee, the reputations that had eluded them during the war. By blaming Longstreet for the Confederacy's failure to win independence, they drew attention away from their own shortcomings. Longstreet was a convenient (and, to their minds, appropriate) scapegoat because after the war he had become a "scalawag," a native white southerner who supported the Republican party during Reconstruction.[42]

Early and Pendleton undertook a variety of projects to memorialize Lee. To raise money, they hired agents to tour the South and give fundraising speeches that blamed Longstreet for losing the battle of Gettysburg, thus freeing Lee from the stigma of defeat. Longstreet's heretical affiliation with the political party credited with freeing the slaves made him a traitor to the white race in the eyes of most of his fellow southerners. Under these circumstances, few questioned either the motives or the historical accuracy of Early and Pendleton's work. Moreover, as southerners embraced this temptingly simplistic explanation for their costly failure, Lee's reputation was magnified to Christlike proportion. Many took solace in their defeat by defending it with cultlike devotion.[43]

For Early and Pendleton, the worship of Lee seems to have given meaning to otherwise empty lives, but Long, Venable, Taylor, and Marshall were not so base in their motivations. They, too, detested Longstreet's postwar politics, but they knew Lee never intended to attack at dawn on July 2. At Longstreet's request, all four provided letters for publication attesting to that fact. Venable even questioned Pendleton's mental health.[44]

Longstreet, however, did not defend his reputation in a subtle fashion. Angered at being frozen out of the circle of Confederate heroes because of his political affiliation, he was not content with publishing the letters from Lee's staff. During the late 1870s and throughout the 1880s, he wrote articles for newspapers and magazines in which he shamelessly exaggerated his own accomplishments and suggested that he had been the brains behind Lee. Horrified by this arrogant presumption, Long, Venable, Taylor, and Marshall soon agreed among themselves that Longstreet had been "fatally late" at Gettysburg, a conveniently vague assertion that allowed them to join forces with Early and assist in destroying Longstreet's reputation. Early welcomed them, despite the fact that the printing of their letters to Longstreet concerning the dawn attack had publicly labeled him a liar. He could hardly do otherwise, as he gained inestimable credibility from their support. With their help, Early became through his publications and prolific private correspondence the dominant force in shaping the way southerners wrote about Lee, Longstreet, and the war.[45] Early took great pains to avoid multicausal explanations of the Confederate defeat at Gettysburg. Through numerous articles, and a private correspondence of astonishing proportions, he reiterated again and again that Longstreet's "betrayal" on July 2 alone explained the South's failure.[46]

Lee's staff officers were remarkably deferential to Early and strayed from his central theme only in relation to Pickett's Charge.[47] Long, Venable, and Taylor insisted that Lee had intended the divisions of McLaws and Hood to advance simultaneously with Pickett's men and that Longstreet's failure to order them forward explained the repulse on July 3. They were unable to produce any documents to support this claim, which ran contrary to Lee's own report. In perhaps the best analysis of this issue, Freeman concludes that Lee's staff officers were either not present with Lee on the

**WILLIAM GARRETT PISTON**

50

morning of July 3 when he gave Longstreet permission to retain McLaws and Hood in place, or failed to hear their entire conversation.[48]

Freeman is probably correct. Longstreet himself admitted that Lee overruled his plans for the morning of July 3 with some emotion.[49] Had Pendleton, Venable, Long, Taylor, or Marshall been privy to Lee's remarks, they certainly would have used them against Longstreet during the postwar controversy. This might have shifted the focus from July 2 to July 3, where Longstreet was actually much more vulnerable to legitimate criticism.

But that did not happen. Longstreet went to his grave defending himself against accusations of tardiness on July 2 and misconduct on July 3 at Gettysburg. Ironically, the falsehoods propagated by his enemies have drawn the attention of historians away from those portions of his conduct on July 2 and July 3 where criticism *is* valid. Any understanding of the Confederate failure in Pennsylvania must confront the confusion that resulted when Lee and his most trusted subordinate worked at cross purposes rather than in harmony toward the common goal of southern victory each man held so dear.

### NOTES

1. Edwin B. Coddington, *The Gettysburg Campaign: A Study in Command* (New York: Charles Scribner's Sons, 1968); Douglas Southall Freeman, *R. E. Lee: A Biography*, 4 vols. (New York: Charles Scribner's Sons, 1934–35), and *Lee's Lieutenants: A Study in Command*, 3 vols. (New York: Charles Scribner's Sons, 1942–44).

2. The three parts of volume 27 of U.S. War Department, *The War of the Rebellion: A Compilation of the Official Records of the Union and Confederate Armies*, 127 vols., index, and atlas (Washington, D.C.: GPO, 1880–1901) (hereafter cited as *OR*; all references are to series 1) contain reports and correspondence pertinent to Gettysburg.

3. *OR* 27(2):298.

4. *OR* 27(2):308.

5. Charles Marshall, *An Aide-de-Camp of Lee; Being the Papers of Colonel Charles Marshall, Sometime Aide-de-Camp, Military Secretary, and Assistant Adjutant General on the Staff of Robert E. Lee, 1862–1865*, ed. Maj. Gen. Sir Frederick Maurice (Boston: Little, Brown, 1927), 179–80.

6. *OR* 27(2):320.

7. *OR* 27(2):318; Coddington, *Gettysburg Campaign*, 374–75.

8. *OR* 27(2):359.

9. Longstreet himself is the only source for this information, but it has been accepted by even his strongest detractors. See James Longstreet, "Lee in Pennsylvania," in *The Annals of the War, Written by Leading Participants North and South* (Philadelphia: Times, 1879), 429; James Longstreet, *From Manassas to Appomattox: Memoirs of the Civil War in America* (Philadelphia: J. B. Lippincott, 1896), 385; Freeman, *R. E. Lee*, 3:105–6.

10. *OR* 27(2):358.

11. For information on Pickett's missing report, see Glenn Tucker, *Lee and Longstreet at Gettysburg* (Indianapolis: Bobbs-Merrill, 1968), 152–54.

12. *OR* 27(2):366–439.

13. Longstreet, "Lee in Pennsylvania," 429.

14. James Longstreet, "Lee's Right Wing at Gettysburg," in *Battles and Leaders of the Civil War*, ed. Robert Underwood Johnson and Clarence C. Buel, 4 vols. (New York: Century, 1887–88), 3:342; Longstreet, *From Manassas to Appomattox*, 385–86.

15. For an analysis of Longstreet's postwar writings, see William Garrett Piston, *Lee's Tarnished Lieutenant: James Longstreet and His Place in Southern History* (Athens: University of Georgia Press, 1987), 137–50, 152–56.

16. Frank E. Everett, Jr., ed., "Delayed Report of an Important Eyewitness to Gettysburg—Benjamin G. Humphreys," *Journal of Mississippi History* 46 (November 1984): 313.

17. The earliest record of Longstreet's claim that he received no orders occurs in a letter he wrote to McLaws in 1873 defending himself against attacks by Early and Pendleton. In it Longstreet presented hindsight as foresight, stating, for example, that he intended on July 3 to seize the Taneytown Road and force Meade to attack him while Lee shifted the rest of the Confederate army south to a position between the Army of the Potomac and Washington. Significantly, Longstreet made no such wild claims in print. See James Longstreet to Lafayette McLaws, July 25, 1873, Lafayette McLaws Papers, Southern Historical Collection, Wilson Library, University of North Carolina, Chapel Hill (hereafter cited as SHC).

18. *OR* 27(2):430.

19. Edward Porter Alexander, "Letter from General E. P. Alexander, late Chief of Artillery First Corps, A.N.V.," in *Southern Historical Society Papers*, 52 vols. and 2-vol. index, ed. J. William Jones and others (1876–1959; reprint, Wilmington, N.C.: Broadfoot, 1990–92), 4:102–3 (hereafter cited as *SHSP*).

20. Edward Porter Alexander, *Military Memoirs of a Confederate: A Critical Narrative* (New York: Charles Scribner's Sons, 1907), 415.

21. Edward Porter Alexander, *Fighting for the Confederacy: The Personal Recollections of General Edward Porter Alexander*, ed. Gary W. Gallagher (Chapel Hill: University of North Carolina Press, 1989), 244. Coddington and other historians have utilized bits and pieces of Alexander's first draft memoirs without fully realizing what they were. Without the context supplied by Gallagher's editing, differences in Alexander's versions of events have been difficult to reconcile—especially in relation to Gettysburg.

22. For details of Alexander's composition, see Gallagher's introduction in ibid., xv–xx.

23. Emory M. Thomas, *Bold Dragoon: The Life of J. E. B. Stuart* (New York: Harper & Row, 1986), 239–41, 252–56.

24. *OR* 27(2):318, 445.

25. Arthur J. L. Fremantle, *Three Months in the Southern States: April–June, 1863* (1863; reprint, Lincoln: University of Nebraska Press, 1991), 260. Lee informed Davis that poor health prevented his exercising closer supervision: "I am so dull that in making use of the eyes of others I am frequently misled." In fact, Lee had followed a loose style of command before his health declined. See R. E. Lee, *The Wartime Papers of R. E. Lee*, ed. Clifford Dowdey and Louis H. Manarin (Boston: Little, Brown, 1961), 590.

26. Quoted in Jay Luvaas, "Lee and the Operational Art: The Right Place, The Right Time," *Parameters* 22 (Autumn 1992): 2.

27. T. J. Goree to S. W. Goree, July 21, 1862, Thomas J. Goree Papers, Louisiana State University, Baton Rouge, La.

28. *OR* 12(2):557, 21:556. In the passages quoted, Lee's praise applied to both Longstreet and Jackson.

29. Because of terrain features and the unexpected advance of part of Meade's army into the Peach Orchard and Wheatfield, McLaws actually attacked at an angle closer to Longstreet's intention than to Lee's; however, even Longstreet's bitterest critics found no fault with him in this connection. See Tucker, *Lee and Longstreet*, 20; Lafayette McLaws, "Gettysburg," in *SHSP*, 7:68.

30. Luvaas, "Lee and the Operational Art," 7.

31. For a discussion of Lee's relationship with Longstreet, see Piston, *Lee's Tarnished Lieutenant*, 22–23, 26–28, 30, 38–39, 64–65, 91–92, 99–100.

32. James Longstreet to Lafayette McLaws, July 25, 1873, McLaws Papers, SHC.

33. In military terms, Longstreet's and Ewell's attacks should be considered simultaneous if they began closely enough together to prevent the shifting of forces from either flank of the Federal army to reinforce the other. Contemporary reports, written at a time of unreliable watches that were never synchronized,

indicate only that Ewell's attack began around dawn and that Lee reached Longstreet shortly after dawn. See Coddington, *Gettysburg Campaign*, 455. Freeman argues that Lee "probably reasoned that if Longstreet did not have faith in the plan it would be worse than dangerous to entrust the assault to his troops alone" and thus adopted the measures that led to Pickett's Charge. See Freeman, *R. E. Lee*, 3:108. If Freeman's analysis is correct, one must question Lee's fitness to command an army. It is difficult to imagine Grant, Sherman, Napoleon, or MacArthur, for example, reaching such a conclusion, but it fits Freeman's thesis that Lee's only flaw was excessive gentility.

34. The best discussions of this issue are in Coddington, *Gettysburg Campaign*, 458; Freeman, *Lee's Lieutenants*, 3:146; and George R. Stewart, *Pickett's Charge: A Microhistory of the Final Attack at Gettysburg, July 3, 1863* (Boston: Houghton Mifflin, 1957), 4–7, 29–30.

35. Coddington, *Gettysburg Campaign*, 547.

36. Whether Longstreet used McLaws and Hood in a way that gave Pickett adequate support is not the question here. Longstreet's advice to Lee was sound.

37. Alexander, *Fighting for the Confederacy*, 252.

38. Edward Porter Alexander to Thomas L. Rosser, April 19, 1901, Thomas L. Rosser Papers, Alderman Library, University of Virginia, Charlottesville, Va.

39. See Thomas Lawrence Connelly, *The Marble Man: Robert E. Lee and His Image in American Society* (New York: Alfred A. Knopf, 1977); Piston, *Lee's Tarnished Lieutenant*; Marshall William Fishwick, *Virginians on Olympus: A Cultural Analysis of Four Great Men* (Richmond, Va.: N.p., 1951); Rollin G. Osterweis, *The Myth of the Lost Cause, 1865–1900* (New York: Archon, 1973); Charles Reagan Wilson, *Baptized in Blood: The Religion of the Lost Cause, 1865–1920* (Athens: University of Georgia Press, 1980); Gaines M. Foster, *Ghosts of the Confederacy: Defeat, the Lost Cause, and the Emergence of the New South* (New York: Oxford University Press, 1987); and Alan T. Nolan, *Lee Considered: General Robert E. Lee and Civil War History* (Chapel Hill: University of North Carolina Press, 1991).

40. Jeffry D. Wert, *From Winchester to Cedar Creek: The Shenandoah Campaign of 1864* (Carlisle, Pa.: South Mountain Press, 1987), 137, 244.

41. John Hampden Chamberlayne, *Ham Chamberlayne—Virginian: Letters and Papers of an Artillery Officer in the War for Southern Independence, 1861–1865*, ed. C. G. Chamberlayne (Richmond, Va.: Dietz, 1932), 134.

42. For a discussion of the actions and motives of Early and Pendleton, see Piston, *Lee's Tarnished Lieutenant*, 118–23.

43. For details on the Lee cult and its astonishing success, see Connelly, *Marble Man*, 27–98.

44. Walter H. Taylor to James Longstreet, April 28, 1875; Charles Marshall

to James Longstreet, May 7, 1875; A. L. Long to James Longstreet, May 31, 1875; C. S. Venable to James Longstreet, n.d., James Longstreet Papers, Emory University, Atlanta, Ga.

45. Piston, *Lee's Tarnished Lieutenant*, 127–31, 133–35, 171; Connelly, *Marble Man*, 73–76, 85–90.

46. A classic example was Early's manipulation of the "Gettysburg series" in the *SHSP*. See Piston, *Lee's Tarnished Lieutenant*, 133–35.

47. See, for example, C. S. Venable to Early, March 13, 1876; A. L. Long to Early, March 12, 1876; Charles Marshall to Early, April 10, 1876, May 24, 1877, March 13, 1878; Walter H. Taylor to Early, May 5, 1876, November 9, 1877, March 12, 1878, Jubal A. Early Papers, Library of Congress, Washington, D.C.

48. Piston, *Lee's Tarnished Lieutenant*, 130; Freeman, *R. E. Lee*, 3:108 n. 4.

49. James Longstreet to Lafayette McLaws, July 25, 1873, McLaws Papers, SHC.

*The Convergence*

*of History and Myth in*

*the Southern Past*

## PICKETT'S CHARGE

*Carol Reardon*

"Longstreet's assault on the third day at Gettysburg . . . has been more
written about . . . than any event in American history. Some of these
accounts are simply silly. Some are false in statement. Some are false in
inference. All in some respects are untrue."[1] So complained one frustrated
southerner in 1888 about the mass of exaggerations, charges, counter-
charges, and outright lies in the historical record concerning an infantry
attack that had become best known as Pickett's Charge. Such dismay is
understandable. During the fifty years between Appomattox and World
War I, the events of a few hours on the afternoon of July 3, 1863, at
Gettysburg became ensnared in a sticky web of selective memory and state
loyalties, charismatic personalities and personal feuds, and the emotional
pull of either the Lost Cause or the cause of national reunion. Indeed,
especially for southerners, memories of Pickett's Charge could express
themselves in wonderfully chameleonlike ways, taking on innumerable
shadings and nuances depending on who told the story and why. In less
than one half-century, Pickett's Charge became both historical event and
emotional touchstone—history and memory—with the demarcation between the two often imperceptible. How and why did this happen? What
insights can Civil War scholars and enthusiasts draw from it more than a
century later?

The historical record provides a solid foundation of indisputable facts.
The original cast of players in this dramatic event is well known, as are

the units and commanders around whom future controversy would swirl. Maj. Gen. George E. Pickett's fresh division of James Longstreet's First Corps, about 4,500 strong, included three veteran brigades, each containing five regiments of Virginia infantry and led by combat-tested brigadiers Richard B. Garnett, Lewis A. Armistead, and James L. Kemper. Pickett's division as constituted at Gettysburg was the only unit of its size in Robert E. Lee's Army of Northern Virginia composed of troops from a single state, a fact of great importance in years to come. Assigned to support Pickett's right flank were Brig. Gen. Cadmus M. Wilcox's Alabamians and three small regiments of Florida infantry under Col. David Lang.

On Pickett's left flank was the division of Maj. Gen. Henry Heth of A. P. Hill's Third Corps. Heth's men had suffered heavy losses opening the battle on July 1; the number of soldiers in the ranks on July 3 wearing bloodied bandages suggested that many of the lightly wounded had been ordered to return to the front. Heth himself had been wounded in the first day's fight, and on July 3, Brig. Gen. J. Johnston Pettigrew was entering only his second day in divisional command. Pettigrew's troops included his own North Carolina brigade, temporarily commanded by Col. J. K. Marshall; Brig. Gen. James J. Archer's brigade of Alabamians and Tennesseans, with Col. B. D. Fry replacing his captured superior; Brig. Gen. Joseph R. Davis's Mississippians and North Carolinians; and Col. J. M. Brockenbrough's small brigade of Virginians. Two North Carolina brigades from Maj. Gen. W. Dorsey Pender's division supported Pettigrew's troops—Alfred Scales's and James Lane's Tarheels under the temporary command of Maj. Gen. Isaac R. Trimble.[2]

Beyond these facts, the historical record reveals little more of which modern students can be certain. Although the total number of soldiers in the attack is unknown, recent scholarship estimates a force numbering between 12,000 and 13,000.[3] Nor is there general agreement on when the preassault bombardment started, how long it lasted, or what time the charge began. For a pivotal moment in military history replete with eyewitnesses, consensus on many aspects of the afternoon's events is surprisingly difficult to reach. An amazingly muddied historical record produces a "fog of war" that promotes an easy blending of legend, myth, and memory.

Certain enduring elements in the story of Pickett's Charge took shape even before Lee's defeated army had recrossed the Potomac. Perhaps because Lee's men knew so little of defeat, the search to explain their reversal of fortune spawned much army gossip. Some viewed the loss as merely

**MAJ. GEN. GEORGE EDWARD PICKETT**
Francis Trevelyan Miller, ed., *The Photographic History of the Civil War*, 10 vols. (New York: Review of Reviews, 1911), 9:215

a fluke. North Carolinian William H. Proffitt, for example, wrote home only that "the fight commenced on the 1st day of July and continued three days when it ceased without either army being routed or driven back. The enemy secured an elevated position and fortified it well which saved them from their usual fate."[4]

Many more of Lee's men, however, seemingly unwilling to credit the Union army with putting up a good fight, looked within their own ranks for a scapegoat on whom to pin the defeat. Even while the Army of Northern Virginia remained north of the Potomac, culprits had been identified. Jedediah Hotchkiss, the great mapmaker, confided to his diary that "we drove the enemy from their works, but our supports were not near enough and the enemy rallied and regained them. Pickett's div. took the hill on the right, but Pettigrew failed to sustain him." Pvt. William Henry Cocke of the 9th Virginia, a survivor of the charge, was more pointed: "Our division charged the enemies breastworks on the heights and suffered severely—the troops which should have supported us failing to do so and running like sheep—thanks to Gracious they were NOT Va. troops."[5]

Similar themes could be found in the diaries and letters of soldiers who were not from Virginia. In the entry for July 3 in his diary, James J. Kirkpatrick of the 16th Mississippi wrote, "Very soon our infantry made their appearance, coming forward to storm the crest. They make a very feeble effort and accomplish nothing. The troops in the movement were mostly North Carolinians." "The distance they had to traverse was nearly a mile,"

BRIG. GEN. JAMES
JOHNSTON PETTIGREW
Robert Underwood Johnson
and Clarence Clough Buel,
eds., *Battles and Leaders of the
Civil War*, 4 vols. (New York:
Century, 1887), 3:429

concluded Kirkpatrick, "there was no intermediate sheltered point to rally at, and the sun's heat was intolerable, is the only excuse that can be plead in their behalf."

Lt. William Calder of the 2nd North Carolina expressed similar sentiments, noting that the assault "was the finest charge of the war and had Pickett's division been supported we could have held the field but Heth's division failing to come up as it should have done they were forced to retire."[6]

The Richmond press reacted to this mass of gossip, accusation, and innuendo amid great confusion in the Confederate capital. Early reports of the battle in Pennsylvania, mostly extracts from pirated copies of New York, Philadelphia, and Baltimore papers about the first day's fight, seemed to promise yet another victory for southern arms.

As early as the evening of July 6, however, although still carrying joyous tidings of victory, the editors of Richmond's five major newspapers began hearing a contradictory story. Wounded men returning from Pennsylvania reported that Pickett's Virginia division had met with disaster three days earlier. Knowing well that many of the families of Pickett's men got their war news from the Richmond papers and that they would demand every shred of information about their kinsmen's fate, editors rushed re-

**MAJ. GEN. ISAAC RIDGEWAY TRIMBLE**
Francis Trevelyan Miller, ed., *The Photographic History of the Civil War*, 10 vols. (New York: Review of Reviews, 1911), 10:104

porters to Winchester, the northernmost point on the telegraph line, to find out what they could. The reports were slow to emerge and confusing at best. Exaggerated claims about great hordes of Union prisoners and wild rumors of many generals killed in both armies mingled with disquieting and increasingly numerous snippets of information about the "reversed Fredericksburg" that Pickett's men had endured.[7]

For nearly two weeks, the dismal story unfolded in bits and pieces of varying accuracy. Among the early reports of the action on July 3, a fanciful description of Confederate victory recalled the ancient battle of Cannae: the fight "was the bloodiest of the war. A. P. Hill fell back in the center which caused the enemy to believe he was retreating. The enemy advanced and the right and left wings of Lee's army surrounded them and took the heights for which we have been contending, capturing 40,000 prisoners, who refused parole. General Pickett's division is now guarding them."[8] The Richmond *Dispatch* exaggerated the charge across less than a mile of open ground this way: "On Friday . . . Longstreet's Corps and 2 divisions of General A. P. Hill's Corps . . . drove the enemy back five miles to the heights which he had fortified. In driving them this five miles we broke through two of their lines of battle formed to receive the onset of our troops and finally charged them to the heights. . . . The charge resulted in repulse but nothing else." Still other accounts gave in to emotion: "Pickett's division . . . commence steadily and in beautiful line to march upon the fatal spot. . . . Our noble boys charge on through shot and shell; their ranks melting away as they advance under the murderous artillery fire of the enemy. . . . Surely none can escape. All must perish before such a murderous volley. What an awful moment."[9]

No detail was too small for Richmond editors to print. Stories of personal heroics were sure to attract readers. Amelia County's Sgt. Leigh Blanton of the 1st Virginia won accolades for rescuing the wounded General Kemper from capture. Maj. Kirkwood Otey of the 11th Virginia offered a stirring eyewitness account along with his unit's casualty list. Armistead's brigade "moved to the charge with regularity and conduct equal to that on dress parade." Indeed, "the heroism of the whole division . . . is beyond praise," and the "celebrated 'charge of the 600' at Balaclava was not more daring and not less entitled to live in history than that of the 5000 Virginians who stormed the heights at Gettysburg." Of his division commander, Otey asserted that "Major General Pickett showed himself fully worthy of the occasion and of the men he commanded. He and his staff were, happily, unhurt."[10]

Friends and families of the many Virginians who did not come through unscathed grew impatient awaiting an explanation for the sacrifice and massacre of Pickett's men. Readers quickly became disillusioned by the incomplete, confusing, and contradictory reporting. One disgruntled Virginian wrote to his nephew that "lying is contagious as well as smallpox, and our editors have caught the disease."[11] One correspondent, "Unus," articulated the concerns of many Virginians when he mused:

> How sad to think that after men have done all that men could possibly do by their valor, won for themselves an immortal name, that some mismanagement should rob them and their country of the fruits of their heroic deeds. Yet their country must ever be grateful to the heroes who there so nobly illustrated Southern valor. And the gallant dead! what pen can do them justice? can express in language

sufficiently mournful the agony and the grief that now brood around many a hearthstone in Virginia. . . . There is fault to be attached to someone; let our high officers, the proper ones, say to whom.[12]

Neither the government nor the army held a formal inquiry into the conduct of the assault, but that did not deter the press from reaching its own conclusions. On July 23, war correspondent Jonathan Albertson's full account of the assault on July 3—the first such comprehensive report—appeared in the Richmond *Enquirer*. Albertson offered convincing answers to the most pressing questions:

> I have never since the war began (and I have been in all the great fights of this army) seen troops enter a fight in such splendid order as did this splendid division of Pickett's. Now Pettigrew's command emerge from the woods upon Pickett's left. . . . I saw by the wavering of this line as they entered the conflict that they wanted the firmness of nerve, and steadiness of tread which so characterized Pickett's men, and I felt that these men would not, could not stand the tremendous ordeal to which they would soon be subjected. These were mostly raw troops . . . who certainly had never been in any severe fight—and I trembled for their conduct. . . . But on press Pickett's brave Virginians[;] . . . they storm the stone fence; the Yankees fly. . . . I see Kemper and Armistead plant their banner in the enemy's works; I hear the glad shout of victory. Let us now look after Pettigrew's division. Where are they now? There, all over the plain, in utmost confusion, is scattered this strong division. Their line is broken; they are flying apparently panic stricken to the rear . . . and Pickett is left alone to contend with the hordes of the enemy now pouring in upon him from every side.[13]

Albertson's sharp indictments rang with authority, and following journalistic practices of the time, papers all through Virginia and the Carolinas lacking their own correspondents with the army reprinted his article widely in the next few weeks. The account provided a durable skeleton for the version of Pickett's Charge embraced by most Virginians after 1863. Unfortunately, not all of Albertson's claims were accurate. His assertion that Pettigrew's division consisted of green troops was patently false. While a few of its regiments had served considerable time along the North Carolina coast and experienced little combat until the Pennsylvania campaign, many more of Pettigrew's men, such as the Tennesseans, had served in every major campaign since 1861.[14] The reporter's inference that Pettigrew's troops were Pickett's missing supports was also incorrect. The after-action reports of both Lee and Longstreet make clear that these troops formed an integral part of the assaulting force.[15] Moreover, Albertson's accusation that the retreat of Pettigrew's men—and that alone—made it impossible for Pickett's troops to take advantage of their breakthrough cannot be proved.

As with most first impressions, these images proved difficult to erase. Other newspaper narratives of the charge would follow, some even longer and, as time would reveal, far closer to what modern scholars of the battle perceive to be the truth. Peter W. Alexander of Savannah probably wrote the best of all, but because his work appeared primarily in papers in Georgia, South Carolina, and Louisiana—states with no troops in the assault and civilians distracted by news from Vicksburg and Charleston—it was soon forgotten.[16]

In the Richmond papers, if anyone cared to notice, survivors of the charge from regiments other than those in Pickett's division tried to remind readers of their parts in the great attack of July 3. Col. David Lang, upset that press accounts omitted the Florida troops who lost nearly two-thirds of their numbers at Gettysburg, sought to right the record: "The men I have the honor to command . . . fight, not for vain dreams of glory, nor yet for newspaper fame, or notoriety, but they are unwilling to stand by in silence and see their deeds go misrepresented to posterity, as to cause their children to blush for shame when they read of them in days to come. All we ask of those who record history, while we make it, is simply justice. Give us this, and we ask no more."[17] The surviving officers of the Tennessee brigade from Pettigrew's division also expressed displeasure over recent press coverage of their actions in the charge.[18]

Most concerned, however, were the North Carolinians of Pettigrew's command, who bristled at the increasingly pointed accusations that they deserved the bulk of the blame for the failure of the assault. The Richmond press had criticized, slighted, or entirely ignored the contributions of Tarheel troops in earlier campaigns, and even as Lee had marched north to Pennsylvania, North Carolina's Governor Zebulon Vance had petitioned the Confederate War Department for permission to send along a correspondent to focus on his state's many units in the Army of Northern Virginia. Permission had been denied, and after the battle, a frustrated Lt.

W. B. Taylor of the 11th North Carolina was only one of many to strike a common chord: "It is said that Pettigrew's brigade ran on the 3rd day at Gettysburg but it is false."[19]

Maj. John T. Jones of the 26th North Carolina, in a letter of condolence to his dead regimental commander's father, expressed astonishment at the differences between the newspaper coverage and his own recollections of the fight. After closing to the right toward Pickett's own troops, he recalled that "At the very moment I thought victory ours, I saw it snatched from our hands." When the order came to fall back, "We did so at the same time with Pickett. The day was lost. You must observe I do not attach any blame to Pickett. I think he did his duty, and if he did, we certainly did ours, because I know we went as far as he did, and I can safely assert some distance beyond, owing to the shape of the enemy works, which ran backwards in our front in the form of a curve, and which compelled us to go beyond where Pickett's men were already at their works in order to reach them ourselves. The color-bearer of my regiment was shot down while attempting to plant the flag on the wall." Jones clearly had described the action around the Angle. Furious with the insinuations of Albertson's article, he fumed that "we were put in the front rank, the post of honor, and not in support, as the Enquirer has it, when there were other troops comparatively fresh, who might have taken our place. Does not this show the confidence of our general in us. . . . We have not even enough left to refute the foul calumny of those who would barely endeavor to pluck from our brows the laurels placed there at the sacrifice of so many of our noble companions."[20]

There would be no recanting, however—the Albertson version of July 3 had become too well entrenched as the standard story. Moreover, by early August editors in Richmond had declared the military situation in the Eastern Theater to be so stable that Gettysburg essentially became old news. The charge already was stepping over the boundary of current history into the realm of cherished memory. An August edition of the *Southern Illustrated News* featured a handsome woodcut of George Pickett along with lengthy extracts of the Albertson piece, reminding readers that "Major General Pickett has earned and will no doubt receive the meed of his country's praise." At a review of Pickett's division in September, a reporter found the men an inspiration from whom the "croakers and faint hearted" could take courage. "Never yet have I seen our soldiers in better spirit or finer condition for fighting," stated this observer, who believed "melancholy and despondent" men could catch a "contagion of buoyant hope and confidence" from Pickett's command, "a splendid body of men . . . notwithstanding their heavy losses in the great charge at Gettysburg."[21]

By December 1863 the press images of July had begun to appear in more substantive literary forms. Edward A. Pollard relied heavily on newspaper reports for his treatment of Gettysburg in *The Second Year of the War*; this book's publication in New York in early 1864 guaranteed that the Virginia version would be the first to make an impact on northern audiences as well. Pollard told a predictable story. Of Pickett's Virginians he wrote, "Never did troops enter a fight in such splendid order." Pickett personally, "seeing the splendid valor of his troops, moved among them as if courting death." But, asked Pollard, "Where is Pettigrew's division—where are the supports? The raw troops had faltered and the gallant Pettigrew himself had been wounded in vain attempts to rally them."[22]

Maj. W. J. Baker of Pettigrew's old brigade feared that Pollard's volume would be just the first of many to discount the contribution of North Carolina troops if something were not done to counter the trend. He wrote to Capt. Louis G. Young of the late general's staff (Pettigrew had been mortally wounded on the retreat from Gettysburg) to complain that Pollard reproduced "the erroneous and unjust accounts of the battle of the 3rd of July, which appeared in the Richmond papers, shortly after the retreat from Gettysburg." Asking Young to do something to correct the record, Baker asked, "Shall these injurious accounts go to the world un-contradicted? Shall they be permitted to be incorporated into the history of the war without protest?"[23] Young began a letter-writing campaign in March 1864 eulogizing Pettigrew and clearing the name of his men, but the articles changed few minds.[24]

In the dark days after Appomattox, when the South first tried to make sense of what had happened to all the dreams of 1861, the story of the assault at Gettysburg found new life. For many, it offered the important lesson that even in trying times there can be honor and dignity. Robert E. Lee provided the model of grace in defeat. His willingness to accept re-sponsibility for the destruction of Pickett's division—"it is all my fault"— and his compassion for the men he sent across the valley of death—"Too bad! Oh, too bad!"—were, to one of Lee's first biographers, "sublime."[25] No less sublime was the sacrifice made by Pickett's division. "The courage of Virginia could do no more," Richmond editor Pollard wrote in yet another work, and still other early postwar histories enshrined Pickett's men as "a solid lancehead of Virginia troops" and "the pride and mettle of glorious Virginia."[26]

But all this attention sometimes proved disquieting. Lee's biographers underscored the general's matchless composure by sharply contrasting his conduct with that of a tearful and disheveled George Pickett seemingly unable to control either his emotions or the remnants of his command. Defeat at heavy cost had been hard enough to bear. Despite Lee's assurances that they had fought the good fight, Pickett's men reflected on the bad luck that followed them relentlessly after Gettysburg. Detached to the Richmond defenses after returning to Virginia, supposedly to refit, they were not recalled to the Army of Northern Virginia during the spring campaign of 1864. Good work in defense of the capital seemed forgotten in the wake of their collapse at a crucial moment at Five Forks on April 1, 1865. Relieved after that fight, Pickett himself stayed with his men to the end, only to have Lee ask, in tones he rarely used, "Is that man still with the army?"[27]

Some of Pickett's men resented any imputation that they had done less than their full duty. It was so important to "the memory of its thousands fallen in imperishable glory, to the living honor of its hundreds of maimed and scarred veterans, to the fortunate few who have honestly won their laurels without these proud, yet painful testimonials," that former division inspector general Walter Harrison wrote *Pickett's Men: A Fragment of War History*. Published in 1870, it was among the first concise unit histories to appear in print on either side. Alluding to the works of Lee biographers and others who had cast Pickett's men as poor soldiers, Harrison hoped his book's quick publication would "correct many misapprehensions and errors into which writers of more extended works have fallen, either through ignorance of actual events, or false information as to the facts material to a fair judgment of its merits."[28]

Although Harrison did not change the historical record as dramatically as he hoped, his book did reinvigorate impressions from July 1863 that Pickett's men were special and merited all praise. Indeed, their actions on the third day at Gettysburg alone sufficed to secure their place in the South's pantheon of heroes. Memories of the debacle at Five Forks or their general's removal quickly evaporated, and pride and pathos mingled freely as Pickett's men began a long period of commemoration and memorialization.

The immortality of the charge "belongs alike to all the Virginians whose heroism made it a great deed," proclaimed an 1871 memorial tribute to Capt. George H. Geiger, one of Kemper's aides who died on the slopes of Cemetery Ridge. Their cause must have been sacred if William F. Cocke of the 19th Virginia, a son of privilege who could have avoided military service, "was content to shoulder his musket and march abreast with men of the humblest grade of life" only to hear at Gettysburg "the voice which said, 'come up hither.'"[29] In the early 1870s, when the remains of more than 2,000 dead southerners were disinterred from trench graves at Gettysburg for reburial in Richmond's Hollywood Cemetery, the special sacrifice of Pickett's men hung over the proceedings. "I cannot dwell upon it," wrote one man, "let others if they can, who feel it less, at all events less bitterly and personally than I." The memories of July 3 and all that followed still seemed like "sitting on one's coffin and gazing into one's empty grave."[30]

Pickett's veterans received help in fashioning their new, more heroic image. Robert E. Lee died in 1870. The leaders of the newly established Southern Historical Society, nearly all from Virginia, began to cast Lee as "the marble man," the flawless symbol of all that was right about the Lost Cause. To do so, they had to relieve Lee of all responsibility for any failure, especially the defeat at Gettysburg. This would be difficult because Lee had accepted the blame publicly, and his first biographers had used it to good effect. Nonetheless, the Lee cult, as they have been called, focused on James Longstreet, Pickett's immediate superior at Gettysburg and the senior officer in Lee's army who was not from Virginia.[31]

Most of the charges against Longstreet centered on his conduct on July 2, but the sacrifice of Pickett's division also became part of the attempt to shift the blame for Gettysburg to Lee's First Corps commander. Walter Taylor, once on Lee's staff, asserted that while Lee had intended to use all three First Corps divisions in the July 3 attack, Longstreet had unaccountably held back two of them to protect his already secure right flank. That left Pickett to advance alone, supported only by Pettigrew's battered troops. "Was it designed to throw these few brigades upon the fortified stronghold of the enemy?" Taylor asked. Clearly he doubted that Lee intended for "those men of brave hearts and nerves of steel" to charge alone, blaming Longstreet for the fate that befell Pickett's men.[32] Throughout the 1870s, under the guise of assisting the Comte de Paris with his history of the Civil War, Taylor and other prominent Virginians, including Jubal Early, Armistead Long, William Nelson Pendleton, and Fitzhugh Lee, wielded their pens like Toledo blades, slicing away at Lee's "Old War

Horse" at every turn and deftly pinning the demise of Pickett's division on Longstreet's insubordinate mismanagement.[33]

Conspicuously missing from all the attacks on Longstreet were George E. Pickett and the members of his official military family. The bonds of friendship and loyalty between Pickett and his former superior refused to break. Still, his silence cast no doubts on his status as a loyal son of Virginia. Even after an uncomfortable, emotion-charged interview with Lee in 1870 that prompted him to tell Confederate partisan John Mosby, "That old man destroyed my division," Pickett nonetheless had served as an honorary pallbearer at Lee's funeral. Indeed, he was chosen president of the Southern Historical Society in October 1874.[34] Pickett did not finish his term, passing away in August 1875 at age fifty. The estimated crowd of nearly 40,000 who viewed his funeral procession provided strong evidence of his fame in the Old Dominion.[35] His men would not forget him or his example in the literary wars ahead.

Just as Lee's death gave impetus to the movement to preserve and even embellish his life and career, some of Pickett's men decided their general deserved no less a tribute. Some time after their commander's funeral, his men formed the Pickett's Division Association. Most active in the 1880s, it preceded the formation of the United Confederate Veterans by several years, and its members became the protectors and promoters of the memory and reputation of their commander and their comrades.[36]

The strong spirit of romanticism that infused much postwar southern literature proved especially useful in helping Pickett's men transform themselves from mere soldiers or even martyrs into something much more enticing—bona fide heroes.[37] As the 1880s progressed, to call them mere heroes was to damn with faint praise. No longer merely "the flower of the Virginia infantry" (an 1863 accolade), when described by Capt. Henry Owen, formerly of the 18th Virginia, they had become the distillation of the finest Old Virginia had to offer: "Nearly every family of honorable mention in the history of the State as a Colony or Commonwealth, had its representative here, either among the officers or among the privates marching in the ranks. [There were] presidents, professors and students[,] . . . graduates of law and medicine, editors and divines—men of learning, of wealth and refinement[,] . . . and in the wake of these proud Cavaliers came the yeomanry of the Old Dominion, the bone and sinew of the land . . . sprung from a warlike ancestry."[38]

Such men stood as more than heroes, and the new image caught on in sometimes unexpected ways and with all kinds of audiences. Pickett's men took center stage in elaborate paintings of the battle of Gettysburg, such as Paul Phillipoteaux's massive depiction still on display at the Gettysburg Cyclorama. They were honored in song and in poetry of widely varying quality.[39] In *St. Nicholas*, the most popular children's magazine of the day, American youth learned that "those on the left faltered and fled. The right behaved gloriously. Each body acted according to its nature, for they were made of different stuff. The one of common earth, the other of finest clay. Pettigrew's men were North Carolinians. Pickett's were superb Virginians."[40]

Delighted by this attention, Pickett's men gave their new image as superior representatives of southern valor still another turn. Despite much criticism from other Virginians, they announced their intention to return to Gettysburg, not merely as ex-Confederates but as Americans committed to ending sectional ill will. In 1887 they accepted an invitation to the dedication of the regimental monument of the 69th Pennsylvania Infantry, part of the Philadelphia Brigade they had faced on Cemetery Ridge on July 3, 1863.

On July 2, 1887, more than 500 Pennsylvania veterans greeted Pickett's men back to Gettysburg. As a northern band played "Dixie" and a Virginia color-bearer waved the Stars and Stripes, the national press hung on every word spoken by Col. William Aylett, once of the 53rd Virginia: "We come as the survivors of a great battle, which illustrated the greatness and glory of the American people. . . . We have come forth from the baptism of blood and fire in which we were consumed, as the representatives of a New South, and . . . over the tomb of secession and African slavery we have created a new empire, and have built a temple to American liberty."[41]

The appeal of Pickett's men quickly transcended regional boundaries. They became national heroes and learned how to use their clout. When denied permission by the Gettysburg battlefield commissioners to build a monument at the site of their deepest penetration into northern lines on Cemetery Ridge, Pickett's men turned to Union veterans' groups to force a compromise. In 1888 a four-foot scroll of New Hampshire granite was placed inside the Angle where General Armistead was mortally wounded—the text of its dedicatory address carefully worded to honor not merely the South but the "glory of the American volunteer soldier."[42] When Pickett's men dedicated their division memorial in Richmond, some Grand Army of the Republic posts sent representatives, while some southern veterans' groups, such as the Richmond Howitzers, refused to supply a delegation. Pickett's men liked to quote Gen. George McClellan, whose stunning eulogy described their general as "the purest type of the perfect soldier" who had earned a place in American history "as nearer to Light Horse Harry, of the Revolution, than any other of the many heroes produced by old Virginia."[43] At every opportunity, Pickett's men wrote or spoke of their noble determination on that fateful day "to win for Virginia and the Confederate States a name which would be handed down to posterity in honor and which would be spoken of with pride by not only Virginia but by all America."[44]

Not everyone enjoyed the elevation to mythic proportions of Pickett's men. Since July 3, 1863, the survivors and friends of Pettigrew's and Trimble's men had chafed at their treatment in the wartime press and postwar histories. They resented the attention lavished on Pickett's troops and eventually decided to wage a literary battle to right the historical record about Gettysburg. What they did not know was how to fight it.

Pettigrew's and Trimble's veterans already understood from wartime press practices that the pen and the sword could be equally deadly, especially to units from states outside Virginia. So long as Virginians held nearly all the important editorial positions on the increasingly authoritative *Southern Historical Society Papers*, the stories of troops from other states had been almost entirely shut out of its pages. Of the antebellum South's three chief literary communities—New Orleans, Charleston, and Richmond—only Virginia had a stake in how the story of the assault on July 3 was preserved. Moreover, their great inroads into the northern, and therefore national, literary mainstream meant that whole new audiences would discover the Virginia version of Pickett's Charge in the writings of such authors as John Esten Cooke and Thomas Nelson Page.[45]

To preserve the history of their own participation at Gettysburg, the forgotten North Carolina troops used the few avenues open to them. They relied chiefly on local newspapers and a number of well-intentioned but underfunded and undersubscribed periodicals. One disgruntled Tarheel complained in 1867 in *The Land We Love* that "it is unfortunate for North Carolina that none of her own sons has attempted a history of the war. There was scarcely a corporal in the ranks of the North Carolina troops, who could not write a more *truthful* history than any yet put forth. He might not be able to adorn it with flowers of rhetoric and ideal descriptions of battles, but he could tell what actually occurred, without drawing upon the fancy and the imagination." Among the most "ridiculous shams" were "the reflections made upon Pettigrew's brigade at Gettysburg," especially because "the object is not to injure the brigade, but to exalt Pickett's division."[46]

North Carolina held a special grudge. "It is not difficult to trace the source of this slander," wrote an editor of a Wilmington newspaper. "Certain newspapers, immediately after the disastrous battle, in their efforts to glorify the deeds of Pickett's Division, misrepresented the facts in regard to the North Carolinians in the division of Gen'l Heth"—with the result that "as gallant a body of men as ever charged a battery or fought for human liberty, have been grossly vilified year after year, and their splendid courage has been turned into arrant cowardice." More pointedly, "The Virginia historians, Pollard, McCabe, *et id omne genus*, set the example of doing injustice to North Carolina soldiers, and we have but little hope that their example will cease to be followed," complained editor T. B. Kingsbury of *Our Living and Our Dead* in 1875.[47]

Not all of Pettigrew's and Trimble's survivors and friends gave in so passively to such pessimism. Although the Old Dominion's grip on Confederate war history had not loosened much by 1886, many Virginians insisted they claimed no honors for themselves due troops from other states. Encouraged by such sentiments, Tennessean William Swallow tried to write an objective narrative about the charge for Louisville's short-lived *Southern Bivouac* magazine. Basing his story largely on discussions with men from both armies wounded in the battle (as he himself was), Swallow strove to be fair to all states and even wrote Gen. James Kemper, Pickett's surviving brigadier, to ask what he recalled of the pivotal moment when Virginians, Tennesseans, and North Carolinians combined forces to break into the Angle. Kemper's answer pained Swallow: "From the beginning to the end of that charge, up to the time when Pickett's Division found itself in the cul-de-sac of death" and meeting "an overpowering fire in front, and raking fire from both the right and left, I never saw any command or any troops on the Confederate side except . . . Pickett's Division."[48]

Stung by the general's response (perhaps unnecessarily—Kemper occupied the extreme right of Pickett's line farthest from Pettigrew's and Trimble's men and genuinely may not have seen them), Swallow spelled out in detail his specific challenges to Virginia's version of the charge. First, he demanded acknowledgment that Pettigrew's and Trimble's commands constituted part of the formal column of attack and not merely Pickett's reinforcements. Second, he asserted that Pettigrew's and Trimble's men neither wavered nor broke early during the charge; he himself had been one of those who "carried the struggle to the very points of the enemy's bayonets." Finally, he argued that "the movement ought more properly be called the 'Assault of A. P. Hill's Corps'" because six of the nine attacking brigades were from Hill's command. Reluctantly, he would accept "Longstreet's Assault," inasmuch as Lee had given him command of the attack, but "it would be a misnomer to call this assault, as many writers have done, 'the charge of Pickett's division.'" Similar comments by fellow Tennessean J. B. Smith worked their way into *Century Magazine*'s Battles and Leaders Series, but neither Swallow nor Smith produced any lasting cracks in the Virginia-crafted story.[49]

One man who would not have been surprised that the Tennesseans accomplished so little was William R. Bond. An ex-Confederate staff officer from North Carolina, Bond had tried since 1881 to break into the national literary mainstream with his opinion that the Virginia version of July 3 distorted the facts. After the Philadelphia *Weekly Times* published a story that repeated "with probably the best intentions the slander which originated in Richmond nineteen years ago," Bond decided to stop the spread of lies still heard all over Virginia and repeated in the North as well.[50] Increasingly obsessed with correcting matters, Bond personally financed in 1888 an inflammatory publication entitled *Pickett or Pettigrew?* Reprinted four times by 1900, and enlarged with more evidence each time, Bond's pamphlet ultimately provided many critics of the Virginia version of Pickett's Charge with ammunition to enter the fray. In time, Bond's was a loud voice, but through the 1890s it alone was not loud enough to make a difference.

Condemning "the trash that passes for Southern history," Bond demanded greater recognition for all North Carolina troops, which had, after all, "shed the first blood, the last blood, and the most blood" of the war. Characterizing the Richmond press as "wonderfully narrow and selfish" throughout the war, he described their editorial policy as one in which if Virginians "were called upon to bleed freely, then . . . troops from some other state were to blame for it." The prevailing image of the charge at Gettysburg reflected the handiwork of Richmond's wartime press. Some commands, Bond noted, had "the habit of 'playing possum'" in tight situations, and Pickett's men ranked among the most guilty. In fact, at Gettysburg the "brave, the magnificent" Virginians really had become "sick of fighting, as the number of surrendered show." Yet as the pampered pets of the Richmond editors, they continued to be portrayed as if "their division stood to Lee's army in the same relation, that the sun does to the Solar system." Bond argued that Pickett's men "did not kill twenty of the enemy at Gettysburg." For that matter, it took the losses of only two North Carolina regiments in the charge to equal the number of dead in all fifteen of Pickett's.[51]

Bond insisted that the Tennessee and North Carolina brigades of Archer, Scales, and Pettigrew went as far and stayed at least as long as any of Pickett's Virginians. Davis's Mississippi brigade, which included the 55th North Carolina, "while charging impetuously ahead of the line was driven back, when it had reached a point about one hundred yards from the enemy. Lane's North Carolinians, the left brigade, remained a few moments longer than any other troops and retired in better order." The only men of Pettigrew's division to disgrace themselves that day occupied the extreme left of the line and broke at first fire—Brockenbrough's Virginians. Any other version of the charge, concluded Bond, especially that told and retold for years by the Virginians, amounted to no more than "libel containing so much ignorance, narrowness and prejudice."[52]

In the thirty years or so after Appomattox, Bond and his allies made little progress in their effort to right the historical record or reshape the popular image of the attack. They fired many single shots but no telling volleys capable of winning a literary war with the Old Dominion. The confident Virginians addressed the chief Tarheel complaints as misguided and irrelevant. In 1882, for example, Virginian ex-cavalryman Fitzhugh Lee offered a comprehensive argument for calling the attack Pickett's Charge, a sore point with many non-Virginians. It was not a demonstration of Virginia bias, Lee insisted, but simply routine military procedure: "The operation of a detached force generally takes the name of the commanding officer. Pickett was the senior officer in rank, and hence the charge has generally been written in the pages of history as 'Pickett's Charge'. . . . If either Heth or Pender had been present and ranked Pickett, the assault would have been known as Heth's or Pender's charge as the case might be."[53]

By the 1890s the Old Dominion's grip on the story of Pickett's Charge was so secure against critics outside the state that Virginians felt free to refine the story in unexpected ways. For more than a decade Virginians actually argued among themselves about what had happened on July 3 at Gettysburg. Several of Pickett's former subordinates fomented the controversy. Still agreed that soldiers in the ranks deserved all praise, they used their memoirs and Virginia newspapers to raise nagging doubts about the personal courage and integrity of their division commander. Kirkwood

Otey of the 11th Virginia—the same officer who had praised Pickett's conduct in 1863 as "fully worthy of the occasion and of the men he commanded"—opened the battle with a sinister suggestion. "Whoever will take the trouble to make inquiries will find that there is an underground rumor, narrative, or whatever you may call it," wrote Otey in the Richmond *Times* in 1894, "that General George E. Pickett did not take part in the immortal performance of his division." Otey had "never heard a positive statement as to where General Pickett was in that charge, never heard him located or placed," and suggested that nobody could place Pickett on the battlefield because he was not there. When Otey had gone to have a hand wound dressed, the surgeon directed him to "get some whiskey to alleviate the pain." At the "whiskey wagon," he saw "two officers of General Pickett's staff (their names can be furnished if desired) . . . standing on the tongue of the surgeon's wagon, each with a tin cup, awaiting their turn for a ration of whiskey. . . . Their presence (the staff officers) naturally suggested that General Pickett might be in the neighborhood."[54]

Otey admitted receiving his "Confederate chloroform" before he actually saw Pickett personally, but any hint of impropriety raised questions of no small matter. Why did Otey wait until the 1890s to voice his complaints? He likely held a grudge over his court-martial shortly after Gettysburg on charges of drunkenness on duty. Found guilty but restored to his command because of the great need for experienced field officers in his division, Otey apparently nursed a grudge against Pickett for some real or imagined ill for thirty years.[55]

Otey's accusations proved damaging. They cast doubt where none had existed before, and even nonparticipants in the charge added fuel to the fire. Cavalryman Thomas Rosser wondered why Pickett did nothing to link up with Wilcox's Alabamians or to counter the flanking movement of Stannard's Vermonters. With no evidence but ample venom—probably linked to unresolved questions about responsibility for the fiasco at Five Forks—Rosser concluded that "Genl Pickett was not on the field when the above conditions were presented, and I have never seen an officer or private soldier (and I have seen many who were in that attack) who was in that attacking column, who says that he saw Genl Pickett after his command emerged from the clouds of smoke . . . and I feel sure that he had been detained in the rear, from some unknown cause, and was not on the field, near enough to command the attacking column, when the enemy was reached." What might that unknown cause be? Virginian John S. Wise provided a clue in his memoirs: Pickett "was a high and free liver, and often declared that, to fight like a gentleman, a man must eat and drink like a gentleman."[56]

Not surprisingly, the majority of Pickett's men refused to believe allegations that sullied their general's name. Under pressure to account for and defend the general, ex-major Charles Pickett, his brother and former adjutant, rallied other staff members to the cause. Just a few years earlier they had compared notes extensively on their actions during the charge to help James Longstreet write his memoirs.[57] Even at this late date, it was easy to find a solid nucleus around which to build a defense of the Pickett name. Charles Pickett, ex-captains Robert Bright, W. Stuart Symington, and E. R. Baird of the general's staff, his courier Thomas Friend, and other veterans of the division quickly answered Otey's accusations. Charles Pickett responded first. His brother unquestionably had been under fire of the enemy. He had sent not one but three staff officers—one at a time—to hurry Wilcox's men onto the field because he "deemed it hardly within the bounds of reason that more than one of them could reach Wilcox as the ground . . . was swept . . . with a deadly hail of missels [sic]." When Charles Pickett had left the general at the Emmitsburg Road to ask Longstreet for reinforcements, he was sure "it was our final meeting in this world." Pickett's former courier was incredulous: "I cannot imagine how anyone, who wore the 'gray' can be guilty of such traitorous lies, particularly against such a man as Gen. Pickett." He swore that "the vile tongue of those base slanderers will never take one laurel from the crown of Gen. George E. Pickett, as long as his Soldiers and his Soldiers Children live."[58]

In December 1894 Pickett's closest allies responded to Otey's charges directly: "Pickett assumed his proper position in the rear and center of his line of battle, moving forward with his division. . . . When the attack failed he personally superintended the withdrawal. . . . That there could possibly have been any doubt as to the facts above mentioned is a matter that will never be comprehended by any man or officer familiar with the facts."[59]

Pickett's men did their commander proud. Martin Hazlewood, head of Richmond's George E. Pickett Camp of the United Confederate Veterans (successor to the Pickett's Division Association), managed to publish in the *Southern Historical Society Papers* the first substantive article on the charge by a participant.[60] Some veterans, such as Captain Baird, went on the United Daughters of the Confederacy lecture circuit.[61] If a Virginia town dedicated a monument to its local southern soldiers, the obligatory address likely included high praise of Pickett and his men.[62] Hoping to prove a pattern of bravery under fire, Pickett's partisans even claimed for him an unduly large share of the credit for breaking the Union line at Gaines's Mill during the Seven Days battles in 1862.[63] In "the interest of truth and history, and in defense of the immortal name of Pickett," his men continued to defend a superior "who is entitled to the praise and gratitude of the land he served, and the admiration of all the brave of the world." Remembering Pickett's silence in the 1870s when the Lee cult attacked his conduct at Gettysburg, James Longstreet repaid his subordinate's loyalty, providing in his memoirs a stirring picture of the moment when Pickett accepted his orders to charge Cemetery Ridge.[64]

The most important new recruit to the literary wars, however, was the general's widow, LaSalle Corbell Pickett. Since the Gettysburg reunion in 1887, where she was introduced as fulfillment of the Old Testament prophecy that "a woman shall crush the serpent's head," Sallie Pickett had committed herself to opposing "hatred, sectionalism, and strife" while promoting and protecting her husband's good name.[65] In the 1890s she determined to use her famous name to market her marginal literary skills in defense of the man she called My Soldier.

Shrewd and insufferably romantic, Sallie Pickett presented a simple message. George Pickett had "the keenest sense of justice, the most sensitive consciousness of right, and the highest moral courage."[66] No doubt still bristling from Otey's charge, she made it seem absolutely clear in *Pickett and His Men* that her husband could not have been drunk at Gettysburg. General Wilcox had tempted him: "Pickett, take a drink with me. In an hour you'll be in hell or in glory." But Pickett had resisted: "I promised the little girl who is waiting and praying for me down in Virginia that I would keep fresh upon my lips until we should meet again the breath of the violets she gave me when we parted. Whatever my fate, Wilcox, I shall try to do my duty like a man, and I hope that, by that little girl's prayers, I shall to day reach either glory or glory." His men had "followed where the flash of Pickett's sword lit the way to glorious victory, or not less glorious defeat." Indeed, George Pickett's heroism was confirmed by an equally great man, Abraham Lincoln, who, although an Illinois congressman, had helped to obtain Pickett's appointment to West Point. While the president viewed Cemetery Ridge before his great address, one man said, "Think of the men who held these heights!" "Yes," Lincoln had replied, "but think of the men who stormed these heights!" Pickett and his men.[67]

Tempered by unexpected attacks from fellow Virginians, Pickett's supporters never again let their guard down. After 1900 complacency was a

luxury they could not afford. They needed all their numbers and more, because at the turn of the century, with deepened commitment, better organization, and a unity of purpose, North Carolina veterans and friends of Pettigrew's and Trimble's men came storming back to challenge Virginia yet again.

North Carolinians formed a state literary and historical society in 1900. William R. Bond, along with Walter Clark and Samuel A. Ashe, all former Confederate officers, oversaw the society's Civil War projects. Among the first endeavors was Clark's ambitious five-volume history of the North Carolina Confederate regiments. Predictably, the sketch of each Tarheel unit in the charge rejected in some way part of the Virginia version of Pickett's Charge. The survivors of the 7th North Carolina advanced only moderate claims—they went as far as any other command, were among the

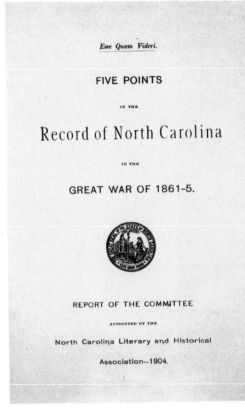

The image on the title page reads:

*Esse Quam Videri.*

FIVE POINTS

IN THE

Record of North Carolina

IN THE

GREAT WAR OF 1861-5.

REPORT OF THE COMMITTEE

APPOINTED BY THE

North Carolina Literary and Historical

Association--1904.

last to withdraw, and left their flag and the wounded color-bearer along with their wounded major near the stone wall.[68] Others claimed much more. The major of the 26th North Carolina recalled that his color-bearer died as he planted his flag on the stone wall itself, adding, "I know we went as far as Pickett did, and I can safely assert some distance beyond."[69]

The famous Angle in the Union line loomed large in North Carolina memoirs. The rock wall facing Pettigrew's front lay about eighty yards farther east, or higher on the ridge, than the point where Pickett's men broke through the Federal position. Regardless of the fact that they had not breached the line, North Carolinians laid a very literal claim to penetrating farthest at Gettysburg. As validation, veterans of the 55th North Carolina offered what they believed to be the clinching, if macabre, piece of evidence: sworn testimony that placed the bullet-ridden corpse of their Capt. E. Fletcher Satterfield farther to the front than any other dead Confederate that day.[70]

North Carolinians saw no reason to restrain their attacks. In addition to the regimental sketches, Clark's volumes included several essays aimed specifically at resolving the controversy in the Tarheels' favor.[71] Why hold back in the fight against the Virginia version of the assault, one North Carolinian wondered. "One shot may accomplish nothing, or two or three, but keep firing [and] it will be pierced at last, and its builders and defenders will be covered" with shame. The state historical society devoted an entire pamphlet to the cause: "North Carolina at Gettysburg and Pickett's Charge a Misnomer." Its pages included the possibly correct claim that some North Carolina soldiers fought inside the Angle with Pickett's men—along with the highly unlikely assertion that the Richmond papers "were willing to slander brave men from five states in the left wing to save Pickett from failing to get promotion" to lieutenant general.[72] By 1904 the historical society seems to have created a new, if unofficial, state motto for North Carolina: "First at Bethel, Farthest to the front at Gettysburg and Chickamauga, Last at Appomattox."[73]

North Carolina did not fight its battle alone. Friends and survivors of Archer's Tennessee brigade stepped into the fray, wielding a different weapon. The Nashville-based *Confederate Veteran* magazine, official organ of the United Confederate Veterans, showed a tendency quite the reverse of the *Southern Historical Society Papers* in seeming to welcome almost any article that was not by or about Virginians.[74] Moreover, its editors rarely checked the veracity of contributors. Ex-captain J. B. Turney of the 1st Tennessee took advantage of the opportunity to write about Archer's men entering the Union lines—ahead of the Virginians. He recalled the scene vividly: "Not until we were within about fifteen steps of the stone wall did I order a charge with bayonets. . . . Another instant, and we were engaged in a desperate hand-to-hand conflict for the possession of the fragile wall of masonry, the sole barrier between combatants." The story proceeded to depart even further from the Virginia version. Observing Turney's precarious advanced position, General Armistead of Pickett's division led his Virginians over the wall in support of the Tennesseans. When Armistead fell mortally wounded, of course Turney was there to catch him before he hit the ground.[75]

Taken to extremes, this could and occasionally did turn into Civil War history in the style of a tabloid. Sgt. Dick Reid of Nashville offered his memoirs to prove that, as the editors proclaimed, he had "been there." He painted a lively picture of lining up for the charge alongside Gen. Robert Toombs's Georgia brigade near some thirty-pounder Parrott cannons. He saw General Armistead, "an old man, seventy years old," mount his horse to lead them into the attack rivaling the fiercest fights Reid had ever seen.[76] None of it was true. No Georgians took part in the charge; Toombs had been out of the army for almost six months by the time of Gettysburg; and the forty-six-year-old Armistead led his men on foot and not on horseback.[77] Still, there was little to prevent publication of such articles, and, at least in its early years, *Confederate Veteran* would be an ally, often unwittingly, of Pettigrew's and Trimble's men.

Friends of Joseph Davis's Mississippi brigade stayed out of the literary war until nearly 1910, but their sentiments were clear long before that. At the 1905 dedication of the Confederate monument in Carrollton, Mississippi, the orator recited a flowery poem about Pickett's Charge. He watched his audience getting restless and then ugly until he finally explained why he chose that particular ode for the occasion. First, it fit his theme of the bravery of southern soldiers; second, it paid splendid tribute to the sublime courage of the men who stormed Cemetery Ridge; and third, he assured his listeners that he knew as well as they that the men who broke through the Union line were really the Mississippians of Davis's brigade, and not Pickett's Virginians at all.[78]

Mississippians also used *Confederate Veteran* magazine to make their case. Sgt. W. D. Reid of the 11th Mississippi asserted without doubt that "I went to that rock fence and was shot down there, and that some of my company and regiment crossed that fence and but few returned." Like North Carolinians, they used the publications of their own new Mississippi State Historical Society to play down the valor of Pickett's Virginians: "The enemy force behind the works in Pickett's front as he approached was in single line, was weaker than the force confronting Pettigrew's division at the point of its attack."[79] Mississippians also borrowed freely from North Carolina's historical literature to argue that Davis's brigade made the deepest penetration of the Union line. The dead Captain Satterfield's 55th North Carolina was, after all, part of Davis's command. Even into the 1930s, friends of the 11th Mississippi continued to press the claim that the regiment's dead could be found in Ziegler's Grove well inside Union lines. They also sought permission, without success, to mark the alleged spot with a monument.[80]

Excluding Wilcox's men, whose presence Pickett's troops missed on July 3, Alabama had provided only a single regiment and an additional battalion for the charge. Few survivors of the 13th Alabama or the 5th Battalion took part in the literary war against Virginia. Ironically, however, an Alabamian helped achieve the principal victory supporters of Pettigrew's and Trimble's men won. Ex-major William McKendree Robbins of the 4th Alabama served for years as the only southerner on the Gettysburg Battlefield Commission. Although not a veteran of the charge itself, Robbins betrayed his sympathies when he contributed a special essay on the July 3 charge to the North Carolina regimental history series. His diaries as park commissioner reveal as well that when prominent southerners, such as Gen. Stephen Dill Lee, asked for information about the battle, Robbins often steered them to North Carolina Historical Society pamphlets.[81]

Responsible for writing the narratives on the metal tablets that mark the step-off points for each of Pickett's, Pettigrew's, and Trimble's brigades, Robbins tried so hard to be objective that he finally refused to read all postwar southern versions of the charge. Relying instead on a valuable collection of postbattle interviews—either the John Bachelder interviews or more likely the government discussions with veterans done in the late 1890s after the establishment of the battlefield park[82]—he concluded finally that Pickett's, Pettigrew's, and Trimble's men advanced equally far. But he also agreed that Pickett's men broke through the advanced portion of the Union line, while Pettigrew and Trimble went almost to— but not across—the more recessed part of the wall north of the Angle. He believed further that some individual Tennessee and North Carolina soldiers—but no organized command from those states—crossed the wall with Pickett's men. He offered no judgment about who broke first or who stayed longest. Even if supporters of Pettigrew's and Trimble's commands did not agree with all his findings, they had to be delighted that Robbins convinced the battlefield commissioners to give the attack the formal name of the Pickett-Pettigrew-Trimble Charge.[83]

Not surprisingly, Pickett's men responded to all of this with yet one more literary frenzy. Having little new to say, they exaggerated their exaggerations, condemned with greater vigor, and polished their idols to an even brighter sheen. They also attacked with a newfound unity. Old squabbles fell away as nearly all Virginians rallied behind Pickett and his men. Memoirs from Captain Bright of Pickett's staff and letters from Pickett's regimental officers began to flood the *Southern Historical Society Papers*; many of the same articles appeared in the Richmond *Times* to reach an even larger audience.[84] James Crocker of the 9th Virginia permitted the *Papers* to print his effusive lectures to the United Daughters of the Confederacy.[85] Rooney Lee's son, grandson of the Confederate commander at Gettysburg, delivered a rousing commemorative address to southern veterans at a Richmond reunion. Elaborate in his praise of Confederate heroes, Lee mentioned only three by name—a Virginia triumvirate made up of traditional figures Stonewall Jackson and Jeb Stuart, and a newcomer to such august company, George E. Pickett.[86]

Nothing connected with the charge seemed too inconsequential to consider. The discovery of General Garnett's sword in a Baltimore pawnshop in 1905 received tremendous coverage.[87] Belated eulogies for Pickett's dead colonels appeared with regularity, and southerners pointed to the return of the sword belt of Col. James Gregory Hodges, 14th Virginia, by a former Union artilleryman as a wonderful sign of how far the spirit of reunion had come. Interested parties even debated the number of officers who rode their horses into the charge against Pickett's explicit orders, a theme carried to its greatest excess by the *Cavalry Journal* in an article entitled "The Equine Heroes of Pickett's Charge."[88]

Above all the Virginians still had Sallie Pickett. Even more than before, she flooded major American magazines with flowery biographical sketches of My Soldier. Respectable literary journals shunned her work, but the editors of newer, more popular magazines printed it. During 1913, the year of the fiftieth anniversary of the great charge, she serialized the story of the Pickett family's wartime adventures in ten installments that boosted circulation of one new women's magazine, *Cosmopolitan*.[89] Literary critics panned her novel *The Bugles of Gettysburg*, a 163-page, tortuous tale of ill-fated romance, friendship, loyalty, honor, death, and Pickett's Charge.[90] Then there was the publication of what Sallie Pickett assured readers were some of her husband's wartime letters to her. The effusive missives in *The Heart of a Soldier, as Revealed in the Intimate Letters of General George E. Pickett, C.S.A.*, contain facts Pickett could not have known when he allegedly wrote the letters. Indeed, modern scholars have proved conclusively that Sallie herself rather than the general authored them. Still, even as fakes they served a purpose. By the time of the fiftieth anniversary of the assault, George Pickett's greatest moment and his place in history were secure.[91]

The fiftieth anniversary ceremonies demonstrated that Virginia's version of events on July 3 had captured the American imagination. A series of photographs told it all. Crossing an open field were old Virginians in gray, waving their canes, white beards and empty sleeves here and there. Waiting for them were old Pennsylvanians in blue, lined up along the stone wall where they had stood fifty years before. Blue and gray met again at that wall, and this time they shook hands.[92] One North Carolinian attending the ceremonies groused that "we boys always called it Pickett's newspaper charge."[93] That was true enough, but it was a charge that Pickett clearly won.

Now, 130 years after Pickett's Charge, it is time to attempt to separate the true from the false, to fill in the omissions, and to rein in the exaggerations. It is not an easy task. Research on Gettysburg is sometimes difficult, especially for July 3 on the Confederate side. For example, the *Official Records of the War of the Rebellion*, so helpful in answering questions about many other battles, are not very useful. Lee and corps commanders Hill and Longstreet treated the charge as just one episode in long campaign reports, and modern readers, like some of the participants, can wonder how much any of the three generals really saw once the firing started. Among reports by division commanders, the story of Pickett's is well known. Lee ordered his lieutenant to destroy it, allegedly because it bluntly blamed others for the failure of the attack. Pickett did not submit another, and if Sallie Pickett really had the original, as she claimed, she never revealed its contents.[94] Pender and Pettigrew lay dead by mid-July, and Trimble was a wounded prisoner. Henry Heth might have said something but limited his comments mostly to July 1 before he was wounded. He and Pickett also were cousins, which may help explain why Heth remained fairly quiet in the postwar years.[95] Of nine original brigade commanders, only Davis and Lane have published reports.[96] Printed regimental reports are also few in number.[97] In the absence of more available official documents, southerners on any side of the controversy could write without fear of authoritative contradiction. For the same reasons, it remains difficult to verify or corroborate eyewitness reports or to separate genuine accounts from fabrications.

The validity of much of the Virginia version remains intact, chiefly because large parts of it seem to have been true all along. Pickett's men did break the Union line. They were the only organized command to do so. They stayed until attacked at least from the front and the right. But why did the charge fail? Who was responsible for it? What made Pettigrew's men fall back and when did they do it? Why did Wilcox's and Perry's men fail to support Pickett? At any given moment in the assault, what were Pickett's *and* Pettigrew's men doing? Emphasis on one or the other command has denied students an understanding of what happened on the *entire* field at any specific time. There is one other pertinent point.

Asked after the war why his men lost, Pickett gave an answer instructive for future military historians: "I believe the Union Army had something to do with it."[98] Not all the right questions have been asked yet.

As historians begin to understand the importance of memory to a people—memory, as opposed to history—it becomes more obvious why all this was of such concern to the war's survivors and their children.[99] The legacy has been handed down even to the present generation. In 1988 an issue of *Blue & Gray Magazine* devoted its front cover to a photograph of a monument erected in 1986 to the 26th North Carolina on Cemetery Ridge, carefully placed outside the Union lines but well up the slope from the Armistead marker located near Pickett's deepest penetration. At the 125th anniversary ceremonies, some reenactors representing that regiment of Pettigrew's old brigade were denied permission to enter the Union position as a cohesive unit. "When told that we North Carolinians could send a contingent of troops over the wall but only under the Virginia flag, we agreed to a man to 'die' in front of the wall rather than to assist the Virginians in perpetuating such a lie," one modern Tarheel wrote.[100]

The dramatization of the great charge in *Gettysburg*, the film adaptation of Michael Shaara's Pulitzer Prize–winning novel *The Killer Angels*, is likely to continue to fan the flames of controversy among North Carolinians. In living color, reaffirming the Virginia version of the assault, Dick Garnett's riderless horse trots rearward after its master falls near the Angle, Lo Armistead leads his men over the stone wall to meet the troops of his friend Win Hancock, and Pickett watches in horror (and apparently far to the front) as his division disintegrates under hot Union fire. Johnston Pettigrew appears only once—to give James Longstreet a copy of a book he wrote. Isaac Trimble storms into several scenes to complain about the errors in judgment other generals made. But neither of these last two senior leaders in the Pickett-Pettigrew-Trimble Charge plays any role in the film's depiction of the grand assault on July 3. The Virginia version still stands strong.

Whether or not a present generation can embrace William Faulkner's observation that for every southern boy there comes a time when it is still just before one o'clock on July 3, the cannonade has not yet begun, and once it does, life will never again be the same,[101] it cannot deny that few moments in American history command such a hold on the national imagination. Virginia's efforts to create such a lasting image and the energies expended by North Carolina and its allies to correct the historical record make the story of Pickett's Charge a peculiarly appealing tribute to what was, after all, simply an infantry assault that failed.

NOTES

1. William R. Bond, *Pickett or Pettigrew? An Historical Essay* (Weldon, N.C.: Hall & Sledge, 1888), 6.

2. The most insightful modern study, which describes in detail all the troops involved on both sides, is George R. Stewart's *Pickett's Charge: A Microhistory of the Final Attack at Gettysburg, July 3, 1863* (Boston: Houghton Mifflin, 1957).

3. Stewart decreased the traditional number of 15,000, first attributed to Longstreet, to approximately 10,500 in *Pickett's Charge*, 159. In *Nothing but Glory: Pickett's Division at Gettysburg* (Hightstown, N.J.: Longstreet House, 1987), 9–13, 226, Kathleen Georg Harrison and John W. Busey place the total closer to 12,000 or 13,000 because they discount the usual assertion that Pickett's command sent fewer than 5,000 men into the charge. Their analysis of division muster rolls puts Pickett's strength at more than 6,200.

4. W. H. Proffitt to Miss R. L. Proffitt, July 9, 1863, Proffitt Family Papers, Southern Historical Collection, Wilson Library, University of North Carolina, Chapel Hill (hereafter cited as SHC).

5. Jedediah Hotchkiss, *Make Me a Map of the Valley: The Civil War Journal of Stonewall Jackson's Topographer*, ed. Archie P. McDonald (Dallas, Tex.: Southern Methodist University Press, 1973), 157; William Henry Cocke to Father, July 11, 1863, Cocke Family Papers, Virginia Historical Society, Richmond, Va. (hereafter cited as VHS).

6. Entry for July 3, 1863, James J. Kirkpatrick diary, 16th Mississippi file, Box 7, Robert L. Brake Collection, U.S. Army Military History Institute Collection, Carlisle Barracks, Pa. (hereafter cited as USAMHI); William Calder to Mother, July 8, 1863, 2nd North Carolina file, Brake Collection, USAMHI.

7. Two of the earliest reports hinting at the disaster that had befallen Pickett's men can be found in the Richmond (Daily) *Dispatch*, July 10, 1863, and the Richmond *Whig*, July 12, 1863.

8. Richmond (Daily) *Dispatch*, July 10, 1863; Augusta (Ga.) *Tri-Weekly Constitutionalist*, July 15, 1863.

9. Richmond (Daily) *Dispatch*, July [?], 1863; Richmond *Sentinel*, July 20, 1863.

10. Richmond *Sentinel*, July 16, 1863.

11. William Norwood to Wm [Tillinghast], July 15, 1863, Tillinghast Family

Papers, William R. Perkins Library, Duke University, Durham, N.C. (hereafter cited as PLDU).

12. Richmond *Sentinel*, July 20, 1863.

13. Albertson, who signed his articles only with the letter *A*, was identified in J. Cutler Andrews, *The South Reports the Civil War* (Princeton, N.J.: Princeton University Press, 1970), 543. Albertson's article appeared in the Richmond *Enquirer* on July 23, 1863.

14. A protest against this charge can be found in the Richmond *Enquirer*, July 29, 1863.

15. U.S. War Department, *The War of the Rebellion: A Compilation of the Official Records of the Union and Confederate Armies*, 127 vols., index, and atlas (Washington, D.C.: GPO, 1880–1901), 27(2):320, 357 (hereafter cited as *OR*; all references are to series 1).

16. Peter Alexander's fine article can be found in the Savannah *Republican* of July 20, 1863, the Mobile *Daily Advertiser and Register* of July 23, 1863, the Charleston *Mercury* of July 23, 1863, the *Daily Southern Guardian* (Columbia, S.C.) of July 31, 1863, and the New Orleans *Picayune* of August 1, 1863.

17. For Lang's letter to editors of the Richmond *Enquirer*, dated July 26, 1863, see Francis P. Fleming, "Gettysburg: The Courageous Part Taken in the Desperate Conflict July 2–3, 1863, by the Florida Brigade," in *Southern Historical Society Papers*, 52 vols. and 2-vol. index, ed. J. William Jones and others (1876–1959; reprint, Wilmington, N.C.: Broadfoot, 1990–92), 27:198–99 (hereafter cited as *SHSP*).

18. Richmond *Enquirer*, August 14, 24, 1863.

19. Glenn Tucker, *Zeb Vance: Champion of Personal Freedom* (Indianapolis: Bobbs-Merrill, 1965), 272; W. S. Taylor to his mother, July 29, 1863, W. P. Taylor Letters in William B. Floyd Papers, SHC.

20. Maj. John T. Jones to Mr. Burgwyn, July 30, 1863, printed as "Pettigrew's Brigade at Gettysburg," in Walter A. Clark, comp., *Histories of the Several Regiments and Battalions from North Carolina in the Great War 1861–'65*, 5 vols. (Raleigh, N.C.: E. M. Uzzell, 1901), 5:133–35 (hereafter cited as *N.C. Regiments*). Jones was later killed in the battle of the Wilderness.

21. Editorial, Richmond *Daily Examiner*, August 1, 1863; *Southern Illustrated News*, August 1, 1863; Richmond *Enquirer*, September 1, 1863.

22. Edward A. Pollard, *The Second Year of the War* (Richmond, 1863; New York: Charles B. Richardson, 1864), 281–83. See also Pollard's *The Third Year of the War* (New York: Charles B. Richardson, 1865), 33–34.

23. Maj. W. J. Baker to Capt. Louis G. Young, December 14, 1863, quoted

in "Pettigrew's Brigade at Gettysburg," *Our Living and Our Dead*, February 1875, 552.

24. Richmond *Enquirer*, March 18, 1864, reprinted in ibid.

25. See John Esten Cooke, *A Life of General Robert E. Lee* (New York: D. Appleton, 1871), 325, who borrows the phrase "perfectly sublime" from British Lt. Col. A. J. L. Fremantle, who had accompanied the Army of Northern Virginia to Gettysburg.

26. Edward A. Pollard, *Early Life, Campaigns, and Public Service of Robert E. Lee* (New York: E. B. Trent, 1870), 113.

27. Douglas Southall Freeman, *R. E. Lee: A Biography*, 4 vols. (New York: Charles Scribner's Sons, 1934–35), 3:129, 4:112.

28. Walter Harrison, *Pickett's Men: A Fragment of War History* (New York: D. Van Nostrand, 1870), 3–4.

29. John Lipscomb Johnson, *The University Memorial: Biographical Sketches of Alumni of the University of Virginia Who Fell in the Confederate War* (Baltimore: Turnbull Brothers, 1871), 435, 450, 455.

30. "A Story of Gettysburg," *Southern Magazine* 12 (1873): 657.

31. See Thomas Lawrence Connelly, *The Marble Man: Robert E. Lee and His Image in American Society* (New York: Alfred A. Knopf, 1977), 26–61, for the rise of the Lee cult.

32. Walter R. Taylor, "Second Paper by Colonel Walter R. Taylor," in *SHSP*, 4:135.

33. See, for example, Armistead L. Long, "Letter from General A. L. Long," in *SHSP*, 4:118–23; Jubal A. Early, "Leading Confederates on the Battle of Gettysburg: A Review by General Early," in *SHSP*, 4:241–81; and Fitzhugh Lee, "Letter from General Fitz Lee," in *SHSP*, 4:69–76.

34. John S. Mosby, *The Memoirs of Colonel John S. Mosby*, ed. Charles Wells Russell (Bloomington: Indiana University Press, 1959), 381; J. William Jones, *Army of Northern Virginia Memorial Volume* (Richmond, Va.: J. W. Randolph & English, 1880), 88, 90. In *The Hero in America: A Chronicle of Hero Worship* (New York: Charles Scribner's Sons, 1941), 301, Dixon Wector described Pickett as one "who sulked upon the outskirts of the Lee cult" because Lee "knew of his occasional lapses with the whiskey bottle."

35. *New York Times*, October 25, 1875.

36. Many of the records of this organization are in the Edward Payson Reeve Papers, SHC.

37. Rollin G. Osterweis, *Romanticism and Nationalism in the Old South* (New Haven: Yale University Press, 1949), 235–39, provides a useful definition of

romanticism. See also Charles W. Coleman, Jr., "The Recent Movement in Southern Literature," *Harper's New Monthly Magazine*, May 1887, 837–55.

38. Manuscript draft of an article that ultimately appeared in the Philadelphia *Weekly Times*, March 26, 1881, Henry T. Owens Papers, VHS.

39. Probably the most enduring poem was Will Henry Thompson's "High Tide at Gettysburg," first published in *Century Magazine*, July 1888, 418–19.

40. Quoted in Bond, *Pickett or Pettigrew?*, 7.

41. Anthony W. McDermott [and John E. Reilly], *A Brief History of the 69th Regiment Pennsylvania Veteran Volunteers, from Its Formation until Final Muster Out of the United States Service, by Adjutant Anthony W. McDermott. Also an Account of the Reunion of the Survivors of the Philadelphia Brigade and Pickett's Division of Confederate Soldiers, and the Dedication of the Monument of the 69th Regiment Pennsylvania Infantry, at Gettysburg, July 2nd and 3d, 1887, and of the Rededication, September 11th, 1889, by Captain John E. Reilly* (Philadelphia: D. J. Gallagher, 1889), 54, 60.

42. Circular to raise funds for the Armistead monument prepared by Colonel Andrew Cowan, adopted by the Philadelphia Brigade on August 12, 1887, for solicitation of funds by the Philadelphia Brigade, Cowan's Battery survivors, and Pickett's Division Association, copy in Reeve Papers, SHC. See also John M. Vanderslice, *Gettysburg Then and Now* (1899; reprint, Dayton, Ohio: Morningside, 1983), 376–79.

43. McClellan's memorial tribute was printed in LaSalle Corbell Pickett, *Pickett and His Men* (Atlanta, Ga.: Foote & Davies, 1899), 425.

44. J. H. Walker, "The Charge of Pickett's Division," *Blue and Gray* 1 (1893): 222.

45. See, for example, John Esten Cooke, "An Old Virginian," *Scribner's Monthly*, July 1881, 453–65; Thomas Nelson Page, "Marse Chan—A Tale of Old Virginia," *Century Magazine*, April 1884, 932–42; and the work of George Cary Eggleston.

46. "The Haversack," *The Land We Love*, June 1867, 155.

47. "North Carolina at Gettysburg," *Our Living and Our Dead*, November 1874, 194; T. B. Kingsbury, "Another Witness—Gettysburg," ibid., October 1875, 457.

48. James L. Kemper to William H. Swallow, February 4, 1886, James Lawson Kemper Papers, VHS.

49. William H. Swallow, "The Third Day at Gettysburg," *Southern Bivouac* 1 (February 1886): 562–75; J. B. Smith, "The Charge of Pickett, Pettigrew and Trimble," in *Battles and Leaders of the Civil War*, ed. Robert Underwood Johnson and Clarence C. Buel, 4 vols. (New York: Century, 1887–88), 3:354–55.

50. W. R. Bond, "Pickett's Men at Gettysburg," Philadelphia *Weekly Times*, 28 October 1882.

51. Bond, *Pickett or Pettigrew?*, 7–8, 11, 13–14, 23–24.

52. Ibid., 28, 7.

53. Fitzhugh Lee to "Editor, Times," n.d. [ca. 1882], Box 5, Brake Collection, USAMHI.

54. Richmond *Times*, November 7, 1894.

55. Confederate States of America, Adjutant General's Department, *General Orders from the Adjutant General's Office, 1862–1863* (Richmond, Va.: War Dept., 1864), 41–42.

56. Thomas Rosser to A. S. Perham, February 2, 1903, copy in A. S. Webb file, Box 4, Brake Collection, USAMHI; John S. Wise, *The End of an Era* (Boston: Houghton Mifflin, 1899), 338.

57. James Longstreet to Charles Pickett, October 5, 1892, Charles Pickett Papers, VHS; Charles Pickett to James Longstreet, October 12, 1892, photocopy in James Longstreet Papers, SHC. See also Robert A. Bright to Charles Pickett, October 15, 1892, and W. Stuart Symington to Charles Pickett, October 17, 1892, in Pickett Papers, VHS.

58. Charles Pickett to editors, Richmond *Times*, November 11, 1894, copy in Box 3, Brake Collection, USAMHI; Thomas Friend to Charles Pickett, December 10, 1894, Pickett Papers, VHS.

59. Charles Pickett, E. R. Baird, R. A. Bright, Thomas R. Friend, Thomas K. Harrison, Rawley Martin, and W. Stuart Symington to editors, Richmond *Times*, December 19, 1894.

60. Martin Hazlewood, "The Gettysburg Charge," in *SHSP*, 23:229–37; Richmond (Daily) *Dispatch*, January 28, 1896.

61. See, for example, Edward Baird's speech to the Essex Chapter of the United Daughters of the Confederacy, Tappahannock, Va., manuscript in the Edward R. Baird Papers, Museum of the Confederacy, Richmond, Va. (hereafter cited as MC), or Captain John Lamb, *Addresses Delivered at the Unveiling of the Monument to the Confederate Soldiers of Charles City County, Va.* (Richmond, Va.: Whittet & Shepperson, 1901).

62. Typical is Captain Lamb's *Addresses at Unveiling of Monument*, 25, in which he asserted that "we may safely affirm had Pickett's Charge been sustained as was expected, or made at the time fixed on[,] the map of America would have changed, and two governments instead of one would be exercising control of the magnificent domain over which the Stars and Stripes float proudly today."

63. J. Cooper, "Pickett's Brigade at Gaines' Mill," *Confederate Veteran* 6 (Octo-

ber 1898): 472–73. Supporters of Cooper's position included George Wise, letter to the editor, ibid. (December 1898): 568–69; among opponents were George Todd, "Gaines' Mill—Pickett and Hood," and N. B. Hogan, letter to the editor, ibid., 565–67, 567–69.

64. Thomas R. Friend to editor, Richmond *Times-Dispatch*, November 24, 1903; James Longstreet, *From Manassas to Appomattox: Memoirs of the Civil War in America* (Philadelphia: J. B. Lippincott, 1896), 392–409.

65. McDermott [and Reilly], *History of 69th Pennsylvania*, 67.

66. LaSalle Corbell Pickett, "General George E. Pickett," in *SHSP*, 24:151–54.

67. Pickett, *Pickett and His Men*, 302, 308, 408.

68. Capt. J. S. Harris, "Seventh Regiment," in *N.C. Regiments*, 1:380.

69. Asst. Surg. George C. Underwood, "Twenty-Sixth Regiment," in ibid., 2:342–68.

70. Charles M. Cook, "Fifty-Fifth Regiment," in ibid., 3:299–300.

71. See, for example, Capt. S. A. Ashe, "The Pettigrew-Pickett Charge," and William McKendree Robbins, "Longstreet's Assault at Gettysburg," in ibid., 5: 137–59, 101–12.

72. Bond, *Pickett or Pettigrew?*, 7–8; "North Carolina at Gettysburg and Pickett's Charge a Misnomer," (n.p., n.d.), points 7 and 15, copy in Walter Clark Pamphlet Collection, MC.

73. The fullest defense of this new slogan is in *Five Points in the Record of North Carolina in the Great War of 1861–5. Report of the Committee Appointed by the North Carolina Literary and Historical Society—1904* (Goldsboro, N.C.: Nash Brothers, 1904).

74. When Virginians claimed *Confederate Veteran* slighted the Old Dominion, editor Samuel A. Cunningham advised them to read articles in the magazine more closely. See *Confederate Veteran* 1 (July 1893): 197.

75. J. B. Turney, "The First Tennessee at Gettysburg," *Confederate Veteran* 8 (December 1900): 535–37.

76. Dick Reid, "Incidents of the Battle of Gettysburg," *Confederate Veteran* 11 (November 1903): 508.

77. Ezra J. Warner, *Generals in Gray: Lives of the Confederate Commanders* (Baton Rouge: Louisiana State University Press, 1959), 11–12, 307.

78. Speech of Walter Clark in *Unveiling of the Confederate Memorial (Carroll County, Mississippi) by the P. F. Liddell Chapter, U.C.V.* (n.p., 1905), 42.

79. W. D. Reid, "Peril by Rock Fence at Gettysburg," *Confederate Veteran* 19 (February 1911): 66; Baxter McFarland, "The Eleventh Mississippi Regiment at Gettysburg," *Mississippi Historical Society Publications* 2 (1918): 558.

80. Maud Brown, author of *The University Grays: Company A, Eleventh Missis-*

*sippi Regiment, Army of Northern Virginia, 1861–1865* (Richmond, Va.: Garrett and Massie, 1940), led the campaign for the monument. For the park administration's refusal, see J. Walter Coleman, superintendent of Gettysburg National Military Park, to Brown, February 28, 1941, in scrapbook at Gettysburg National Military Park Library, Gettysburg, Pa.

81. Robbins, "Longstreet's Assault at Gettysburg"; William McKendree Robbins Journals, July 12, 1901, William McKendree Robbins Papers, SHC.

82. The John Bachelder Papers are at the New Hampshire Historical Society, and the Gettysburg National Battlefield Park Commission studies are in RG 94, National Archives, Washington, D.C.

83. Robbins Journals, March 17, 1904, Robbins Papers, SHC. Robbins wrote to Edward Porter Alexander on November 11, 1903: "The simple truth is they both went equally far, their line of dead marking the point they reached; and Union officers who viewed the grounds that same evening have told me often that Pettigrew's dead west of the wall and Pickett's dead east of the wall formed one straight north and south line" (Edward Porter Alexander Papers, SHC).

84. Robert A. Bright, "Pickett's Charge," in *SHSP*, 31:228–36 (reprinted in Richmond *Times-Dispatch*, February 7, 1904); Rawley White Martin and Capt. James Holmes Smith, "The Battle of Gettysburg," in *SHSP*, 32:183–95 (reprinted in Richmond *Times-Dispatch*, April 10, 1904); Joseph Mayo, "Pickett's Charge at Gettysburg," in *SHSP*, 34:327–35 (reprinted in Richmond *Times-Dispatch*, May 6, 1906).

85. J. F. Crocker, "Pickett's Charge—My Personal Experiences in Taking Up Arms," in *SHSP*, 33:111–35; Crocker, *Gettysburg, Pickett's Charge and Other War Addresses* (Portsmouth, Va.: W. A. Fiske, 1906; enlarged and reprinted in 1915).

86. James Armstrong, *Grand Gathering of the Men Who Wore the Gray at the Capitol of the Confederacy* (Charleston, S.C.: n.p., 1906), 5.

87. Winfield Peters, "The Lost Sword of General Richard B. Garnett," in *SHSP*, 33:26–32, and Baltimore *Sun*, November 4, 1905.

88. William Henry Stewart, "Colonel John Bowie Magruder," in *SHSP*, 28:203–10; J. F. Crocker, "Colonel James Gregory Hodges," in *SHSP*, 37:184–87; "Equine Heroes of Pickett's Charge," *Cavalry Journal* 24 (November 1913): 482–83.

89. Mrs. General George E. Pickett, "The Wartime Story of General Pickett," serialized in *Cosmopolitan* 55 and 56 (1913). The battle of Gettysburg is discussed in *Cosmopolitan* 56:611–22.

90. LaSalle Corbell Pickett, *The Bugles of Gettysburg* (Chicago: F. G. Browne, 1913).

91. See Gary W. Gallagher, "A Widow and Her Soldier: LaSalle Corbell Pickett

as Author of the George E. Pickett Letters," *Virginia Magazine of History and Biography* 94 (July 1986): 329–44.

92. "Gettysburg Fifty Years After," *Review of Reviews* 48 (1913): 177–83, and pictures scattered throughout Lewis Beitler, comp., *Fiftieth Anniversary of the Battle of Gettysburg* (Harrisburg, Pa.: William Stanley Ray, 1915).

93. John C. McInnis to Marcus C. S. Noble, July 24, 1913, Marcus Cicero Noble Papers, SHC.

94. Glenn Tucker, "What Became of Pickett's Report of the Gettysburg Campaign?," *Civil War Times Illustrated* 6 (October 1967): 37–39.

95. Henry Heth, *The Memoirs of Henry Heth*, ed. James L. Morrison (Westport, Conn.: Greenwood Press, 1974), 177–78, 237.

96. *OR* 27(2):650–57 (Davis), 664–69 (Lane), 616–21 (Wilcox), 631–33 (Lang).

97. *OR* 27(2):385–87 (19th Virginia), 642–55 (26th North Carolina), 646–48 (7th Tennessee). Some regimental reports for Kemper's brigade are in the George Pickett Papers, PLDU.

98. A frequently repeated story, one version of which can be found in LaSalle Corbell Pickett, "My Soldier," *McClure's*, 1908, 569.

99. For a useful examination of this concept, see Edward Tabor Linenthal, *Sacred Ground: Americans and Their Battlefields* (Urbana: University of Illinois Press, 1991), 87–126.

100. See Jeff Stepp to the editor, *Blue & Gray Magazine* 6 (October 1988): 6.

101. William Faulkner, *Intruder in the Dust* (New York: Vintage, 1972), 194–95.

*The*

*Parallel Lives of*

*Two Virginia Soldiers*

## ARMISTEAD AND GARNETT

*Robert K. Krick*

What did Maxcy Gregg and Thomas R. R. Cobb have in common? Why do Paul Semmes and William Barksdale fit together in Confederate imagery? Or Abner M. Perrin and Junius Daniel, John M. Jones and Micah Jenkins, Lawrence O'Bryan Branch and William E. Starke? The men in those pairs stand together, of course, because they fell together, Confederate general officers killed at the same time and place. Lewis A. Armistead and Richard B. Garnett seem to make a matched pair in that deadly fraternity, but in fact, unlike others on the list, the two Virginians had experienced remarkably parallel lives during virtually their entire shared four and one-half decades on earth.

The biographical roads that led Perrin and Daniel to adjacent graves at Spotsylvania Court House were very far from identical, but Dick Garnett and Lewis Armistead wound up dead in July 1863 at Gettysburg, victims of the same ill-starred charge, after following astonishingly similar paths. Their common threads included an identical birth year; well-placed Virginian ancestry; close relatives occupying powerful positions in the U.S. Army, with ties that got the young men into the U.S. Military Academy; mutual discomfort at West Point; two decades of antebellum military service in the same Sixth U.S. Infantry, without ever deviating from commissions in that unit; extensive common experience with Mexicans, Indians, and Kansas in the tumultuous 1850s; a transcontinental adventure through the Mormon War and across the Sierra Nevada to

**THIS PREWAR PHOTOGRAPH** of Lewis Addison Armistead is published here for the first time through the kindness of two leading authorities on Confederate images, Bill Turner and Lawrence T. Jones. The view was taken at a St. Louis gallery operated by T. Harry Hughes. The original print, together with twenty-six other rare images, fell victim to a ring of Postal Service thieves looting registered parcels in Dallas, Texas, in 1988.

gold rush California; service in the unfriendly Colorado River desert; and nondescript opportunities for distinction as Confederate officers before July 1863.

Lewis Addison Armistead was born at New Berne, North Carolina, on February 18, 1817, the son of Elizabeth Stanley and Walker Keith Armistead, an army officer from Virginia. The boy's father was one of five brothers who had fought in the War of 1812. His uncle, Maj. George Armistead, had commanded Fort McHenry in September 1814 when its resistance to British attack inspired Francis Scott Key to write "The Star-Spangled Banner." Another uncle was killed in Canada that same month. Walker Keith Armistead held the rank of lieutenant colonel at the time of Lewis's birth. The next year he became a full colonel and was brevetted to brigadier general when Lewis was eleven years old.[1]

The family name of the prominent and militarily inclined Armistead family was pronounced at some variance from the obvious phonetic version, in typical Virginian fashion. A scholarly treatise on Virginia language patterns, with a list quaintly titled "Some Virginia Names Spelt One Way and Called Another," identifies the correct nineteenth-century pronunciation as Um'sted.[2] Whether or not one accepts the vowel switch to open the pronunciation, the *i* in the middle of the word clearly was silent.

Walker Keith Armistead's position as one of the handful of general officers in the U.S. Army unquestionably was pivotal in securing admission for Lewis to the military academy. The elder Armistead wrote directly to the secretary of war on January 24, 1833, "to solicit for my son . . . a cadet's warrant" and signed himself as "Brig'r Genl." He added the arrant misstatement that the boy was a splendid student. Less than two months later young Lewis was writing to the secretary of war, from Winchester, to acknowledge his acceptance to West Point. He was one of ten boys from the rather small Armistead clan who applied to the military academy during the four decades before the Civil War.[3]

Richard Brooke Garnett also was born in 1817, in Essex County, Virginia, one of twin sons delivered on November 21 to Anna Maria Brooke and William Garnett. Richard's twin brother, William Henry, died in the 1855 yellow-fever epidemic in Norfolk. Seven of his nine other siblings had also died by 1861. Two of Dick Garnett's sisters married Virginia Military Institute professors, Thomas H. Williamson and John Mercer Brooke (whose second wife was Sandie Pendleton's widow, née Kate Corbin). Anna Garnett died in 1854 and was interred in the plot next to that where Thomas J. "Stonewall" Jackson would be buried nine years later. Her brother George Mercer Brooke was a general in the U.S. Army,[4] who would replicate for young Dick Garnett the role that W. K. Armistead played in securing appointment to West Point for the next generation.

A final Garnett family connection has led to a great deal of confusion among modern students endeavoring to identify Confederate photographs. Richard's father, William Garnett, had a younger brother named Robert Selden Garnett. R. S. Garnett's fourth child and first son, who bore his father's full name, became the first Confederate general killed during the Civil War. Long after the wartime deaths of the cousins, a photograph of a dark-bearded man appeared in print labeled as Richard B. Garnett. Another photograph of a beardless, but apparently dark-haired, man was identified as that of Robert S. Garnett. According to turn-of-the-century family members, neither image was Richard. The late Eleanor Brockenbrough of Richmond, an incomparable and virtually infallible authority on Confederate matters, knew the family members involved and concluded that no likeness of Dick Garnett survives.

The photograph still universally identified today as that of Dick Garnett, wrote a family member in 1908, "can and will be vouched for by any member of [the] family as an authentic likeness of Robt. S. Garnett, and not Richd. B. Garnett, of whom there is no picture in existence so far as known. R. B. Garnett was a man of just the opposite type, having light hair and blue eyes, and he wore no full beard." The family believed that the second photo also depicted Robert S. Garnett. They had no doubt that neither was Richard and offered several witnesses to that effect, inside the family and out. An amusing modern eruption over the photographs actually became a court case in Essex County in 1986, the result of an attempt to seek legal redress over the labeling of portraits of the two generals on that county's courthouse walls.[5]

ROBERT K. KRICK

The prospects for photography of any sort, to say nothing of quarreling over its results, had not troubled Dick Garnett when he undertook in 1833 an attempt to secure admission to the U.S. Military Academy. The effort took three years to succeed. Richard wrote a letter of supplication to the secretary of war in December 1833, in a mature and dignified style and smooth penmanship. His private tutor certified in the same month that the teenager was "rigidly moral" and exuded an "ardent desire" to do well scholastically—a textbook instance of damning with faint phrase. The ardent desire bore some fruit in "Vulgar & Decimal Fractions" and some other oddments, but apparently far from universally. Henry A. Wise wrote in support of Garnett's cause. So did various friends and kin, often alluding to Dick's uncle-general and to his prominent family, "one of the most worthy & respectable" in a state conscious of such things. The boy's own father wrote to the secretary of war about Dick and added in a bizarre postscript that the applicant "is in his 16th year & may possibly be in fact 16 years old though of that I am not certain." Historians enamored of psychohistory may well be able to find something to amuse them in a father who had little idea of the birthdate of twin sons.

More correspondence during 1834 sought admission to West Point for Dick Garnett, but in vain. The turning point came the following year when Uncle George intervened. George Mercer Brooke, Dick Garnett's mother's brother, had been a brigadier general in the tiny U.S. Army of the period for more than a decade. He was accordingly one of the most powerful men in the nation's military establishment. General Brooke wrote in September 1835 to President Andrew Jackson in a personal vein, addressing his old acquaintance as "Dear General." Brooke reminded Jackson that this was "the first personal favor I have asked" and noted that, although he had been in service for twenty-seven years, no relative held any office on the basis of his influence. After making his plea on behalf of his nephew, Brooke chatted about a mutual acquaintance. The letter worked. Jackson scribbled and initialed a penciled endorsement on the back directing that Richard Garnett be admitted to West Point the following year and charged against a special fund "alloted to the . . . Territories." A few months later General Brooke wrote to the secretary of war to assure him that nephew Richard had been studying diligently. When the hard-won appointment finally arrived in April 1836, General Brooke acknowledged it in a personal note.[6]

Lewis Armistead reached West Point three years before Richard Garnett arrived there, despite having the same birth year. Their time at the military

**GARNETT FAMILY MEMBERS**
identified this likeness as
Robert Seldon Garnett, and it
has been printed over that
caption many times. They were
emphatic that neither this nor
the other Garnett photograph,
taken from the opposite profile
and showing an individual
with full dark beard and
different hairstyle, depicted
Richard Brooke Garnett. A
1986 court case in Virginia
investigated the controversy.
Francis Trevelyan Miller, ed.,
*The Photographic History of the
Civil War*, 10 vols. (New York:
Review of Reviews, 1911),
10:147

academy fell in a period during which a remarkable array of young men
who would become famous as Civil War generals were in attendance. Garnett failed one year; Armistead failed two before being expelled during
his third assault on the school's academic bulwarks. In consequence both
had multiple sets of classmates at different times. The star-studded array of
cadets who shared classes with Armistead or Garnett included Richard S.
Ewell, William Tecumseh Sherman, George H. Thomas, Josiah Gorgas,
John F. Reynolds, H. G. Wright, Don Carlos Buell, cousin Robert S.
Garnett, J. M. Jones, P. G. T. Beauregard, Alexander R. Lawton, E. O. C.
Ord, Edward Johnson, H. H. Sibley, Braxton Bragg, Jubal A. Early, John
Sedgwick, Joseph Hooker, Arnold Elzey, and John C. Pemberton. Other
contemporaries of Armistead, Garnett, or both were James Longstreet,
Earl Van Dorn, Lafayette McLaws, Richard H. Anderson, William B.
Franklin, Roswell S. Ripley, Alfred Pleasonton, Simon B. Buckner, Alex-

ander Hays, Winfield Scott Hancock, J. R. Anderson, George G. Meade, and U. S. Grant.[7]

Armistead mastered neither the scholastic rigors of West Point nor its conduct requirements. By October 1833 his father was obliged to ask the secretary of war that Lewis be allowed to resign because "his recent sickness" had left him in an "unprepared state" for his classes. The resignation was accepted on November 21. The following April, Lewis had been accepted again for another try at the first-year curriculum. He lasted the year this time but stood fifty-second among fifty-seven cadets and was judged deficient and turned back for yet another year. Armistead's new attempt should have gone smoothly that fall, if it ever would, because he was taking the same courses for the third time. Even so, in November 1835 he stood fortieth in mathematics and twenty-seventh in French.[8]

Whether Armistead ever could have conquered his first-year classes must remain problematical, because his checkered career foundered on disciplinary shoals. There is no record of conduct difficulties during his first brief venture at West Point. A few months into his second fall, however, he was court-martialed for answering at muster on behalf of a missing friend and for standing guard for the same fellow. The court found Lewis guilty in part and sentenced him to standing four extra Sunday guard tours. At the end of the 1834–35 year, which Armistead failed academically, he stood 201 among 240 cadets in all classes in conduct. Jubal A. Early, who would be Armistead's nemesis in a clash the next winter, finished 223rd among the same group, with 189 demerits—only 11 short of mandatory expulsion. In the fall of 1835, as Armistead essayed the same classes for a third time, he earned 22 demerits in one month, putting him on a course for automatic dismissal by spring.[9]

Armistead's accumulation of demerits became moot on January 16, 1836, because a ruckus in the mess hall on that day led to his final departure from the military academy. A member of George E. Pickett's staff, who knew Pickett's brigadier well, wrote soon after the Civil War that he had "been told" that the "youthful escapade" involved "the partial cracking of Jubal A. Early's head with a mess-hall plate" by Armistead. One family history accepts that version (a second declares that Armistead graduated), and so does the only published sketch of the plate-wielding cadet.[10]

There is no reason to doubt the story, but pinning down the particulars in contemporary records proved to be a frustrating undertaking. The oversized manuscript document recording cadet offenses as they occurred has been folded in eighths for a century and a half, with one crease right atop Armistead's entry for January 16. Everything beyond "Disorderly conduct" has crumbled and vanished. A surviving battalion order dated the next day placed "Cadet Armistead . . . in arrest charged with disorderly conduct in the Mess Hall. . . . Limits his room." A fire that leveled a main academy building in 1838 destroyed the registers of delinquencies for the period 1830–37, together with much correspondence.[11] Jubal Early apparently was in Florida at the time, so devotees of conspiratorial theories of history can hardly blame him for the fire.

Because the cadet hospital records are extensive and explicit, one might expect to find Jubal Early entered in the register with a notation about skull repairs, even if he had suffered only the "partial cracking" of record. Register number 603 shows Early as a frequent patient at the hospital through 1834, with eight visits for seven different complaints. During the same period Armistead only visited the dispensary three times. Evidently Armistead was hardier than Early, liked laudanum less, or perhaps just needed class time more. Lewis was one of the last cadets to succumb to the rampant influenza epidemic in November 1834. Come January 1836, however, the hospital register is missing. Judging by the numbering system, it has been lost for a century or more. Early's post-Armistead cranial adjustments must remain shrouded in mystery.[12]

Although details of the January 16 fracas remain uncertain, there can be no doubt that Early was not a model cadet in deportment. In February 1836 he was nearly halfway to the mandatory dismissal total for demerits, and he finished his second-class year that spring with 196, four short of expulsion. By then Armistead was long gone. His father's shadow won for him the slender privilege of resigning to avoid the embarrassment of being expelled. The superintendent of the academy wrote to his superior that Armistead, "through imprudence," faced dismissal and had on January 29 "presented his Resignation, which on account of his father I hope will be accepted." It was, on February 2, to take effect on the fifteenth.[13]

While Dick Garnett's term at the military academy was not so riotous as Armistead's (neither broken crockery nor cracked heads appear in his surviving record), his stay was not always smooth. Garnett was arraigned by the always busy West Point court-martial system in April 1838 and December 1839. His felony in the first instance was "Hallooing in the Barrack Hall." At the end of his five years at the academy, with enrollment average about 220, Garnett rated in conduct at ranks of 164, 132, 201, 198, and 190. That lower-third showing in deportment mirrored his general academic standing. Toward the end of his second year, for instance, in a class that finished with fifty-eight members, Garnett ranked forty-fifth in mathematics, fortieth in French, and thirty-sixth in drawing. During Garnett's third year, ending in 1839, he failed and withdrew. Taking the same courses again during the next term, he finished fourteenth among his new classmates, then graduated in 1841 standing twenty-ninth among fifty-two graduates. His cousin Robert S. Garnett of the debatable image graduated with Richard and just two academic ranks away.[14]

Had Lewis Armistead survived his third tilt with the military academy, he would have been commissioned as a second lieutenant on July 1, 1839; having failed to complete even a single year, he was not commissioned until July 10, 1839, and that directly from civilian life. He had lost all of nine days in rank. The influence of family connections to the army continued to pave the way for Lieutenant Armistead. The newly minted officer and gentleman left promptly for Florida to campaign against the Seminoles. He served there for a time under his father's command but fell sick and had to leave Florida's enervating climate about the middle of July in 1840. The lieutenant's education in the ways of bureaucracies everywhere included a frightened scramble to straighten out quartermaster accounts he had signed over while heading for sick leave. An entirely inflexible quartermaster general in Washington was unimpressed by surgeon's orders or anything other than the paperwork that ruled his staff existence. Armistead survived his educational brush with headquarters rigidity and won promotion to first lieutenant in March 1844, after five years in grade.[15] The antebellum army was like that.

For Dick Garnett the Old Army, as it came to be known, was even more grudging with rewards. His commission as second lieutenant on graduation in 1841 remained in force for six years, even longer than Armistead's. Both young officers held their rank in the same Sixth U.S. Infantry. The regimental commander in the early 1840s was Zachary Taylor. Their assignments were to the distant frontier and sometimes beyond. In 1844 Garnett's Company F was posted at Fort Smith, Arkansas, and Armistead's Company I was at Fort Towson, C.N.—in the Cherokee Nation. Both men spent a great deal of time on leave during their two decades with the Sixth Infantry. Without a careful review it is impossible to state definitively that they were away more than their peers who were bereft of friends in high places; however, a first survey of the regimental records suggests that conclusion, especially for Armistead. Dick Garnett's long absence from the Sixth Infantry in the middle of the decade came as the

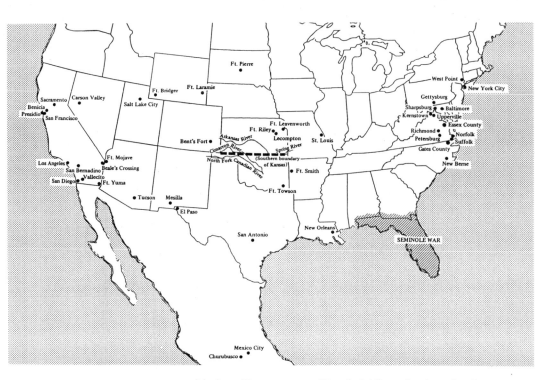

**SITES ASSOCIATED** with the military careers of Lewis Addison Armistead and Richard Brooke Garnett (Map by George Skoch)

result of orders: he was detached to serve as aide to his uncle-general in late 1844 and again beginning in October 1845. Garnett remained with General Brooke through the Mexican War, during which time Brooke served extensively at the New Orleans port of embarkation. Brooke received promotion to major general in 1848 for "performance of his duties in prosecution of the war." Nephew Richard became a first lieutenant in February 1847, while under his uncle's command.[16]

Lieutenant Armistead served with the Sixth Infantry in Mexico in frequent combat and with distinguished results. He won a brevet to captain for gallant and meritorious conduct at the battles of Contreras and Churubusco on August 20, 1847, and another to major for similar distinction in action at Molino del Rey three weeks later. In the August action, the advancing line included troops under Armistead, Hancock, Longstreet, Buckner, and Sedgwick—all West Point comrades and all destined for 1860s fame. A few days later at the storming of Chapultepec, it was said that Armistead was the first man to leap into the ditch, while George E.

Pickett planted an American flag nearby. Two accounts have Armistead wounded at Chapultepec.[17]

Henry Heth, who graduated from West Point in 1847, reached Mexico in time to serve with the Sixth Infantry beside "dear old Lewis [Armistead], a kinsman of mine." Heth and Armistead and Winfield Scott Hancock, of whom Armistead was particularly fond, formed a congenial junior officers' mess. Armistead and his chum Hancock explored the region in tandem, climbing the peaks soaring above Mexico City. In his cheerful and anecdotal memoirs, Harry Heth preserved an interesting perspective on his thirty-year-old superior officer. "Armistead was a good-natured man," Heth wrote, "and I am afraid we teased him too much." Hancock particularly guyed his friend and messmate about his appetite, in a tale often told to fellow officers. Armistead customarily carved the meat. By Hancock's account, "When we had a turkey, chicken or duck for dinner, Lewis would give us a very small piece and then say, 'Boys, I will take the carcass.'"[18]

Because Garnett and Armistead both served steadily and long—very long—with the Sixth Infantry, the roll of that regiment's leaders offers an interesting idea of the sort of patrons and tutors with whom the young officers would be in frequent contact. In stark contrast to the long roster of familiar names among their military academy peers, the list of Sixth Infantry field-grade officers is uniformly unfamiliar. When Zachary Taylor commanded the regiment in the early 1840s, Garnett's and Armistead's colonel was about as impressive a man as the army had to offer. The rest of the dozen men who held such roles were of quite another sort. Who has heard of William Hoffman, Albemarle Cady, J. V. Bomford, John Greene, Gustavus Loomis, Francis Lee, George Andrews, Henry Atkinson, Newman Clarke, Washington Seawell, and William Davenport?[19]

In the early 1850s Lt. Richard B. Garnett came into unfriendly contact with some Miniconjou Sioux near Fort Laramie and figured in the opening stages of one of the U.S. Army's least successful Indian encounters. In June 1853, while Garnett commanded at Fort Laramie, a quarrel arose between some of the Miniconjou and a nearby ferry operator. When a sergeant from the fort intervened, one of the Sioux fired a musket at him. Garnett sent two dozen men under Lt. H. B. Fleming to apprehend the man who had fired the shot, but the Indians ran for cover and opened fire. In the fight that followed, three Sioux were killed and two captured. The next summer, not long after Garnett had left Laramie for detached duty,

Fleming responded to a similar incident (the pièce de résistance this time being a cow) in like fashion. The result was the famous Grattan Massacre.[20]

Garnett was involved with at least one Indian under decidedly different circumstances. Early in 1855, near what is now Wheatland, Wyoming, an Indian named Looking Woman gave birth to a son by Lieutenant Garnett, who meanwhile had been assigned to recruiting duty in the East. Any uncertainty about parentage that the Virginia Garnetts may have experienced apparently found resolution, because they acknowledged the kinship. Louis Garnett of the Essex County, Virginia, line addressed William ("Billie") Garnett, the son of Richard and Looking Woman, in a letter as "Dear Cousin." Louis told his cousin that "most of the admirable persons of whom I write you are your blood relations. . . . Your grandfather and mine were brothers. We trace back to the same ancestor . . . Muscoe Garnett of Essex County, Va." Billie Garnett spent much of his life working as a scout and interpreter. He was employed by the noted Baptiste Pourier, accompanied a delegation of chiefs to Washington, met U. S. Grant, served at the Dull Knife battle in November 1876, and witnessed the death of Crazy Horse. Billie died in South Dakota in 1928.[21]

Lewis Armistead had been married in more traditional style since about 1844 to Cecilia Lee Love. Cecilia was a granddaughter of Richard Henry Lee, a signer of the Declaration of Independence. The couple apparently had two children with them on the Kansas plains in 1855, but only one son is mentioned in the family history. That boy, named Walker Keith Armistead after his grandfather, married a granddaughter of Daniel Webster.[22]

In March 1855 Brevet Major Armistead won promotion to regular rank of captain, his last advancement before the onset of the Civil War. The new rank came on the heels of a series of letters to Washington on his behalf. One referred to Armistead's gallant record in Mexico and reminded the secretary of war that the first lieutenant was "the *oldest* in the service" at that rank. Another lauded Armistead's distinguished Virginia connections and impractically urged a regular line majority or even lieutenant colonelcy for him. In December 1854 Armistead went so far as to write to Adj. Gen. Samuel Cooper, albeit with becoming modesty, on his own behalf.[23]

Almost immediately after the promotion arrived, disaster struck the Armisteads on the hostile frontier. Armistead commanded at Fort Riley, Kansas Territory, while that post went through the pangs of establishment and construction. At the beginning of August 1855 the major led his company up the Smoky Hill River, leaving his wife and children behind.

On August 3 Cecilia Love Armistead died suddenly, one of fifteen victims (fourteen of them civilians) who fell prey on that single day to a virulent cholera epidemic that swept the post. Lewis hurried back to Riley in response to an emergency summons. He arrived to find his wife a corpse prepared for burial by friendly women, and the civilian workmen threatening mutiny in terror of the epidemic. His two motherless children, the eldest a ten-year-old boy, posed an enormous domestic problem in that alien landscape. Armistead built a wooden trellis over Cecilia's grave and persuaded vines to grow around it, but by the early twentieth century the site was lost and only remembered by old-timers. Despite the ordeal, the major resumed military operations almost at once in the midst of the campaigning season. By the end of the month the grieving husband and his company had marched to Bent's Fort. At the end of September they were back at Fort Riley, and Armistead was preparing for five months of leave in which to undertake the sad task of realigning his bereft family's living arrangements.[24]

Lewis Armistead's connection with Fort Riley extended into 1857, when he was commanding the post at the time of an apparent Cheyenne threat in July. With only one company of infantry at his disposal, Armistead feared an onset too powerful for him to resist. His appeal to Col. Philip St. George Cooke for support from the colonel's dragoons brought help, but no attack developed. The modern biographer of Henry H. Sibley in describing this affair called Armistead "the incompetent commander of Fort Riley." Anyone who has examined the career of Sibley to book-length extent certainly should recognize incompetence with pellucid clarity; but there is no other contemporary comment so derogatory about Armistead, and none of his superiors recorded major or recurring faults against him.[25]

Richard Garnett caught up to Armistead in regular rank when he became captain in May 1855, just two months after his longtime comrade's promotion to that rank. Garnett remained in the East, mostly in New York, on recruiting duty, however, for more than a year after the promotion. Both men saw vast swaths of the Indian frontier as captains and company commanders during the mid-1850s. Between the spring of 1855 and that of 1858 Garnett's end-of-the-month postings included these exotic locales: Fort Pierre, Nebraska Territory; Camp Bacon; on board steamer *Clara*; Fort Leavenworth; Northern Boundary, Kansas Territory; Lecompton, K.T.; Spring River, K.T.; Arkansas River, K.T.; Cimarron River; Willow Creek; North Fork Canadian River; and Camp Bateman (near Leavenworth). On September 3, 1855, Garnett's Company K of the

Sixth Infantry participated in Harney's big attack on the Sioux, but the captain was not with his company at the time.

During the same three-year span, Armistead's postings included these far-flung locations, in addition to Fort Riley: Smoky Hill, K.T.; Bent's Fort; Pole Creek; Laramie River; and Republican Fork, N.T. Their intimate friends of West Point and Mexican War days, Winfield Scott Hancock and Harry Heth, remained with the Sixth during this period. Hancock was a lieutenant in Garnett's company for a time, then for years served as the regimental adjutant. Heth held down the post of regimental quartermaster for the Sixth. An interesting example of the rigors of frontier campaigning, and of the responsibilities borne by company commanders, can be seen in the operations of Armistead's company in July, August, and September of 1856. During the first of those blazing hot months, his company of foot soldiers covered 423 miles. During August it covered 296 more miles, and during September another 323. Because it is not clear how late in July the company began this hegira, nor how early in September it finished, it is impossible to compute a precise average march rate per day. Even if the march began on July 1 and ended on September 30, which seems unlikely, covering 1,042 miles of trackless wilds on foot in 92 days must have taken enormous perseverance. Leading a trek of that sort cannot be claimed as a precisely apt preparation of Lewis Armistead for command of a Civil War infantry brigade, nor for charging into the hail of lead and iron pouring from Cemetery Ridge near Gettysburg, but it surely must have made him a sturdier man and a better leader of men.[26]

Captain Garnett's experience equivalent to Armistead's long march came in the delicate arena of Bloody Kansas. During the winter of 1856–57, Garnett and his company were stationed at such tense spots as Lecompton, whose name was synonymous with constitutional quarrels. The next May Lt. Col. Joseph E. Johnston received the unenviable assignment of surveying the debatable southern boundary of Kansas. He took along six companies. Dick Garnett accompanied Johnston as the senior infantry commander. Johnston's private journal reveals Garnett struggling to keep his foot soldiers up with the mounted troops, vainly chasing Indians suspected of murder, parlaying with Indians in Mexican dialect, jury-rigging a ferryboat out of metallic wagon beds, and scouting ahead with Johnston and small parties of officers.[27]

Soon after he completed this difficult trip, Captain Garnett wrote in some disgruntlement on his own behalf to the secretary of war. He pointed out that his military academy standing was second best among those assigned as infantry officers (who always came from the lower-ranking graduates). The one higher-graduating infantryman had since died. Now he had been "not only outstripped by my classmates in the race for promotion, but by many who had left the academy several years subsequent to my graduation." What was "still more mortifying" was that the recent increase in the number of army regiments had at once catapulted twenty-four juniors over Garnett's head, leaving him "*deeply* humiliated." What seemed to be "the harshness with which I have been treated" had been as bad as though "*calculated to destroy all soldierly feeling and pride*." Although this heartfelt plea did no good, it provides an important window into the unhappy military soul of Captain Garnett.[28]

The theater of operations of the Sixth Infantry, and therefore of Armistead and Garnett, changed dramatically in 1858. The regiment and its components left the Great Plains and headed for Utah Territory to augment the army units arrayed in what became popularly, if inaptly, known as the Mormon War. A show of force in Utah in 1857 under Col. Albert Sidney Johnston required renewed strength the next year to maintain its role. In January 1858 the War Department decided to send Johnston "the reinforcements he would need to confront a people in arms." The Sixth Infantry made up about one-fourth of the total reinforcements, which moved west in May and June. Both Armistead and Garnett were carried on the regimental return for the end of May as "En Route for Utah." Long before the troops reached Utah, peace commissioners had wrung an accord from the charged atmosphere. Fortunately for everyone involved, there was no war to be fought by the time the Sixth neared Utah.[29]

With peace triumphant in Utah, the War Department distributed the troops accumulated near the troubled points to other duty. The Sixth Infantry received orders to march to Walla Walla, Washington Territory, to deal with Indian troubles reported there. The best route to Walla Walla seemed to be across the mountains to Benicia, California, and thence up the coast by steamer. The Sixth Infantry left Fort Bridger, Wyoming, on August 21, 1858, to begin that roundabout journey. Since snow "lay eight inches deep at Bridger" late in August, the prospects for crossing the big mountains en route to California must have seemed somewhat daunting. The infantry marched into the Sierra Nevada late in October from Nevada's Carson Valley, not far ahead of the schedule that a dozen years before had resulted in the notorious commissary quandary for the Donner party in those same mountains.[30]

The combination of hardships, remarkable scenery, and curiosities that greeted Armistead, Garnett, and their comrades in that spectacular wilderness comes vividly across the years from the letters and journal of an enlisted man who marched in the column. "We had hard times in the mountains," he wrote two weeks after the ordeal ended. The men floundered "in many places" through snow piled "two or three feet deep." The infantryman marveled at the tallest trees he had ever seen and "six feet in diameter," at brooks that "flow—no, they leap—down the mountain . . . forming high waterfalls," and at "deep declivities and steep precipices." Once out of the towering mountains the Sixth Infantry observed with wonder the frantic scenes in California's gold country. The regiment reached Sacramento on November 11 and Benicia four days later, where it stood for an elegant review attended by civilians from all around the San Francisco region.[31]

The last leg of the journey to Walla Walla never came about because events elsewhere deflected the Sixth Infantry to a very different corner of the West Coast. A party of emigrants bound from Iowa to California had been beset on August 27 by Mojave Indians as the pilgrims attempted to cross the Colorado River in the vicinity of modern Needles, California. By killing a dozen travelers, wounding that many more, and pillaging the wagon train, the Indians drew on themselves the wrath of the army. Much of the Sixth Infantry headed to southern California to go after the Mojaves. The rest of the regiment remained near San Francisco. As a result, Lewis Armistead and Dick Garnett would spend the remainder of their pre–Civil War careers in California, primarily in the barren wastes east of San Bernardino.[32]

Armistead was at the Presidio in San Francisco at the end of December 1858, and Garnett was at Benicia. Two months later both men were on or near California's southeastern border. Lewis Armistead's trip to the desert involved a great deal of waterborne hazard. On February 11, 1859, his Company F was one of four companies of the Sixth Infantry that left San Francisco aboard the steamship *Uncle Sam*. The ship's cargo included 300 mules and all of the infantrymen's weapons and baggage. *Uncle Sam* ran into "a perfect hurricane" near midnight and nearly foundered. Most of the cargo went over the side to lighten ship, under direction of the Sixth's officers, who managed to maintain discipline amidst the chaos. Just as the decision had been made to pitch the mules overboard as well, the winds suddenly ceased, as though by a miracle. Only two men died in the episode.[33] The loss of weapons during the storm would have an impact on Armistead's career in August, when he fought a battle against the Mojaves.

Both Armistead and Garnett were at Fort Gaston in southern California at the end of March 1859. One month later Armistead had reached Fort Mojave (spelled *Mohave* on almost every contemporary document at this period, as was the Indian tribe's name), where he remained through the blazing summer. Most of the time he commanded at the post. Garnett's location during the same months was at San Bernardino, at Camp Prentiss (near San Bernardino), and then at Fort Yuma. Armistead's post lay in the most desolate country imaginable, away from the nearest wagon track and starkly isolated from any news or other human contact. Fort Mojave was about thirty miles north of Beale's Crossing, which is where Interstate 40 crosses the Colorado River today. The fort was on the east bank of the river and as a result geographically in the Department of Utah, but the Department of California administered it. Fort Yuma was somewhat less isolated, though hardly any more Edenic. It stood on a high bluff just across the river from Yuma, Arizona, where Winterhaven, California, now stands.[34]

Bvt. Maj. Lewis A. Armistead commanded a battlefield for the first and only time in his long military career on August 5, 1859, when he led fifty infantrymen in action against 200 or more Mojave Indians a dozen miles into the desert below Fort Mojave. In campaigning against the Mojaves, Armistead very likely took the lead role because his company was the best armed of those in the vicinity. With his brevet rank of major, Armistead doubtless was able to lay claim to such rifles as remained available after the *Uncle Sam* disaster. His men, he wrote on August 6, "had, with few exceptions, the new musket." Some of the companies had to make do with smoothbores—and poor smoothbores at that, converted to percussion from flintlock firing systems. Armistead's well-equipped company surely would be the aggressive maneuver element of choice under almost any circumstance. The Indians he chased carried bows and arrows, with which they could match quite well against smoothbores. The Mojaves, a Paiute people, lived in a warrior society, one of the few California tribes so configured.[35]

Major Armistead led twenty-five picked men of his Company F out of Fort Mojave during the night of August 4. His object was "to surprise the Indians by keeping around on the mesa, and in that way get below them." Lt. Elisha Gaylor Marshall, a New Yorker, left the fort the next morning with two dozen more troops selected from his Company I of the Sixth. Marshall's role was to move ostentatiously and directly toward the suspected Mojave stronghold. The ploy worked. Armistead's clandestine march put him within reach of hostile Indians before they knew he was near. The major personally crawled close enough to fire the first shot at three braves and killed one of them. "The firing," of course, "soon raised the whole valley." Armistead hurriedly picked a strong position behind a backwater of the Colorado River, which he described variously as "a small slough" and as "a Lagoon." The Mojaves swarmed around the infantrymen "very bravely," but Armistead repulsed them steadily.

After about thirty minutes of hot firing, Lieutenant Marshall reached the scene, and the Indians drew off. Twenty minutes later they surged back again "as boldly as before." This onslaught lasted about fifteen minutes before the Mojaves again broke off contact. Major Armistead concluded after a long pause that his enemies "had had enough," and formed his fifty-man force into column for the return to the fort. The infantry had not marched far before the Mojaves fell on them once more, "this time more boldly than ever." Away from Armistead's carefully selected defensive position, the ground suited the Indians better than it did the column from the Sixth Infantry. Terrain "full of little sand hillocks" and complicated by "the dense nature of the chaparral" gave the attackers ample cover close to their goal. "They stood our fire very well," Armistead wrote a few hours later, "coming up to within twenty and thirty paces, but in about thirty minutes they had to run. This time they were apparently so well satisfied as to omit their whoop of defiance, which had accompanied their other retreats."

By now the Indians had in fact had enough, and Armistead led his victorious troops back to Fort Mojave, having won one of the sharpest encounters fought by any part of his regiment during the two decades that he served with it. He did not estimate Indian numbers at the time, saying only, "I do not know how many Indians there were—there were a great many." Later he gauged the hostile strength at 200. Lieutenant Marshall thought that there were about 300 Indians in the attacking force. Both officers agreed that the twenty-three enemy dead they had counted did not constitute an accurate total, because many others must have been hidden in the same dense chaparral that covered the attack. Losses in the two companies of the Sixth Infantry totaled only three men. A regimental summary of the action written three weeks later concluded with both magnanimity and accuracy that "the Indians fought with great bravery, repeatedly charging the troops." On August 6 Armistead completed his handwritten report, the heat of the march and the fight still on him, with an embittered plea for relief from the ineptitude of the army's quartermasters. His men faced campaigning in that unforgiving, hard country without shoes. Armistead had been forced to seek the partial expedient of buying all footgear in the stores of the post sutler, without authorization, and billing the government.[36] Whether or not commanding 50 infantrymen against 200 Indians prepared Armistead for his duties as a Confederate general, struggling against a maladroit supply system unquestionably foreshadowed what he would face in Virginia during the Civil War.

Less than a month after his victory on the Colorado River, Major Armistead was granted sixty days of leave—perhaps as a reward for his successful campaigning. Before the end of the two months Armistead's leave was extended for another six months, then for four more beyond that, and finally for an additional two months. The modest leave that began on September 3, 1859, eventually carried Armistead into October 1860. Two more months of absence, on detached service, finally ended that December. When he rejoined Company F at New San Diego, where he also assumed command of the post, Armistead had been away more than thirteen months. The major and his company remained at San Diego through April 1861. He resigned on May 26 in response to the secession of his home state of Virginia.[37]

Dick Garnett, meanwhile, saw a great deal of the same deserts but without the action that won credit and broke the monotony for Armistead. While his longtime mate fought the Mojaves and then departed on extended leave, Captain Garnett remained at Fort Yuma through the blistering summer of 1859. On September 20 he was sick enough to have to relinquish command of his Company K for a full month. In November 1859 Garnett moved to Armistead's old post, the remote Fort Mojave. He and his company languished there until September 1860, when they returned, doubtless joyfully, to Benicia. Garnett was at Benicia at the end of April 1861. Eighteen days later he resigned in order to follow his native state out of the Union.[38]

A Special Order dated June 12, 1861, put Lewis Armistead on leave during the interval while his resignation was being processed. Three days later he took part in a lachrymose farewell that has come to symbolize the wrenching impact of civil war on the officer corps of the Old Army. A group of southerners heading home for Confederate service gathered on June 15 for a final sad evening with their northern friends who had determined to stay with the Union. The setting was Camp Fitzgerald, an army post on the outskirts of Los Angeles. The camp's location shifted several times during this period, so its precise site on June 15 cannot be established. Albert Sidney Johnston, the ranking officer present and about to start for his native South, escorted his wife to the farewell meeting. Armistead's special friend Winfield Scott Hancock played host at his quarters; Hancock's wife, Almira, left a vivid account of what she called "a never-to-be-forgotten evening."[39]

As midnight drew nigh, Colonel Johnston's wife sang some romantic songs with a deep emotion that moved the whole group. "The most crushed of the party," Almira Hancock remembered, "was Major Armistead, who, with tears, which were contagious, streaming down his face" told Hancock feelingly, "Good-by; you can never know what this has cost me." The Virginian gave Almira Hancock a satchel full of souvenirs with instructions to send them to his family if he should die. A little prayerbook among the mementos was for Mrs. Hancock. On the flyleaf Armistead had written his name and the motto "Trust in God and fear nothing."[40]

Lewis Armistead began the long trek toward the seat of the new war as part of the most famous group of military emigrants moving in that direction. Albert Sidney Johnston went with the party and was its best-known member, so it often has been identified as his. In fact the leader was Alonzo Ridley, northern born but of southern sympathies. Ridley later became a Confederate major commanding the 3rd Arizona Cavalry. Because Union sympathizers and troops were watching the southern officers closely, and there was talk of arresting them, the party resorted to subterfuge to get away from Los Angeles. The southerners gave out June 25 as their departure date, but in fact they moved east on June 16, the morning after the farewell at the Hancocks' quarters. Armistead remained behind for some reason, but he caught up at Vallecito on June 30. When the whole party assembled, it numbered eight resigned officers and twenty-five civilians. Four of the eight officers heading into the desert were destined to die in battle for the Confederacy. The two ill-fated men, in addition to Johnston and Armistead, were Richard Henry Brewer, killed as a major at the battle of Piedmont, and Francis Mallory, killed at the head of the 55th Virginia at Chancellorsville.[41]

Armistead, Johnston, Ridley, and their thirty compatriots arrived at Yuma on July 4. As Armistead stood watch outside the encampment one night, one of the men of his old company approached him from the direction of Fort Yuma and proposed that the emigrants join him and his disaffected mates in overthrowing the fort and splitting the plunder. Armistead of course had a quite different sort of rebellion in mind. The route through southern Arizona in July led the party into some of the hottest terrain on the continent. The mercury soared above 120 degrees with discouraging regularity. The travelers reached Tucson on July 18 and left that place on the twenty-second. They passed the horrifying scene of a massacre perpetrated by Cochise's Indians at Apache Pass and reached Mesilla, Arizona (now New Mexico), on the Rio Grande just north of El Paso on July 28. The caravan broke up at Mesilla soon thereafter, but Armistead and Johnston remained together at least to El Paso, and perhaps farther. They had covered 800 miles to reach Mesilla and faced nearly that great a journey to reach San Antonio.[42]

The details of the rest of Armistead's epic trek are not readily available. In December 1861 he recalled having arrived in Richmond "about the 15th of September last." None of the particulars of Dick Garnett's journey to Confederate soil have come to hand, but it must have ended almost simultaneously with Armistead's, because Garnett's first Confederate regular commission bore the date September 14. Despite their concurrent arrival at the capital city, and in the face of secondary accounts that place him in the Ridley-Johnston-Armistead column, it is clear that Garnett did not make the trip in that company. He began from Benicia, far north of Los Angeles, and apparently traveled on his own. The September 14 commission was to the rank of major of artillery. On the same day Garnett accepted a commission in the provisional army as lieutenant colonel, assigned to Cobb's Georgia Legion; it was to take rank from September 2.[43]

Lieutenant Colonel Garnett spent two busy and successful months serving as second in command of the Cobb Legion. Col. Thomas R. R. Cobb, whose querulous style prompted him to criticize savagely almost every officer around him, thought that Garnett was wonderful—"a perfect gentleman" and "an excellent officer." Gentleman Dick Garnett saw little action but gained valuable experience in handling troops in larger numbers than his familiar company of regulars. Perhaps his most exciting moment with the Georgians came on the morning of November 13, 1861, when the green soldiers opened fire on friendly pickets, killing their own major and wounding three other Confederates. Garnett's horse was shot from under him in this typical early war exchange of friendly fire. So fond of Garnett was the irascible Cobb that he fumed in his best egocentric style when his subordinate was promoted to brigadier general on November 14 (not, presumably, for valor the preceding day). Cobb insisted in all seriousness—he had no other métier—that Jefferson Davis had promoted Dick Garnett just to spite Cobb: "I think Davis meant this as a lick for me." Cobb was too big a man to be beaten down, though, because "thank God, I have patriotism enough to despise his malice and still work for my country."[44]

Despite their smooth early collaboration, Dick Garnett doubtless was well away from the perennially unhappy Cobb. It is easy to imagine that General Garnett enjoyed his promotion to brigadier without any anxiety about supposed ulterior motives in the Confederate White House. Unfortunately for everyone concerned, however, the new general was about to step into the path of Thomas J. Jackson. He would suffer grievously at the hands of that inflexible, if legendary, officer. Dick Garnett inherited the famous Stonewall Brigade, which had been Jackson's own. At the battle of Kernstown on March 23, 1862, Jackson miscalculated on the basis of bad information, and his little army suffered a sound tactical whipping. During the early phases of the withdrawal Garnett made decisions that seemed necessary, and probably were, as he sought to discharge the functions of a general officer. Jackson disagreed with the decisions, and his extraordinarily narrow view of leeway available to subordinates compounded his unhappiness. The result was the most famous Confederate court-martial in Virginia. Garnett's colonels all supported him unswervingly. Jackson's charges included some silliness and some misunderstandings mixed in with the substance of his complaint. When the court finally met in August, Jackson seemed to be losing his case. After barely a single day of the hearing, the trial was suspended as the army lunged across the Rapidan River in a move that led to the battle of Cedar Mountain. The court never reconvened.[45]

Jackson had written in stern derogation of Garnett to his favorite member of the Confederate congress in May, suggesting that his hapless subordinate was completely incompetent. "I wish that if such appointments are continued," Jackson wrote in remarkably disrespectful temper, "that the President would come in the field and command them, and not throw the responsibility upon me of defending this District when he throws such obstacles in my way." Despite Jackson's fine scorn, Dick Garnett received a new assignment as a brigade commander outside Stonewall's command, in George E. Pickett's division. His brigade contained five Virginia infantry regiments, the 8th, 18th, 19th, 28th, and 56th. Garnett led his new troops at South Mountain in September 1862, where he reached the vicinity of

Turner's Gap late in the day. Then he fought the brigade again at Sharpsburg on September 17. Most of the men came to respect and admire their new commander, but the colonel of the 8th Virginia, who was given to opinionated pronouncements, damned Garnett with mixed faint praise: "While he was not a man of much mental force, he was one of the noblest and bravest men I ever knew." The month after Sharpsburg, General Garnett assumed command for a time of the Virginia brigade of wounded William Mahone, in another division.[46] His assignment to the brigade in Pickett's division became permanent, however, and he remained at its head until Gettysburg.

Lewis Armistead's Confederate career, like the rest of his life, paralleled Garnett's experiences in several ways, particularly in its lack of opportunity for major or steady distinction. Armistead reached Richmond in mid-September 1861 impoverished, widowed, and with an orphan son on hand. "I never was a man of any wealth," he told the adjutant general of the Confederacy, "and the little I had was all sacrificed when I left the U.S. Army." Armistead successfully solicited a cadetship for his boy and then threw himself into Confederate military affairs. His first commission—as was Garnett's—was as major in the regular army dated—as was Garnett's—September 14, 1861. For a few days Armistead commanded sixteen companies of Texas volunteers, the nucleus of what would become the enormously renowned Hood's Texas Brigade. Then on September 25 the War Department promoted Armistead to the rank of colonel and assigned him to command of the 57th Virginia, "just organized at Camp Lee," near Richmond. Colonel Armistead would become General Armistead in a few months, but he never would be separated from the 57th during the rest of his life.[47]

For several months at the end of 1861 Colonel Armistead and his 57th Virginia manned quiet defensive posts in the vicinity of Richmond. In January 1862 they were stationed at Howard's Grove near the capital city. A few weeks later, on February 14, 1862, Armistead received orders to "proceed without delay to Suffolk, Va., and report for duty to Major-General Huger." For the next two months Armistead's correspondence was headed either from Suffolk or from nearby Fort Dillard, North Carolina. Although he had seen no action during any of these Confederate assignments, the colonel's prewar training and experience prompted the government to tender him the wreath and stars of a brigadier general, effective the first day of April.[48]

General Armistead's new brigade included the 14th, 53rd, and 57th Virginia infantry regiments together with the 3rd Georgia. He soon added the 9th and 38th Virginia to his strength and lost the Georgia regiment to Jefferson Davis's compulsion to align brigades homogeneously by states. The five infantry regiments from Virginia soon blended their identities into Armistead's brigade, which remained intact for the rest of the general's life. As might have been expected of a hard-bitten veteran of long service in the Old Army, Lewis Armistead brought stern notions of duty to the task of molding soldiers out of the citizens he commanded. Armistead was anything but a "holiday soldier" or "carpet-knight," according to the colonel of the 53rd Virginia. "He was a strict disciplinarian, but never a martinet. Obedience to duty he regarded as the first qualification of a soldier. For straggling on the march or neglect of duty on the part of his men, he held the officer in immediate command strictly responsible. The private must answer to the officer, but the officer to him."[49]

During his first months in command, Armistead faced the same range of problems and challenges that beset the entire Confederate military establishment during that troubled period. He weeded out unfit subordinates, sometimes facing the tacit opposition of Richmond bureaucrats in the process. He sought to unite understrength commands into effective fighting units. He fought the insidious threat posed to undermine his regiments by appeals for infantrymen to switch to the good-time arm by joining the cavalry ("if countenanced it will do the service incalculable injury"). More than any of those administrative woes, General Armistead grappled with the need to implement the fantastic law passed by the Confederate congress that established conscription while mandating furloughs and election of officers. The notion that enlisted men should elect their commanders was unsettling enough; lack of direction from headquarters on how to execute the remarkable new law exacerbated the problems. On April 19, Armistead pointed out to Richmond a number of conundrums: Who elected field officers (state law was more specific than, and a bit divergent from, the new national law)? Who supervised the election process? and To whom should the returns go? The seasoned Old Army regular clearly wanted the central bureaucrats to do their job more thoroughly. Nine days later he had received no answer. The confusion was demoralizing the troops. Answers were badly wanted and new questions loomed. Could elections go forward immediately, or must each command await the arrival of the new conscripts—who, after all, were the object of the law and the cause of the confusion in the first place?[50]

Whether organized in conformance with the new law and its ramifications or not, Armistead and his Virginians headed for the seat of the war within a few weeks of his appointment. On April 27 and 29 his headquarters were at Sandy Cross in Gates County, North Carolina. By May 15 he had reached Petersburg, Virginia. Two weeks later Armistead led the brigade into his first battle as a Confederate officer when it faced the enemy at Seven Pines on June 1, 1862. The brigade performed poorly despite its general's personal bravery. D. H. Hill reported that "Armistead's men fled early in the action, with the exception of a few heroic companies, with which that gallant officer maintained his ground against an entire brigade." George E. Pickett "discovered Armistead's brigade had broken and were leaving the field pell-mell." An early postwar sketch of Armistead deftly described the distinction between the general's demeanor and that of his men: "Gen. Armistead was first engaged with his brigade (or a portion of it rather) at . . . Seven Pines . . . where he personally distinguished himself for extreme gallantry." One measure of Armistead's exposure to hostile fire survives in the form of a voucher for reimbursement of $250 for his black horse, killed in action under the general at Seven Pines.[51]

Precisely one month later, on July 1, Armistead again led his brigade into action and again finished the battle with only a fragment clinging to the colors. After desultory skirmishing through most of the Seven Days the brigade fought at the battle of Malvern Hill, where things went badly for the Confederates in almost every particular and in every sector of the field. A Georgian serving with the brigade next to Armistead's insisted that the Virginia general earned an unusual nickname because of this episode: "I know that General Armistead was drinking, for I was behind the same poplar tree that he was behind, when he took out a brandy bottle and took a long pull at it." Because of this incident Armistead was known ever after as the "Poplar General," according to the Georgian, who used that nom de guerre to identify him throughout the rest of his reminiscences. Armistead's troops belonged to Benjamin Huger's division still, which meant that they did not receive alert high-level support. Before the Confederate attacks at Malvern Hill, Gen. James Longstreet examined Armistead's ground and promised to send support; none ever arrived. The excited and overwrought Gen. John B. Magruder personally ordered Armistead's brigade forward in a forlorn assault. Armistead took 1,200 men into action and reported the loss of 50 killed and nearly 300 wounded; he was fortunate to have escaped without even greater hurts. The morning after the battle Gen. Jubal A. Early came upon Armistead with about a dozen men and asked "where his brigade was." Armistead answered: "Here are all that I know anything about except those lying out there in front."[52]

Lewis Armistead and his brigade saw only the fringes of the Second Manassas campaign; he reported only two men killed. On the eve of R. E. Lee's advance into Maryland, the Confederate commander designated Armistead as the army's provost marshal for the campaign beyond the river. Between September 6 and 26, Armistead discharged that difficult chore during the most damaging period of straggling and poor discipline in the army's entire history. Details of his performance do not survive, but he must be adjudged an abject failure as provost marshal because of the chaos that afflicted the Army of Northern Virginia. It is more than likely that no one could have succeeded in the task at that time and place. Armistead's brigade did not accompany him to his provost functions. It fought at Sharpsburg and was one of the two unfortunate brigades that fell into Gen. William Nelson Pendleton's inept hands during fighting over the recrossing of the Potomac near Shepherdstown. The brigade lost five men killed and thirty wounded in the Maryland campaign and its aftermath.[53]

When the army returned to Virginia and Armistead resumed command of his brigade, no doubt delighted to be shed of the thankless provost job, they were assigned as a permanent component of George E. Pickett's division. There Armistead found his old friend Dick Garnett newly in command of the brigade that previously had been Pickett's. The two presumably resumed their decades-old military association without missing a step. Pickett's division held a deep reentrant angle in the Confederate line at Fredericksburg in December 1862, so neither Garnett nor Armistead participated in that one-sided victory. Later that month Armistead found himself at war with his own military establishment, however, over an incompetent subordinate. Col. David Dyer had succeeded Armistead in command of the 57th Virginia through seniority. The general had shown the strength of will necessary to force Dyer before an examination board to determine his adequacy—egregious inadequacy, in Armistead's view ("I believed him to be *entirely unqualified*")—to hold regimental command. The board, coincidentally, was headed by Brig. Gen. Richard Brooke Garnett. Dyer resigned instead of facing the board, claiming ill health. The Adjutant and Inspector General's Office in Richmond demanded a surgeon's certificate rather than cheerfully accepting this pragmatic result. To complete this bureaucratic farce, the regimental surgeon declared Dyer's health to be good. General Armistead's harried letter to the Richmond officials should be required reading for anyone prone to considering Confederate military matters at the purely tactical or strategic level. Dyer finally resigned unconditionally, without the medical subterfuge he had sought, and Armistead at last could retool his old regiment.[54]

Lewis Armistead's difficulties with Colonel Dyer may have originated in, or at least been exacerbated by, the general's stern military personality. Twenty years of hard-bitten duty as a company officer no doubt had deposited a crust of crackling terseness atop any surviving residue of native Virginian courtliness. Armistead admitted as much in a frank endorsement that he wrote concerning another regimental commander with whom he stood at odds. On February 15, 1863, Col. John Grammer, Jr., of the 53rd Virginia submitted his "immediate & unconditional resignation." He complained to Richmond that "on every occasion Brig. General Armistead's manner & tone are so offensive & insulting that I can but believe he . . . wishes to force me to resign." Grammer felt certain that he soon would be provoked so greatly as "to be cashiered for insubordination." Armistead approved the resignation with relish, declaring, "I do not believe Col Grammer competent for the position he holds," but denying any intention to insult him. The general's revealing endorsement stated a case that no doubt prevailed in many instances throughout an army of prickly civilians commanded by curt veterans: "I have felt obliged to speak to him as one military man would to another and as I have passed nearly all my life in camps my manner may not be understood or appreciated by one who has been all his life a civilian."[55]

Because of his assignments and details, Armistead had fought in only two big battles (Seven Pines and Malvern Hill) before he approached Gettysburg with Pickett's division in 1863. Most recently the division had been among the detachment under James Longstreet that had missed Chancellorsville while rounding up commissary stores in southeastern Virginia. One of Armistead's last communications, dated July 2, 1863, suggests that he was not necessarily on comfortable terms with division headquarters. Answering a note from Maj. Charles Pickett, the general's brother and staff member, Armistead denounced as a lie the statement that "a majority of the men seen committing depredations in the neighborhood" belonged to his brigade. "There must be some error in the reports," Armistead insisted, since "no cases of plundering by them have come to my knowledge." Furthermore, "Previous to the receipt of your note I had ordered three daily drills with the view of keeping the men in camp."[56] Within a few hours everyone—generals, nepotistic staffers,

ARMISTEAD AND GARNETT

119

and depredating enlisted men—would be cast into a cauldron that would make such petty concerns disappear from view.

Armistead's and Garnett's appointment with destiny took them across the deadly open field in front of Gettysburg's Cemetery Ridge on July 3 and into the teeth of murderous infantry and artillery fire. Armistead exhorted his men with a reminder of their families and firesides and then, according to one of the brigade, led them forward from a position twenty paces to the front. Part of the way across the bloody field Armistead, "glorying in the conduct of his men," said proudly to a fellow officer, "Look at my line; it never looked better on dress parade." The image of Armistead reaching the Federal line waiting behind its famous stone wall, his black felt hat carried on his raised sword, is one of the most familiar and evocative Gettysburg vignettes. As he led his surviving Virginians into the midst of the Federal cannon, the general went down. A member of the 14th Virginia recalled that Armistead had reached a second set of guns before he fell. "The squad that killed Armistead," the Virginian wrote years later, "was just about where the monument of the 71st Penn. is located." One northern artillerist saw Armistead "yelling something to his men," then he "caught holt of the left wheel of the [cannon] and fell right there."[57]

A sergeant from Philadelphia must have been the first Federal to reach the prostrate Armistead, because he claimed the general's sword as a trophy (it was returned to Virginia in 1907). Lewis Armistead and Dick Garnett had been attacking troops commanded by their dear friend Winfield Scott Hancock, himself the victim of a grievous wound by the time the southern infantry closed on his position. Armistead asked to see his old comrade Hancock, but because of his own wound and his continuing responsibilities, the Union officer sent Capt. Henry H. Bingham of his staff. Bingham, later a member of Congress and a recipient of the Congressional Medal of Honor for bravery at the Wilderness, "ministered to Armistead's requests and had him removed to the hospital of the Eleventh Corps." After the war Bingham identified the site for a marker locating Armistead's wounding.[58]

A myth enchanting to some northerners insists that Armistead, having fallen mortally wounded at the head of his veterans, suddenly and eagerly recanted his Confederate heresies. The nonsense about a deathbed conversion gained widest circulation from that paragon of inaccuracy and misrepresentation, Abner Doubleday. In Doubleday's dreadful 1882 book, *Chancellorsville and Gettysburg*, he professed to know that "dying . . .

ROBERT K. KRICK

120

**An example** of the many artistic representations of Lewis A. Armistead leading his Virginia soldiers against the Federal defenses on Cemetery Ridge. Louis Shepheard Moat, ed., *Frank Leslie's Illustrated History of the Civil War* (New York: Mrs. Frank Leslie, 1895), p. 418

[Armistead] saw with a clearer vision that he had been engaged in an unholy cause, and said . . . 'Tell Hancock I have wronged him and have wronged my country.'" Earlier in the same sentence, Doubleday had displayed his historiographical colors by announcing that Armistead—ever uncertain of his loyalties—"had fought on our side . . . at Bull Run" before being "seduced" away.[59] Armistead of course had been at Tucson, Arizona Territory, on July 21, 1861, a location readily distinguishable from Prince William County, Virginia, at any time of the year and particularly during the Sonoran desert summer.

After his encounter with Captain Bingham, and completely unaware that he would fall prey to the twisted spirit of Abner Doubleday, Armistead came under the care of a succession of surgeons at the Eleventh Corps hospital. Surgeon Henry C. Hendrick of the 157th New York Infantry described the general's wounds as being in a leg and in his left arm.

Neither had resulted in a broken bone. "He had lost quite a great deal of blood, but," the surgeons thought, "the wounds were not necessarily fatal. He never rallied, however, and died a little past noon on the Fourth of July."[60]

Lewis Armistead walked to his death at the head of his brigade. His friend Dick Garnett had preceded him onto the deadly field on horseback. Garnett was mounted because he could not walk. During the march toward Gettysburg, the general had run afoul of Pickett's headquarters staff even more painfully than had Armistead. A "fiery steed" belonging to Capt. Robert Anderson Bright "slashed out and kicked Gen. Garnett on the ankle." The general's last known correspondence, dated June 25, 1863, makes clear the effect of his injury. Writing from Chambersburg to "My dear Mrs. Dandridge," Dick Garnett complained that his leg was "still quite sore" and was only "improving slowly." At that date he could not even ride on horseback and feared he would "not be able to do so for a week or more." Eight days later he was killed on horseback. Despite his own physical woes, Garnett exuded confidence in the army's commander, whom he referred to as "General Robert," and in the "fine condition" of the army.[61]

Garnett attacked at the head of the left half of Pickett's front line on July 3. Maj. Charles Stephens Peyton of the 19th Virginia, who fell wounded in the assault near Garnett, called the general "our cool, gallant, noble brigade commander" and described his final attack vividly: "Never had the brigade been better handled. . . . There was scarcely an officer or man in the command whose attention was not attracted by the cool and handsome bearing of General Garnett, who, totally devoid of excitement or rashness, rode immediately in rear of his advancing line, endeavoring, by his personal efforts . . . to keep his line well closed and dressed. He was shot from his horse while near the center of the brigade, within about 25 paces of the stone wall." Sometime early in the fighting, Garnett's dark bay mare was killed outright. The general then mounted his best horse (valued at $675 as compared with $550 for the mare), a bay gelding "of fractious spirit." Both Garnett and the gelding went down near the wall. Lt. Col. Norborne Berkeley of Garnett's brigade, lying wounded and awaiting capture, saw the horse badly wounded next to the dead general and "unable to move from the spot."[62]

Astonishingly, Dick Garnett's body disappeared. He had been the cynosure of thousands of eyes on both sides as he led the dramatic attack on horseback and as he fell, but no one ever identified his remains. The next day his Old Army friend, Union general Henry J. Hunt, "made diligent search in person, for Garnett's body . . . but could not identify it." Years later Confederate general George H. Steuart came across Garnett's inscribed sword in a Baltimore shop, bought it, and kept it. After his death a more thoughtful relative gave it back to the Garnett family. Dick Garnett's bones doubtless went back to his native state after the war, together with thousands of other unidentified bodies from Gettysburg, for burial at Richmond's Hollywood Cemetery. Interested historical students dedicated a monument to Garnett's memory at Hollywood in 1991.[63]

The peculiar and inexplicable disappearance of Garnett's corpse probably constituted a more dignified end than that to which Armistead's was subjected. Alfred J. Rider of the 107th Ohio buried Lewis Armistead's remains near the Eleventh Corps hospital on the George Spangler farm, about two miles southeast of the point where he had been mortally wounded. Approximately a month later a Dr. Chamberlain of Philadelphia hunted up Rider because "he thought Armistead[']s friends would pay a good price for his body." Rider showed the venal Pennsylvanian where he had buried the general. Chamberlain dug up the "Rough box" containing the body and embalmed poor Armistead's remains for sale to grieving family members. The Baltimore branch of the family saw to burial of the general's body in their vault at the Old St. Paul's Cemetery in Baltimore beside his Uncle George, the hero of Fort McHenry. Confusion developed in the twentieth century about where Armistead had gone, but he has been in Baltimore since 1863.[64]

Whether Lewis Armistead saw his companion-in-arms Dick Garnett fall to his front, or knew of it before his own death, cannot be known. Certainly he might have. As Armistead lay dying in enemy hands, did he reflect on the long road that he and Garnett had trod together for so many years? No two Confederate general officers experienced anything remotely like the steady propinquity shared by the two men for fully a quarter-century. The two youngsters who joined the Sixth U.S. Infantry and followed it across the continent, against Indians and Mormons and Kansans and mountains and weather, had become seasoned campaigners in the process. Death on adjacent bits of blood-soaked ground in Adams County, Pennsylvania, yielded a final common thread, that of indignity: Lewis Armistead's corpse wound up hostage to petty human greed, while Dick Garnett's disappeared entirely.

## ACKNOWLEDGMENTS

The author would like to acknowledge Susan P. Walker of the United States Military Academy Archives, whose cheerful and efficient assistance met the highest standards of the archival profession, and the late Eleanor Brockenbrough of the Museum of the Confederacy in Richmond, Virginia, who did as much for Confederate history as any single individual who ever lived; she is very sorely missed.

## NOTES

1. Virginia Armistead Garber, *The Armistead Family* (Richmond, Va.: Whittet & Shepperson, 1910), 66; James E. Poindexter, *Address on the Life and Services of Gen. Lewis A. Armistead* (Richmond, Va.: [R. E. Lee Camp, No. 1, Confederate Veterans], 1910), 1; Francis B. Heitman, *Historical Register and Dictionary of the United States Army*, 2 vols. (Washington, D.C.: GPO, 1903), 1:169. The Poindexter pamphlet also exists in an undated (ca. 1950s) version with variant collation.

2. Bennett W. Green, *Word-Book of Virginia Folk-Speech* (Richmond, Va.: Wm. Ellis Jones, 1899), 13.

3. W. K. Armistead to Secretary of War, January 24, 1833, and Lewis A. Armistead to Secretary of War, March 21, 1833, both in "U.S. Military Academy Application Papers, 1805–1866," RG 94, M688, Roll 87, National Archives, Washington, D.C. (hereafter cited as NA). The index to this collection reveals ten Armistead surnames among the applicants during the period.

4. James Mercer Garnett, *Genealogy of the Mercer-Garnett Family of Essex County, Virginia* (Richmond, Va.: Whittet & Shepperson, c1910), 35–38. Richard Lewis of Lexington, Va., called Anna Garnett's gravesite to the author's attention.

5 G[arnett] B. Waggener to "Dear Miss Harrison," August 4, 1908 (two letters of that date), Museum of the Confederacy, Richmond, Va. (hereafter cited as MC); manuscript notes in Eleanor Brockenbrough's hand in the Garnett file, MC; Daniel P. Baker, "Pitched Battle over Civil War Portraits," *Washington Post*, April 25, 1986; Christine Reid, "Pictures Present a Hairy Problem," Richmond *Times-Dispatch*, October 13, 1985; Christine Reid, "Question of Beard to Be Settled in Court," Richmond *Times-Dispatch*, March 1, 1986; Robert Freis, "Were Generals' Names Switched?," Fredericksburg *Free Lance-Star*, April 19, 1986. A summary of the court squabble, including correspondence from the most actively involved modern descendant, is in *Blue & Gray Magazine* 3 (June–July 1986): 27. Discussions with Eleanor Brockenbrough confirmed for the author the question of Garnett's identity. Firm contemporary confirmation about Richard Garnett's

appearance comes from a letter written by Lt. James Henry Langhorne of the 4th Virginia on the day that Garnett assumed command of the Stonewall Brigade. "He is a man about 42–3 years old [Garnett had been 44 for two weeks] light hair blue ey[e]s & lig[h]t complexion, & has rather a pleasant face," Langhorne told his father. See J. H. Langhorne to "Dear Pa," December 7, 1861, in Langhorne Family Papers, Virginia Historical Society, Richmond, Va.

6. The correspondence concerning Garnett's application is in "U.S. Military Academy Application Papers, 1805–1866," RG 94, M688, Roll 91, NA. It includes these items, all to the secretary of war unless otherwise noted: letters from Edward S. Young, a tutor, December 13, 1833; Richard B. Garnett, December 17, 1833; William Garnett, December 19, 1833; Henry A. Wise, December 26, 1833; Robert S. Garnett, December 6, 1834; Gen. George M. Brooke to President Andrew Jackson, September 1, 1835, with endorsement signed "A. J." on September 29; Gen. George M. Brooke, March 29 and April 18, 1836.

7. *Register of the Officers and Cadets of the U.S. Military Academy . . . June, 1841* (New York: J. P. Wright, 1841). The partial listing of contemporaries of Armistead and Garnett is taken from this publication for the years 1835–41. The last year, as cited here, is the first to show an imprint; the earlier years are all n.p., n.d.

8. W. K. Armistead to Secretary of War, October 29, 1833, and Lewis A. Armistead acceptance of reappointment, April 12, 1834 (from Upperville), both in "U.S. Military Academy Application Papers, 1805–1866," RG 94, M688, Roll 87, NA; *Register of the Officers and Cadets . . . 1835*; Armistead resignation, November 21, 1833, in "Engineer Department Records Relating to the United States Military Academy, 1812–1867," M91, Roll 26, p. 349, NA; "Monthly Consolidation of the Weekly Class Reports including the Conduct Roll . . . U.S. Military Academy," for November 1835, RG 94, NA.

9. "Engineer Department Records Relating to the United States Military Academy, 1812–1867," M91, Roll 26, pp. 364, 367, NA, contains the Armistead court-martial particulars; "Monthly Consolidation of the Weekly Class Reports . . . U.S. Military Academy," November 1835, RG 94, NA; *Register of the Officers and Cadets . . . 1835*.

10. Walter Harrison, *Pickett's Men: A Fragment of War History* (New York: D. Van Nostrand, 1870), 33; Garber, *Armistead Family*, 67; Poindexter, *Address*, 1. Mary Selden Kennedy, *Seldens of Virginia and Allied Families*, 2 vols. (N.p., 1911), 1:191, is the family history (Armisteads loom large among the eponymous allied families) that mistakenly reports Lewis's graduation.

11. "Roll of the Cadets who have been punished for offences Committed from the 1st to the 31st January 1836," USMA Records, Conduct Rolls, Entry 232, 1836, RG 94, NA; "List of Orders Relating to Cadet Lewis Addison Armistead,

Extracted From 'Post Orders/No. 6, 1832–1837/U.S. Military Academy,'" U.S. Military Academy Archives, West Point, N.Y.; letter of Susan P. Walker, USMA Archives, to Robert K. Krick, February 21, 1992.

12. Cadet Hospital Register, Book No. 603, State of New York, March 1834 to January 1835, and Book No. 604, beginning in mid-1836, RG 94, NA.

13. "Monthly Consolidation of the Weekly Class Reports including the Conduct Roll . . . U.S. Military Academy," February 1836, RG 94, NA; *Register of the Officers and Cadets . . . June, 1836*; Lewis A. Armistead to Supt. [R. E.] De Russy, January 29, 1836, with endorsement dated February 2 by C[harles] Gratiot; R. E. De Russy to Charles Gratiot, January 29, 1863. The last two documents are in "Records of the Office of the Chief of Engineers, Letters Received," 1836, No. D-1777, RG 77, NA.

14. "Monthly Consolidation of the Weekly Class Reports including the Conduct Roll . . . U.S. Military Academy," April 1838, RG 94, NA; *Register of the Officers and Cadets . . .* for the years ending in 1837–41. Garnett's April 1838 court-martial is summarized in the armywide listing of courts (M1105, NA), but the later one does not seem to be recorded.

15. Heitman, *Historical Register*, 1:169; Poindexter, *Address*, 2; L. A. Armistead to Quarter Master Genl Thomas S. Jesup, September 23, 1840, "Records of Office of Quartermaster General," Entry 225: QM Consolidated Correspondence File, RG 92, NA.

16. Heitman, *Historical Register*, 1:248, 447; Clement A. Evans, ed., *Confederate Military History*, 12 vols. (Atlanta: Confederate Publishing, 1899), 3:597. The record of the Sixth Infantry and its lieutenants before the Mexican War is summarized from "Returns From Regular Army Infantry Regiments, 1821–1916," M665, NA, for the years 1844–46.

17. Heitman, *Historical Register*, 1:169; Glenn Tucker, *Hancock the Superb* (Indianapolis: Bobbs-Merrill, 1960), 41; Frederick Tilberg, "The Military Life of Lewis A. Armistead," Lewis A. Armistead Papers, North Carolina Archives, Raleigh, N.C.; Kennedy, *Seldens of Virginia*, 1:191; C. P. Keith, "Armistead Family," *William & Mary Quarterly* 6 (January 1898): 169; Cadmus M. Wilcox, *History of the Mexican War* (Washington, D.C.: Church News Publishing, 1892), 637.

18. Robert Ryal Miller, ed., *The Mexican War Journal and Letters of Ralph W. Kirkham* (College Station: Texas A&M University Press, 1991), 100; Henry Heth, *The Memoirs of Henry Heth*, ed. James L. Morrison (Westport, Conn.: Greenwood Press, 1974), 56, 66.

19. Heitman, *Historical Register*, 1:92–94.

20. William Y. Chalfant, *Cheyennes and Horse Soldiers* (Norman: University of

Oklahoma Press, 1989), 27–28. Chalfant's excellent book cites a number of contemporary manuscripts.

21. John C. Burns, "Dick Garnett's Boy," Torrington (Wyo.) *Telegram*, January 3, 1986; Eddie Herman, "Couple Credited with Heroism Lie Buried in Unmarked Graves," Rapid City (S.D.) *Journal*, November 26, 1950; letter of Louis Garnett to William Garnett, and other related correspondence, in the files of Gettysburg National Military Park Library, Gettysburg, Pa. (hereafter cited as GNMP). The Herman article includes a good photograph of Billie Garnett.

22. Garber, *Armistead Family*, 68; letters of Thelma M. (Mrs. Lewis Addison) Armistead to Frederick Tilberg, January 20, 27, 1939, in the files of GNMP. Mrs. Armistead noted that in 1939 her son Lewis Addison Armistead, the general's great-grandson, was twenty-one years old.

23. Heitman, *Historical Register*, 1:169; W. A. Gorman to Secretary of War Jefferson Davis, from Executive Office, St. Paul, February 9, 1854; L. A. Armistead to Col. S. Cooper, from Jefferson Barracks, Missouri, December 11, 1854; Law. Taliaferro to Secretary of War Jefferson Davis, from Bedford, [Va.], March 7, 1855. The three letters are in "Applications for Army Promotions," 15W3, Row 11, Compartment 5, Shelf A, Box 58, RG 107, NA.

24. "Returns From Regular Army Infantry Regiments, June 1821–January 1901," April–October 1855, M665, Roll 68, NA; Woodbury Freeman Pride, *The History of Fort Riley* (Fort Riley, Kans.: U.S. Government, 1926), 68, 70, 73–75, 93.

25. Jerry Thompson, *Henry Hopkins Sibley: Confederate General of the West* (Natchitoches: Northwestern Louisiana State University Press, 1987), 135. See also p. 132 for an Armistead comment about frontier campaign gear.

26. "Returns From Regular Army Infantry Regiments, June 1821–January 1901," January 1855–April 1858, M665, Roll 68, NA.

27. Nyle H. Miller, ed., "Surveying the Southern Boundary Line of Kansas," *Kansas Historical Quarterly* 1 (February 1932): 107–27. The original diary, which is reproduced intact in this source, is at the College of William and Mary.

28. R. B. Garnett to the Honorable Secretary of War, from Camp Bateman, December 22, 1857, in "Applications for Army Promotions," 15W3, Row 11, Compartment 5, Shelf A, Box 59, RG 107, NA. The same collection includes a March 26, 1855, letter to Jefferson Davis from M. V. Harkin[?] urging promotion for Garnett.

29. Norman F. Furniss, *The Mormon Conflict, 1850–1859* (New Haven: Yale University Press, 1960), 171–72; "Returns From Regular Army Infantry Regiments, June 1821–January 1901," April–May 1858, M665, Roll 68, NA.

30. Eugene Bandel, *Frontier Life in the Army, 1854–1861* (Glendale, Calif.: Arthur H. Clark, 1932), 55–56, 236–37.

31. Ibid., 56, 237–40.

32. Ibid., 57–58.

33. "Returns From Regular Army Infantry Regiments, June 1821–January 1901," December 1858–February 1859, M665, Roll 68, NA; Bandel, *Frontier Life*, 264–65. Much of the description of the ordeal of *Uncle Sam* is quoted in Bandel from the San Francisco *Herald*, February 13, 1859.

34. "Returns From Regular Army Infantry Regiments, June 1821–January 1901," February–July 1859, M665, Roll 68, NA; telephone conversation on February 13, 1992, between the author and the impressively knowledgeable George R. Stammerjohan, historian for the California Department of Parks and Recreation. Stammerjohan supplied particulars on the locations and circumstances of Forts Yuma and Mojave.

35. Stammerjohan conversation; Armistead's report of fight with Mojave Indians, dated August 6, 1859, in Letters Received, AGO, Main Series, C250, 1859 encl., f/w C 318 1859, RG 94, NA.

36. Armistead's report, August 6, 1859, NA; "Returns From Regular Army Infantry Regiments, June 1821–January 1901," August 1859 and December 1859 annual summary for Sixth Infantry, M665, Roll 68, NA. The three paragraphs narrating Armistead's battle are taken almost entirely from his manuscript report. A handful of the quotes are from the regimental return for August and the annual summary.

37. "Returns From Regular Army Infantry Regiments, June 1821–January 1901," September 1859–June 1861, M665, Roll 68, NA.

38. Ibid.

39. "Returns From Regular Army Infantry Regiments, June 1821–January 1901," M665, Roll 68, NA; Almira Russell Hancock, *Reminiscences of Winfield Scott Hancock* (New York: Charles L. Webster, 1887), 69. The information about Camp Fitzgerald's peripatetic existence is from the Stammerjohan conversation.

40. Hancock, *Reminiscences*, 69–70; Tucker, *Hancock the Superb*, 64–66.

41. William Preston Johnston, *The Life of Gen. Albert Sidney Johnston* (New York: D. Appleton, 1878), 277–80; Robert K. Krick, *Lee's Colonels* (Dayton, Ohio: Morningside, 1991), 260, 423, 476. Ridley's Confederate unit also was known as the 3rd Texas Cavalry, Arizona Brigade.

42. Johnston, *Albert Sidney Johnston*, 281–84, 287, 289, 290–91.

43. Lewis A. Armistead to Genl. S. Cooper, December 2, 1861, in Walker Keith Armistead's Compiled Service Record [hereafter CSR], M324, Roll 62, NA; Richard B. Garnett's CSR, M331, Roll 103, NA.

44. William B. McCash, *Thomas R. R. Cobb: The Making of a Southern Nationalist* (Macon, Ga.: Mercer University Press, 1983), 256, 270–71; Garnett's CSR, NA.

45. Official transcripts of Confederate courts have not survived, but Garnett's copy, together with a great deal of related correspondence, is at the MC. For a summary of the case that quotes extensively from the manuscript record, see Robert K. Krick, "The Army of Northern Virginia's Most Notorious Court Martial," *Blue & Gray Magazine* 3 (June–July 1986): 27–32.

46. T. J. Jackson to A. R. Boteler, May 6, 1862, in the Boteler Papers, William R. Perkins Library, Duke University, Durham, N.C. (hereafter cited as PLDU); Eppa Hunton, *Autobiography of Eppa Hunton* (Richmond, Va.: Privately printed, 1933), 84; Petersburg *Express*, October 16, 1862. The Jackson letter unfortunately is missing its signature page but is unmistakably in the general's awkward hand.

47. Lewis A. Armistead to Samuel Cooper, December 2, 1861, in Walker Keith Armistead's CSR, M324, Roll 62, NA; Lewis A. Armistead's CSR in M331, Roll 9, NA; *Special Orders of the Adjutant and Inspector General's Office, Confederate States*, 5 vols. (n.p., n.d.), 1:110, 117, 296; Lewis A. Armistead's CSR in M324, Roll 980, NA.

48. Armistead's CSR in M324, Roll 980, NA; Confederate States AIGO, in *Special Orders*, 2:64; Armistead correspondence of various dates with the Confederate AIGO in Roll 3 of M473, "Letters Received by the Confederate Adjutant and Inspector General," NA; Armistead's CSR in M331, Roll 9, NA.

49. Harrison, *Pickett's Men*, 34; Poindexter, *Address*, 2. The colonel testifying was Rawley White Martin.

50. Armistead correspondence in "Letters Received . . . ," M473, Roll 3, dated March 28, April 19, 28, and May 15, 1862; Roll 4, dated July 15, 1862; and Roll 10, dated January 19, 1862, NA.

51. Armistead correspondence in "Letters Received . . . ," M473, Roll 3, dated April 27 (two), April 29, and May 15, 1862, NA; U.S. War Department, *The War of the Rebellion: A Compilation of the Official Records of the Union and Confederate Armies*, 127 vols., index, and atlas (Washington, D.C.: GPO, 1880–1901), 11(1):945, 982 (hereafter cited as *OR*; all references are to series 1); Harrison, *Pickett's Men*, 34; Armistead's CSR, M331, Roll 9, NA.

52. Manuscript reminiscences of W. B. Judkins, U.D.C. Collection, Carnegie Library, Rome, Ga.; *OR* 11(2):504, 817–19; Jubal A. Early, *Lieutenant General Jubal Anderson Early C.S.A.: Autobiographical Sketch and Narrative of the War between the States* (Philadelphia: J. B. Lippincott, 1912), 83.

53. *OR* 12(2):568, 19(1):143, 812, 831, and (2):596; Armistead's CSR, M331, Roll 9, NA.

54. Harrison, *Pickett's Men*, 35; Lewis A. Armistead to G. Moxley Sorrel, December 28, 1862, and other documents in David Dyer's CSR, M324, Roll 982, NA.

55. John Grammer's CSR, M331, NA. The colonel's subsequent career as a surgeon accounts for the unusual placement of this document, in a service record grouping having nothing to do with the 53rd Virginia nor even Virginia troops.

56. L. A. Armistead to Major C. Pickett, July 2, 1863, RG 109, Entry 450: Miscellaneous Items, July 1, 1863, NA. The date of the note may be July 1, as the document is docketed that way, but both the numeral and the superscript suffix suggest July 2. Armistead identified Charles Pickett's note as dated June 30.

57. Poindexter, *Address*, 5; D. B. Easley to Howard Townsend, July 24, 1913, in the Military History Research Collection, U.S. Army Military History Institute Collection, Carlisle Barracks, Pa.; Marsha Rader, "Armistead's Fall Remains a Mystery," Washington *Times*, November 16, 1991.

58. Kennedy, *Seldens of Virginia*, 1:191–93; W. C. Storrick, "The Armistead Marker," typescript at GNMP. The souvenir hunter is identified as Sgt. Michael Specat in a 1907 account printed in Kennedy, *Seldens of Virginia*, 1:192, but I have been unable to identify a man of that name. The confusion probably results from the mistranscription of handwriting to typeset print that is so familiar to historians working on nineteenth-century subjects.

59. Abner Doubleday, *Chancellorsville and Gettysburg* (New York: Charles Scribner's Sons, 1882), 195. Doubleday is best remembered today for having invented baseball—something, entirely appropriately to his historical credentials in other matters, with which he had absolutely no connection. Evidence about Armistead's demeanor when wounded ranges widely in several directions. Three good sources are "Interesting Note on General Armistead," Gettysburg *Star and Sentinel*, July 11, 1893, typescript at GNMP; R. W. Martin letter in Armistead C. Gordon, *Memories and Memorials of William Gordon McCabe*, 2 vols. (Richmond, Va.: Old Dominion Press, 1925), 2:72–74; David Gregg McIntosh manuscript memoir of a visit to the battlefields, 131–32, No. M-1889, Southern Historical Collection, Wilson Library, University of North Carolina, Chapel Hill. The unmistakable evidence about Armistead's desert whereabouts in July 1861 is presented earlier in this essay.

60. "Interesting Note on General Armistead," Gettysburg *Star and Sentinel*, July 11, 1893. The article is quoted from Hendrick and one James T. Long.

61. H. T. Owen, "Error in Hon. James W. Boyd's Speech," *Confederate Veteran* 12 (January 1904): 7; R. B. G[arnett] to "My dear Mrs. Dandridge," June 25, 1863, from Chambersburg, in the Bedinger-Dandridge Family Correspondence, PLDU.

62. Evans, *Confederate Military History*, 3:598; Garnett's CSR, M331, NA. The Confederate bureaucracy demanded thorough confirmation to pay claims for dead private horses. As a fortuitous result, Garnett's CSR includes depositions from

several officers about dead and wounded horses, which coincidentally shed valuable light on human affairs.

63. Harrison, *Pickett's Men*, 184–85; Winfield Peters, "The Lost Sword of Gen. Richard B. Garnett, Who Fell at Gettysburg," in *Southern Historical Society Papers*, 52 vols. and 2-vol. index, ed. J. William Jones and others (1876–1959; reprint, Wilmington, N.C.: Broadfoot, 1990–92), 33:26–31; Steve Davis, "Requiescat in Pace: Richard Brooke Garnett," *Grave Matters* 6 (Fall 1990). Davis's fine summary of information on Garnett's death and disappearance served as part of the preparation for the Hollywood memorial marker, which Davis spearheaded. The sword is at the MC.

64. A[lfred] J. Rider to John B. Bachelder, October 2, 1885, at GNMP; Poindexter, *Address*, 7; Tilberg, "Military Life." The Armistead Papers at Raleigh contain some family correspondence about the burial location and circumstances, and the files of Gettysburg National Military Park hold much more. Unseemly confusion about where Lewis Armistead is buried, which still recurs intermittently, provides renewed opportunities for amazed discovery and delighted resolution. Rader, "Armistead's Fall," for instance, declares so recently as 1991 that the mystery has only been solved through "recent efforts by [a] Baltimore area researcher." This writer saw Armistead's casket inside the mausoleum when the crypt was opened briefly in 1968.

*Sergeant Ben Hirst's*

*Narrative of Important Events,*

*Gettysburg, July 3, 1863*

## FREDERICKSBURG ON

## THE OTHER LEG

*Robert L. Bee*

The other contributors to this volume have focused on important leaders, Confederate reactions to Gettysburg, and postbattle collective ideologies. This essay will move downward through the ranks and analytical levels to look closely at a single Union infantry sergeant's portrayal of the third day's fighting. Fate and Gen. Winfield Scott Hancock had placed this man about a hundred yards from where Brig. Gen. Lewis Armistead's spearhead momentarily penetrated the Union line along Cemetery Ridge. Less concerned with what actually happened than with how Sgt. Benjamin Hirst of Company D, 14th Connecticut Volunteer Infantry constructed those events for his reading audience at home, this analysis addresses such questions as What did he emphasize? What did he ignore? And why *this* particular constructed reality rather than some alternative? The object is to use the sergeant's narratives to understand his worldview: his attitudes, beliefs, morals, and knowledge, forged in his prewar existence but tempered by almost a year of hard army service. This understanding in turn offers some glimpses of the culture of Company D and of the Connecticut mill town where virtually all the company's members had lived before joining.

The essay aims at a point between two types of literature about common soldiers: it is neither an annotated verbatim transcript with little editorial intrusion nor a generalizing comment about the behavior and thoughts of the "typical" Civil War soldier.[1] It seeks to reverse the analytical thrust of these latter, generalizing studies by using their conclusions to illuminate why Ben Hirst wrote as he did. Surely one of the major contributions of the general studies is to allow a better understanding of the context within which specific persons of interest—the Ben Hirsts or the Sam Watkinses—formed and displayed their behavioral and ideological patterns.

The most important insights into Ben Hirst's worldview come, however, from the letters and journal he wrote before the third day's battle, as he worked to construct—or perpetuate—a composite social image as male, husband, and household head in the minds of his readers back home.[2]

Benjamin Hirst was born in 1828 in Southport, England, where his father labored in the textile mills. In the late 1840s the Hirst family emigrated to Chester, Delaware County, Pennsylvania, where the father again went to work in the textile mills. There were four Hirst brothers by then—Ben was the oldest, then Joe, John, and Bill. In 1852 Ben married Sarah Quinn of Chester. Sometime before the war Ben and Sarah went to New England to seek work in the textile mills, first perhaps to Dedham, Massachusetts, then to Rockville, Connecticut. There Ben found work as a weaver, probably as a skilled laborer and perhaps a lower- or middle-level supervisor, given his prior experience. The couple was joined by Ben's brothers Joe and John, who also were millhands. Ben bought a house with enough land for a garden and some hogs; he and Sarah may well have provided room and board for Ben's younger brothers. The Hirsts had no children at the time, but there was a pet dog named Curly. Ben stood 5 feet, 7 inches tall. He had a light complexion and wore a goatee, perhaps in an effort to elongate his roundish face.[3]

He enlisted in Company D of the 14th Connecticut Volunteer Infantry, the company being raised by Capt. Thomas Burpee of Rockville.[4] On August 20, 1862, he was mustered into Federal service as a sergeant. Joe and John Hirst volunteered with him and were mustered in as privates. Three-quarters of the men in the company hailed from Rockville.[5]

Ben wrote most of his letters to his wife, Sarah, but he assumed she would show them to others. He instructed her to preserve all his letters from the front "as they may be of use some day." He also started a journal, where he kept track of Important Events. Unfortunately, no letters from

**SGT. BENJAMIN HIRST,** probably photographed on March 13, 1863. Charles D. Page, *History of the Fourteenth Regiment, Connecticut Vol. Infantry* (Meriden, Conn.: Horton Printing Co., 1906), p. 193

Sarah have survived. They would have been hard to preserve under field conditions. After passing them around for other men from Rockville to read, Ben and his brothers probably put them away in their knapsacks. For the 14th Connecticut this was not a good idea; its knapsacks kept getting lost.[6]

Ben's narrative of Gettysburg written in October ("Date no matter") was packaged as a letter to his wife but was clearly intended for a wider readership. "Important Events" is his phrase and capitalization. In his constructed reality Important Events invariably were portrayed in heroic prose, as were those of most soldier-writers who struggled with words lofty enough to match their experience.[7] His Important Events were virtually all battles. There were three other categories in his ordering of reality for the home folks: There was more routine information that required a different, less reflective or heroic style. There were occurrences he deemed generally uninteresting and barely worth describing. And finally there were some topics to be left out of letters altogether—eroticism, for example, or details of how he sought diversions from the monotony of winter camp.

**JOHN HIRST**, *right*, with friends David Whiting, *center*, and Elbert Hyde, *left*, in an image taken during early September 1863. Hyde lost an eye fighting near Petersburg in June 1864; Whiting was killed at Ream's Station in August 1864. Charles D. Page, *History of the Fourteenth Regiment, Connecticut Vol. Infantry* (Meriden, Conn.: Horton Printing Co., 1906), p. 106

The Hirsts' Gettysburg letters are here presented in chronological order. The first is from Ben's brother John to Sarah—probably his first letter to her (Joe, the middle brother, had been severely wounded in the legs during the regiment's assault on Marye's Heights at Fredericksburg). Ben always before had served as the correspondent on behalf of all the brothers. The somewhat peremptory tone of John's brief note was almost certainly at Ben's specific dictation: Ben earlier had repeatedly told Sarah not to try to visit him in the field "as it is no place for a woman" and reassured her that he would send for her if he needed her help. Goaded by anxious impulse after Fredericksburg, however, she unwisely had come to find Ben without his permission.[8]

The elapsed time between Ben's two letters is an important consideration here. Both focus on the third day's battle but were constructed under very different conditions for different purposes and readerships. The October 1863 letter reflects his postbattle ruminations and represents his best efforts at appropriately conveying Important Events.[9]

∗ ∗ ∗

July fourth Near Gettysburg 1863

Dear Sister i write you these few lines to let you know how we are as i know you must be very much excited out here as i expect you have had Great rumours by they time this reaches you we have had a very sharp engagement but you need not believe every thing that you here ben Got bruised on they right Shoulder but it is not Dangerous so take my advice and stay at home untill you here for certain where he is as he may be on his way home by they time you Get this i walked him down to they Hospital and he was in very good spirits and said if he could he should come home it was some pieces of Stone that struck him as he was laying behind a stone wall firing at they rebels we give them a good whipping but some of our boys suffered Brigham Got pretty badly wounded also frank stoughton and John Julian them three i am afraid of william Goodell got shot dead as he was loading is gun. Slightly wounded David Whiteing their was others Just got touched but not to mount to anything we got [sic] i am allright at present but tired we got four colours from they enemy our regm Got them but they division Got some more but i dont know how many now take my advice and do as i tell you Stay at home untill you here from ben as he told me he should write as soon as he could i must close this for now your affectionate Brother John Hirst Hirst [sic]
  Now do as i tell you as ben aint hurt very Bad


July 5.th 1863
Near Gettysburg, Pa

Dear Sarah, I write you these few Lines, so that you can see that I am yet kicking, and am thank ful that I got off so well. The 14.th Conn is covered with Glory having got 5 Rebel Colors in our Posession besides a [word obliterated] . . . of Swords and other Trophys of War [words obliterated] . . . the greatest Battle I have seen for the time we were at it and we Routed three times our number with great Slaughter I wish i could write you all about it, but my shoulder is too lame to attempt it at present. I Shal be all right in a few weeks, altho I had some narrow escapes. our Company and Co B was out Skirmishing when the Rebels opened about 100 Canon upon the Height our Corps occupied. us Skirmishers had to lay where we were while Shot and Shell was bursting among us from both sides. it was here that John Julian got wounded (and I fear Fattaly) Dave Whiting had a narrow escape, a piece of Shell cut his cap and the tip of his ear. at the same time a piece of Shell struck me on the uper part of the Left thigh. I thought it was all up with me, for a minuet or two, until I opened my eyes to look at the Hole and it wernt there. the place is a little black and stiff but that is all. our Guns were after a while silenced, and our Skirmishers drove in then I saw the Rebels in 3 lines of Battle moving to attact us. we had but one line to oppose them with but we had a low Stone Wall behind which we laid, until the Rebels got within 30 Rods of us, then such a Volley of rifles we gave them you cannot imagine. soon the first line was Shattered to pieces, and with shouts of Derision we awaited for the next, served them the same way and soon the whole were Flying from whence the [sic] came, leaving behind them Hundreds of Killed and Wounded, if our Artillery could have helped us but very few would have got away. as it was the 14th alone took more Prisoners than our own Regt number beside the greatest number of Rebel Flags of any Regiment Engaged. after a while the Rebel Batterys opened again to cover their Routed men and a piece of shell or shot knocked a stone from the Wall which struck me on the right shoulder Blade, and with a yell I thought I was gone for sure. John helped me up and to the Hospital when he examined me and found I was not hurt as bad as might have been expected. Corp Wm Goodel was instantly Killed by a Musket Ball. Brigham was Shot in the Body the Ball runing around a Rib came out of his back. Poor Frank Stoughten is shot just below the neck and is in a very Critical condition. we had two more in our Company very slightly wounded. the Regimental Loss is as far as known 56 out of about 180. I have just heard that our Troops are again on the move. John is all right, and kept by me all the time until he saw me comfortable here. I think we shal be moved from here in a day or two, when I will write you again. give my respects to all. I remain your Affectionate

Husband Benjamin Hirst

This account of the Battle
of Gettysburg was written by
me, entirely from my own
experience of what I saw of
it. October. 1863.

Mower U.S.A. Hospital, Philad. Pa.
Benj Hirst. Date no matter.

Dear Sarah,

I believe the last letter I wrote you in the Field was Dated at Union Mills, Md.[10] and that we were then expecting to march to meet the Rebels somewhere within a few miles of that place; [on June 29, 1863] the day before I wrote you those few lines we had made one of the greatest marches of the War. . . . We passed through Mt. Pleasant a very nice little village, but the Inhabitants were not to be seen, then passed through Liberty and when about sunset we arrived at Union Bridge we began to think we had done for one day, but no; Close up is still the word, and we passed through the Village as if the Devil was after us. . . . Now we have marched 27 miles since sunrise, and still no sign of Camping ~~and~~ now we ~~they~~ begin to Growl and to fall out first one gives up, then another, then they begin to fall out in twos and threes, but still I move along as best I can. By and by whole Companies seem to drop out, officers and men together, but still no one can answer the often asked: how much further & ~~Ilebe~~ ["ilebe" inserted above the stricken "Ilebe" here] Damd if I can go any further, and away goes my Gun over the [?] fence and for a few minuets I give way to bitter thoughts as I rest my head upon my hands. Who is to blame for thus marching us Past all endurance, oh it is our new Corps Commander (Gen. Hancock) who wants to show that we can outmarch as well as outfight anything in the army. But no that cannot be it. It is the cursed Rebels, who not daring to attackt us where we could chastise them have stole a march upon us and now threaten to carry the War to our own Homes. Yes that is it and with the thought I get my Gun again and trudge along for a few more weary miles and I got rewarded for my perseverance for I soon saw that the advance were encamped for the rest of the night, and me and John were soon asleep by the road side, having marched with 3 days rations and 60 rounds of amunition over 34 miles. . . . [On] July first we heard heavy firing at some distance from us, it did not take us long to pack up (for most of us had nothing to pack) and soon we were on the march to Gettysburg, about 8 A.M. we marched through Uniontown and took the road to Tanneytown arriving there we heard that the first Corps was engaged at Gettysburg and that our own Hancock was hurrying to the Front to supply the place of Reynolds who was killed we pushed along as rapidly as posible the inhabitants along the route helping us all they could, they handed us water and cheered us on at every step. . . . Never before did I see the men march along so gayly as we whent this day, our own little Co of Rockville Boys keeping well to gather, and joking with the rest, towards evening we began to see traces of the Battle. Artillery was passing rapidly to the front and others from the Front, now we would see a small squad of Rebel prisoners coming to the rear, and then the stories we heard from the Skulkers, Shirks, and Camp followers who lined the road side was a caution. . . . In the mean time we pushed ahead as fast as posible but night overtook us before we got into position, our Regiment was sent to Picket on the Baltimore turnpike where we passed a very quite night.

July 2nd We fell in just at daylight and were marched of without having a chance to cook our Coffee the only Luxury a Soldier has on active service. We soon joined our Brigade and were soon lost in the thousands and thousands of Gallant men marching to the Front; this was a Great sight to Witness, the long Trains of Artillery were going some ahead, others to the right and Left, while Division after Division took its position for Battle. As far as the eye could reach from Round Top, to Cemetary Hill it was nothing but men Forming for the Decisive Conflict inaugerated the day before. We soon joined our own Proud Corps, just taking position a little to the Left of Cemetary Hill. We got one good look at the Spires of Gettysburg and could just discern the long Rebel lines to the right and Left of the City. Away of to our right fighting had already commenced and our skirmishers were thrown out as soon as we got in Position. The first Deleware of our Brigade doing that duty in our imediate front, they were driven back with some loss, and the Rebels occupied a house and Barn from which they could Pick of our Artillery men at their Guns, then we sent out a part of the 12 New Jersey to clean them out which they did in gallant style, losing quite a number in Killed and wounded, but they inflicted equal Loss upon the Enemy besides capturing a large number in the Barn. The same house and barn was again occupied by the Rebels, when the 108th N.Y. supported by the first Delewares again cleaned them out. In the mean time the Rebels made a many desperate attempts to break our lines, but in each case failed. . . . During the Evening our Regt. changed its position a little to the left and in support of Arnolds (2nd R.I. A) Battery. Companies A and F were sent out as Skirmishers and this closed our operations for the Day.

July the Third

At early dawn we quietly took our Position in Line, and our Co with Co B were sent out to relieve Co A and F and to push back the Rebel skirmishers who were a little too near our lines for our comfort, however we advanced in good order and took the required position in good shape. This was the first time our Company had been thus engaged, and when I was sent with 10 men, to relieve some other ones further to the Front, I felt a little timid about walking erect, with the Ball whizing about my ears from the Rebel Sharp Shooters. But I made out to Post the men (I found one of the men I was to relieve Dead at his Post, he was shot through the Head and from his position he seemed to be taking aim at a Rebel. I did not know he was Dead until I put my hand upon his shoulder, and spoke to him) and we were soon popping away as lively as Crickets. (I will here tell you of one incident which goes to show how soon we get insensible to danger; my Gun becoming foul, I got a Ball stuck in the Barrel so that I could not get it home or take it out, in this Dilemma, I placed it before me with the Butt resting against a fence rail, and with my shoe string I pulled the trigger fully expecting it to burst, but it came out all right and I was soon firing away again.) In the mean time the Rebels again occupied the House and Barn I before mentioned, and the remainder of our Regiment were sent to drive them out, and to hold it, which was done in as Gallant a Style as could well be. The Regt held on until they got orders to Burn them down, and the Boys soon had a Fire that effectualy kept the Rebels out for the rest of the Battle. In this affair the Regt lost quite a number of good men, and one or two officers were wounded, and thus the forenoon wore away. [At about 10 A.M. Ben and his squad were relieved on the advanced skirmish line and returned to the skirmish reserve posted along the Emmitsburg Road.] [11] About noon commenced the Fiercest Canonading I ever heard, the shot and shell came from Front and Right and Left. It makes my Blood Tingle in my veins now; to think of. Never before did I hear such a roar of Artilery, it seemed as if all the Demons in Hell were let loose, and were Howling through the Air. Turn your eyes which way you will the whole Heavens were filled with Shot and Shell, Fire and Smoke.

The Rebels had concentrated about 120 Pieces of Artilery upon us and for 2 long hours they delivered a Rapid and Destructive fire upon our Lines, Principally upon the old Second Corps whom they desired to attack. To add to all this was our own Batteries in full Blaze, every shot from which seemed to pass over our heads; it was a terrible situation to be in between those two fires; how we did Hug the ground expecting every moment was to be our last. And as first one of us got Hit and then another to hear their cries was Awful. And still you dare not move either hand or foot, to do so was Death. Once I ventured to look around and just then I saw one of our Cassions blown up, while the same moment a Rebel one was blown up from the same Battery. But all this could not last much longer, our fire began to lose its vigour for want of Amunition, and as the Smoke lifted from the Crest we saw our Guns leaving one after the other and soon a terrible stillness prevailed so that you could almost hear your heart thud in your bosom. But what means that shout of derision in our Front. Up men the Rebels are upon us, there they come a Cloud of Skirmishers in front, with one two, three lines of Battle, stretched all along our Front with their Banners flying, and the men carrying their Pieces at trail Arms. It was a Glorious Sight to see, Rebels though they were. The[y] seemed to march as though upon Parade, and were confident of carrying all before them. But away up that mountain slope in our Rear we knew that (biding their time) as Gallant a body of men as ever Rebels could dare to be were awaiting for them. Yes behind that long, low stone Wall is our own Glorious Second Corps so soon to Imortalise themselves by hurling back that Rebelious Crew who brought their Polluting footsteps to our own dear North. Steady men, and Rally on the Reserve cries our Leader, as we take to our feet; we are driven in, but not in confusion. Sometimes we about Face and return their Skirmishers fire. But still we fall back up the Hill and over the Wall bringing our wounded with us. And now we have a short breathing spell and can Note the Intense anxiety depicted on every countenance. You can see that: One is looking at the Far off Home He will never see again. Another one is looking at his Little ones, and he mechanically empties his Cartridge Box before him determined to part with Life as Dearly as possible. Other ones you can see are communing with Him before whom so many of us will have to shortly appear. We must hold this Line to the Last Man. The Fate of the whole Army now rests with you. Don't Fire until you get the order, and then fire Low and Sure. It is the Clear Voice of Gen Gibbon as he rides along the Line, and gives a word of cheer to each Regiment as he goes along.

A few more words from Gen Hayes, and our own Gallant Col Ellis and there runs along the Line Ready, up with our Flags, Aim, Fire. And time it was too, for the Rebels seemed to me to be within 150 yards of us, and we could hear their Officers pressing them on to the charge, Fire, Fire, Fire all along our Line. There opened upon them such a Storm of Bullets, Oaths and Imprecations as fully satisfied them we had met before, under circumstances a little more favourable to them. Give them Hell x x x . Now We've got you. Sock it to the Blasted Rebels. Fredericksburg on the other Leg. Hurah, Hurah, the first Line is broken. Never mind who is Hit. Give them Hell again. And soon the second Line is sent Howling back after the first one. Right Oblique Fire, Left Oblique Fire, and the supporting Colums are thrown in disorder and soon seek safety in Flight. Then you ought to have heard the Exhultant Shouts of our Brave Boys as the whole Rebel Force gave way in utter confusion leaving thousands and thousands of Killed, Wounded and Missing in our hands. What a sight it was, where but a short time before had stood the Flower of the Rebel Army in all the Pomp of Pride and Power was now covered with Dead in every conceivable Posture, and such a Wailing Cry, mingled with Groans of the Dieing [later changed to "Dying" in pencil] is past conception. Oh for a thousand or two fresh men to charge upon the discomfited Foe, and push them Home. Could this have been done the Southron Army might have been Anhiliated. As it was they suffered a Tremendous Defeat. Our Corp alone Captured 30 Stand of Colers, our Division taking 13 of them, 6 of which were captured by our own little Regt, besides this we took more Prisoners then we numbered men. I did not have the oppertunity to see the whole Fruit of our Victory, but I saw a part of them brought in amid the Exhultant shouts of the Boys, and while i was rejoicing with them I was sent rolling in the Dust being Hit for the third time upon this Eventful day and was this time Dabled [disabled?] for ever carrying a Gun in Active Service ~~again~~ [later crossed out in pencil]. After this I saw but the usual Hospital scenes, which is not very interesting to relate. One thing I ought to do this thank the Citizens of Hanover, Pa. Baltimore, Md and Willmington, Del for their kindness to us in coming from Glorious Gettysburg.

∗   ∗   ∗

In his October version, Ben was careful to portray himself and his behavior under fire in ideal—and above all courageous—terms, according to a prewar Yankee mill-town, respectable working-class image of manliness that prevailed in his time.[12] By the time of Gettysburg, Company D of the 14th Connecticut had been hardened and winnowed by almost a year of combat, including Antietam, Fredericksburg, and Chancellorsville. The regiment and the entire Army of the Potomac hoped for a solid victory after the debacle of Fredericksburg and the humiliation of Chancellorsville. Ben's experience and conduct in these earlier battles helped to shape his narrative. The interplay of the ideal image of manly courage and the reality of combat experience thus guided his prose—that dynamic, plus a Victorian working-class notion of appropriate style for portraying Important Events.

Ben always had been concerned about his manly self-image among readers of his wartime letters. His first attempt at the Important Events genre came in his telling of the battle of Antietam. His construction of that battle played up his aggressive coolness under fire. He bellowed "like a mad bull" at his men for foolishly firing into the regiment in front of them in some tall corn near the Roulette farm. Shortly thereafter he barely escaped capture: he and a pair of comrades were left exposed when too bravely preoccupied with shooting at the enemy to notice that the 14th had pulled back. They rejoined the regiment coolly, in good order. Then he helped a wounded friend named Wilkie to the rear during a lull in the fighting, immediately returning to the regiment after leaving Wilkie along a fence line and apparently out of harm's way. He considered this last act part of his rightful duty, was proud of it, and mentioned it in all his subsequent accounts of the battle. Sadly, Wilkie died later from infection.[13]

This Antietam narrative, actually three narratives written to his wife, to friend Luther Morse, and for his journal, became the stylistic and thematic prototype for those to follow. He was complimented on it by Mrs. Morse, who passed the praise to him via Sarah.[14] In it he owned up to some anxious moments but dared not mention fear. He underplayed his feelings in tight situations. It made him "uncomfortable," he wrote, to watch enemy gunners load pieces he knew were aimed at him while he lay just behind the ridge of a low hill to the northeast of the Sunken Road (Bloody Lane).[15] This narrative revealed the pride he and others felt about their regiment's conduct at Antietam. Of the many major battles the 14th fought, only the account of Gettysburg receives more space in the regimental history.

Fredericksburg was quite another matter. As with the Antietam narrative, Ben wrote first of the buildup: the march from camp at Falmouth to the vicinity of the Lacy House, the hurry-ups and waits, the artillery bombardment. Chronology and the location of the regiment were important. He used subdued prose with a strong dose of first-person pronouns. But when he moved into telling about the assault on Marye's Heights, he switched to the familiar heroic third-person style reserved for Important Events. The regiment did this, went there; their "gallant colonel" (Sanford Perkins, whom Ben had earlier reviled as a martinet) fell while urging his men on. In his account the regiment—or most of it—behaved gallantly in a doomed effort. But there was virtually nothing of what Ben himself did or thought during the assault, leaving the implicit impression among readers that his own conduct was a microcosm of the regiment's gallantry.[16]

Ben's public image at home came under severe attack about three weeks later. Albert Towne, Sr., a grieving father who went from Rockville after the battle in a vain effort to recover his son's body, had returned home with news that Ben and some other noncommissioned officers had behaved badly under fire. Company D had gone into the assault with less than thirty men, led by their first sergeant Frank Stoughton (their officers, Ben disgustedly noted in his Important Events accounts, played sick to get out of the action). Ben and another sergeant fell out of position and called for two other men to help them move a wounded corporal and a private back to the hospital. Instead of returning to the line, now pinned in front of the wall of fire from the rebel muskets beneath Marye's Heights, Ben and the other sergeant stayed in the hospital with the wounded men until the regiment had fallen back to the relative protection of the city's buildings. While Ben was in the rear, his brother Joe was hit in both legs. Presumably he was brought back by the third Hirst brother, John, when the regiment withdrew from the line.[17]

Again, Ben's Important Events narratives of Fredericksburg conveyed nothing about helping the wounded. For that matter, there was no mention of his brother Joe being hit. The behavior of his two brothers under fire was left completely out. He communicated his and John's safety and Joe's fate in a hastily scribbled note to Sarah five days after the fight.[18] This last was not an Important Events narrative but a quick reassurance of their survival—almost identical to the letter John wrote to Sarah after the third day's battle at Gettysburg.

When Sarah wrote him about the gossip, Ben first deemed it laughable and unworthy of serious consideration. But in the same letter he quickly turned to self-righteous indignation. He had indeed, he admitted, taken a man back to the hospital—because he had felt so keenly Wilkie's death at Antietam and concluded that if he had taken Wilkie to the hospital instead of laying him along the fence, Wilkie might have survived. He had resolved before Fredericksburg never to let that happen again.[19]

The allegations persisted, however, and evidently caused Sarah some anguish back in Rockville. Ben finally asked his first sergeant, Frank Stoughton, to write to Mrs. Stoughton in Rockville verifying that he had kept the first sergeant fully informed of his whereabouts during the action—implying that Stoughton tacitly approved of Ben's action.[20] Yet he continued to brood about the charges. They were a direct attack on the very manhood he had constructed so carefully and no doubt lived up to in harrowing circumstances, but they also made him out to be a ridiculous hypocrite in view of his earlier scornful attacks on skulking company officers. Gerald Linderman aptly characterizes Ben's predicament as confronted by other soldiers North and South: "One of the few standing orders more heeded than ignored was the one forbidding soldiers to drop out of the charge in order to aid wounded companions. It was observed because courage was at issue, and to help another might easily be construed as a cowardly attempt to escape combat."[21] Ben's efforts to control the situation at home from afar continued for about three weeks. Either he was succesful, or Sarah simply decided to bear the indignity without bothering him further about it. This last would not have been typical of her.

Ben and Company D were at Chancellorsville the following spring. In his accounts of that battle he again imposed his Important Events style, implicitly arguing that his courageous reputation had been redeemed even if the army's had not. He remained on the line, he reported, and declared dramatically that "I would have been shot, rather than have given way at the moment we did" when the regiment was evidently flanked during action west of the Chancellor House on the morning of May 3. Their leaders had let them down again, Ben dourly noted in an unoriginal conclusion: "We were simply out Generaled."[22] Would this narrative suffice to restore his ideal social image in Rockville? He could not have known for certain because the regiment and the army had in fact been whipped twice in succession. After a defeat, boasting of one's courage and blaming one's leaders are a dubious antidote for skepticism.

Within these general and personal contexts emphasizing courage as the fundamental value and his social image in Rockville as vitally important to him and Sarah, Ben took up pen to construct the third day's battle at Gettysburg.

As usual, he began with an extensive place-and-time narrative of the events leading up to the climax. This was an important segment of the telling of the battle, a requisite setting of the stage; infantrymen wanted to keep track of how far they had marched and what towns they had marched through. In this prelude he portrayed himself as the steadfast but critical soldier, doing his duty manfully even though it was harsh. Samuel Fiske, an eloquent captain in Hirst's regiment, wrote that it was not proper to complain but declared that soldiers got a special dispensation for "soldierly grumblings" or what Ben called "growling."[23] Ben growled here, in this portion of the telling.

The bright victory of the day gave him and hundreds of others free rein to seize heroic words and phrases to describe it for readers afterward. Some of these were in his enthusiastic note to Sarah on July 5, but they came in a gush in his more reflective October narrative. "Gallant" and "brave" were among the most popular. These he used to embellish his theme of personal and collective courage.

He fashioned the detailed description of the skirmish line as his first-person centerpiece of the account. Events during the rest of the day he generalized to the more heroic editorial third person. This particular skirmish line, he wrote, was not a healthy place to be. Its advanced position was along a post-and-rail fence about 200 yards west of the Emmitsburg Road, toward the Confederate line. The reserve for the skirmishers lay beneath another fence along the Emmitsburg Road itself, which at the time formed a slight depression offering some protection from enemy fire. The road was in turn about 200 yards in front of the 14th Connecticut's main line behind a low stone wall on Cemetery Ridge. That morning the strength of each of the two skirmisher companies—B and D—was about twenty men. Each was divided into two reliefs or squads that rotated at intervals between the advance line and the reserve. In posting his relief on the advance line, Ben discovered the dead corporal of Company B still poised as if to fire at the rebels to his front.[24]

Waist-high wheat covered the ground between the advance line and their reserves. Ben wrote that he "felt a little timid" about walking erect through the field, leaving readers to wonder whether in fact he courageously but foolishly did so. A corporal from Company B, Elnathan B. Tyler, was more explicit: "Those of us detailed to go out on the [advance]

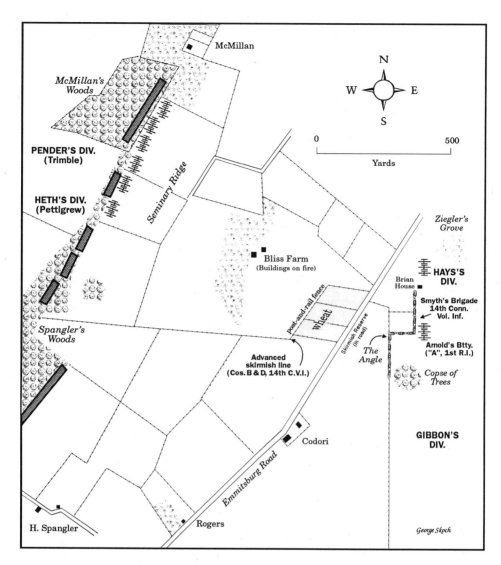

**SITUATION AT 12:30 P.M.**, July 3, 1863, on the portion of the field where Benjamin Hirst and the 14th Connecticut fought

line *crawled* out across the wheat field to the fence beyond." [25] Men on the advance line lay two or three fence posts apart, more or less hidden from enemy sharpshooters by the wheat behind the fence. In this concealment it was dangerous to keep up a desultory fire against enemy sharpshooters; the puff of gray smoke from a skirmisher's rifle or musket instantly revealed his position to the vigilant and very effective rebel marksmen. Thus when Ben wrote that "we were soon popping away as lively as crickets" once he reached the advance line, he was sending an additional message about his courage.

But in case readers at home missed his point, he underscored it with the anecdote about his fouled musket. He had been popping away so often that black powder residue clogged his gun barrel (soldiers were issued special "clean-out" bullets to reduce the problem, but these were unpopular and often thrown away). His aside also tells us more about the armament of the 14th Connecticut in the battle. Companies A and B originally had been issued Sharps breech-loading rifles with a much higher rate of fire than the standard muzzle-loading rifle-musket. Regimental strength on the third day was below 200, meaning that if all the Sharps originally issued had been available, every man would have been using one. But Ben still had his muzzle-loader, as did about half the men then in the regiment. Its veterans recalled years afterward the effectiveness of the Sharps in the defense of the 14th's main position later that day.[26]

The house and barn Ben referred to were the Bliss farm buildings located about 800 yards to the right front of the regiment's main defensive line. They were about 250 yards to Ben's right front as he lay on the advance skirmish line. He and his men undoubtedly took fire from rebel sharpshooters in the barn. But the Confederates were more interested in Union artillerymen serving the guns on Cemetery Ridge. It was a long shot, yet the rebel marksmen were good enough. Before noon the enemy were driven out "for good," and the buildings were burned by the other eight companies of the 14th. The fires were still billowing smoke as the Confederates stepped out on their assault in the afternoon.[27]

Linderman notes that the valued courage was a cool courage, and certainly Ben's narrative stressed his coolness on the skirmish line. After the barrage lifted, the coolness was again manifest in the withdrawal of Ben and the other Federal skirmishers in the face of the Confederate attack. The skirmishers fell back in good order, bringing their wounded with them and turning to fire occasionally at the advancing enemy. This was exactly how a defensive skirmish line should behave, even though it was the first time Ben's company had served in that capacity in combat.

The courage was also a steadfast courage. Ben lay still with the artillery projectiles flying over him. Although he did not mention it, the sun beating down and the lack of breeze must have added immensely to his discomfort. At that same time the regiment's sergeant major back on the main line recalled grimly watching as sweat pouring from his face made puddles in the dirt where he lay; he was regularly showered by gravel, shaken by concussions, and assaulted by clouds of powder smoke as one of the guns of Arnold's battery just behind him joined the barrage.[28] But he silently endured it. Once Ben himself was back behind the low wall on the main line, he noted that men resolutely emptied their cartridge boxes in front of them. This permitted greater speed in loading but also symbolically declared their brave intention to hold their position at all hazards. Did he, too, empty his cartridge box?

Under emphatic orders, the 14th coolly and steadfastly held its fire until the attacking line came up against the fences along the Emmitsburg Road. The portions of the fences still standing were too stout to be broken easily, and the Confederates were forced to climb over them—thus exposing themselves even more to Federal musketry and canister.[29]

Then came Ben's wound, after the Confederate charge had been broken. He wrote on July 5 that he was "thank ful" to come out so well after his close calls. At that time he and his brother wanted to assure Sarah that Ben was not seriously hurt. His brother John wrote that Ben "was in very good spirits" as they both walked to the hospital. Compare this with a generalizing comment by Confederate artillerist William M. Dame, quoted by Linderman: " 'Wounded men coming from under fire are, as a rule, cheerful, often jolly. Being able to get, honorably, from under fire, with the mark of manly service to show, is enough to make a fellow cheerful, even with a hole through him.' "[30] But there was no hole through Ben. In fact it was the classic million-dollar wound. He was moved to a hospital near his old home of Chester; Sarah could visit him there. Three months later he was certain it would keep him from coming back into combat, but the constraints of the courageous ideal prevented his conveying a sense of relief—assuming that was one of the emotions he was experiencing. Still, an ambivalence must have persisted as the war went on and other men with apparently much more serious wounds—First Sgt. Frank Stoughton, for one—returned to combat after recuperating. Ben also lacked the visible scar that could be worn as the lasting emblem of his courage. The wound was honorably won, however, and in view of the strength of his passion to preserve his self-image among readers, it is understandable why he decided retrospectively that he was hit not twice but three times that day.[31]

Ben's October narrative showed some shifts in attitudes and behavior from his earlier heroic accounts. One of these was his discussion of fear. Again, in the earlier narratives he always attributed fear to others and never called it by its name. Instead he used euphemisms then popular among soldiers and civilians alike—these others had "blanched faces," "pale faces," "tight faces."[32] In his October account he came closer—as close as he would come—to describing his own terror. "I felt a little timid about walking erect"; "It makes my Blood Tingle in my veins now; to think of"; and "how we did Hug the ground expecting every moment was to be our last." In his July 5 note, intended for a smaller group of readers, he wrote that "I thought it was all up with me, for a minuet or two, until I opened my eyes to look at the Hole and it wernt there," and "with a yell I thought I was gone for sure." But these examples hardly add up to a dramatic shift. Mostly he continued to characterize fear as something others were experiencing. His persistent avoidance of the first-person singular in his constructions made fear a more generalized, less focused presence. His own face remained almost invisible to readers at home.

Still, even this slight change suggests that in Ben's view his honorable behavior and wounding at Gettysburg had not only restored but enhanced his manly social image at home and had thus given him the right to claim, albeit opaquely, personal emotions that might have compromised that image earlier. Soldiers had special dispensation to growl; soldiers with honorable wounds had dispensation to sidle up more closely to admissions of fear.

His reasons for leaving his brother almost entirely out of the October narrative are not clear, but this, too, was a persistent feature of his Important Events style. John and the others out there on the line with him are anonymous. When the bedlam allowed, did Ben and John call back and forth to each other to be sure each was still all right? Others on that same line did, as they recalled in the regimental history. Ben knew the dead corporal on the picket line but did not give his name in the October account, nor did he identify the killed and wounded of his own company. This was deliberate. But why? Were the details considered too personal, too laden with selfish emotion? If so, then why the detailed discussion of himself on the skirmish line? In his view, was heroic prose to be elevated beyond the first-person singular because it was heroic, larger than one man, or two, or three? Was the "Date no matter" heading another way of saying the Events described were too Important to be bothered with the specific dates of the description itself? Were they too important to be dragged down by descriptions of the blood and bustle of a field hospital after the fight? Were these, in short, largely stylistic decisions, or were they another example of emotional distancing, removing of one's innermost and less-controllable self from readers by using a series of more anonymous constructions?

A more major shift in his Gettysburg narratives was his relative lack of concern about the "shirks" and "skedadlers"—those who, in his opinion, lacked the requisite measure of courage. Again, much of this invective in his earlier Important Events was aimed at company and regimental officers, but he also had been constantly vigilant for shirking among his fellow soldiers and mentioned by name those whom he felt had not measured up. This interest was driven not only by the prevailing courageous ethic but also by a sergeant's need to know which of his men were dependable in combat. In his October narrative he flashed this earlier contempt for "Skulkers, Shirks, and Camp followers" but concluded they were more ridiculous than threatening. They were not from his company or regiment, and besides, this time they could not be portrayed as contributors to a major defeat.

Nor did he follow his earlier pattern of criticizing the behavior of officers. In his October narrative he turned an apparent criticism of Gen. Winfield S. Hancock, his new corps commander, into a blast against rebeldom. His company and regimental officers were his favorite targets in the past; some of them, at least, deserved it. But by Gettysburg most of the inept and cowardly officers had been weeded out along with the shirks in the enlisted ranks, and there was probably little for Ben to growl about in the conduct of the hardened remainder on the third day—even if it had not been a Union victory. He mentioned the calm, reassuring comments by Gens. John Gibbon and Alexander Hays. Almost certainly Hays did more than give them "a few . . . words" as the Confederate battle lines approached. His colorful language, stentorian voice, and high-pitched physical excitement in combat were to become well known to the men in the regiment. (They would also come to despise him for his brash foolishness at the battle of Morton's Ford, where his drunken orders may have caused some of them to be killed or wounded needlessly.) [33]

Linderman notes a close connection between courage and godliness in the soldiers' worldview.[34] Yet Ben mostly left God or religiosity out of his earlier correspondence to Sarah, including the Important Events genre. In his October letter he alluded to God and religious conviction only once. He had faith, and he strove to avoid profanity in even his routine correspondence: "ilebe Damd" was as coarse as he got, and then only to add unusual emphasis. His first regimental commander, whom Ben despised, was portrayed as a "damd Nincompoop." Reid Mitchell has traced the parallel between religious belief and conduct of the war in the worldviews of many soldiers.[35] In marked contrast to these others, including some in his own regiment, there is nothing to indicate that Ben saw God's work in the outcome of battles.

The restraint on profanity is most noticeable in his characterization of the "Oaths and imprecations" that rose to a roar as the two sides drew closer and the men loaded and fired as quickly as they could. George Stewart notes that at about this time in the assault the men's roars and curses could be heard above the din of musketry[36]—yet Ben alluded only to shouts of "Give them Hell x x x ." Surely with adrenalin pumping and mortality in the balance, some men would have been coarser than that despite prevailing sentiments, especially at home, against swearing. It was, of course, ungodly to swear. But it was also indicative of an unseemly loss of manly control, another crucial component of the social image Ben was striving to maintain.[37]

In this passage he did succeed in communicating something of the emotional pitch of combat and the pervasive sense that the 14th Connecticut and the Second Corps were not simply whipping the attacking Confederates but were paying them back for past humiliation inflicted, most profoundly at Fredericksburg. This last battle was also much on the minds of other Federal units during Longstreet's assault. Men of the 20th Massachusetts just south of the Angle were shouting "Fredericksburg!" while firing at the attackers to their front.[38] Yet, as in his portrayals of prebattle anxiety, Ben gives no clear statement of what he himself was doing. Was Sgt. Benjamin Hirst yelling invective as he pumped bullets into the onrushing gray lines? Was "Never mind who is Hit" something *he* shouted? And if so, was it an order to distracted privates or an exultant public notice that the Fredericksburg incident was now behind him?

The most dramatic difference between Ben's October narrative and his earlier Important Events is his characterization of the rebel enemy. Always before he had referred to them simply as "the enemy" or "rebels" or "Grey Backs." But in his October letter he labored at unflattering descriptors: "that Rebellious Crew" with "Polluting footsteps"; Cursed Rebels; Blasted Rebels; the second line sent "Howling" back after the first one. Why this shift? Mitchell describes a series of fundamental alienations experienced by Federal soldiers from their communities, from their surroundings, and from the enemy. This last was bolstered by the pattern of characterizing the enemy as "savage"—that is, unmanly, uncontrolled.[39] To see opponents as such strengthened the soldier's conviction that he fought for a righteous cause and eased qualms about killing fellow human beings. To portray the enemy thus for readers bolstered *their* conceptions that the soldier was doing his manly, patriotic duty. While Ben unquestionably was concerned about this last idea, it is not clear why he did not use the same literary technique in his earlier narratives, when his image was somewhat less secure. It would not seem so necessary to strengthen alienation if he was not returning to combat. Although his brother John never was caught up with the Important Events prose to the same extent as Ben, John continued to refer simply to "the enemy," "Johnnies," or "rebs" for the remainder of the war (the last year as regimental colorbearer). Ben here simply may have been imitating prose he admired in other accounts of the Gettysburg battle. Or it may have been alienation working in an opposite fashion to that characterized by Mitchell: Ben felt a measure of identity with enemy infantrymen as long as he was sharing the front with them and they were a constant presence.[40] Once removed from that landscape, their humanness became less palpable to him—hence more easily questioned in heroic hyperbole.

Still, in none of his narratives did he report killing an enemy soldier—whether or not he could be sure he had done so in the swirl of combat. Like other heroic accounts of Longstreet's assault, Ben's reflected his respectful awe at the Confederate steadfastness and discipline in their moving lines of battle. His and the others' reports used virtually identical imagery: the enemy marched "as though upon Parade." The postbattle distancing from the Blasted Rebels was not total.

He also sought to spare Sarah the details of men's deaths and wounds. This was a persistent feature of all his correspondence to her—routine letters, journal entries, and Important Events. Ben invoked the dead skirmisher and the comments on his posture at the fence line to underscore the dangers there. He described the location and severity of wounds to his Rockville chums—whom Sarah knew—in his July 5 letter, but without vivid details. There were no accounts of the effects of canister or shell on massed ranks of attackers, or of frothing or jagged wounds among those brought into the hospital. In his earlier letters he had been concerned about Sarah's health, particularly her bouts with extreme depression that left her unable to work in the garden.[41] He may well have felt that graphic detail of the effects of battle would simply add to her misery. Yet he certainly preserved such detail in his memory and years later recalled an anecdote for the regimental history about a man having "the top of his head blown off" at Antietam.[42]

There were two other, tactical preoccupations in Ben's narratives that do not reflect his prewar worldview. One is the count of enemy flags captured. In stressing this he was typical of the soldiers of his time, for whom a regimental battle flag was the embodiment of the regiment's life-stuff and, as Mitchell observes, that of the home communities as well. The 14th Connecticut officially captured five of them; four men risked their lives to do so, one was wounded in the effort, and three received Medals of Honor. The regimental history perpetuates the rumor that a sixth flag was taken—a "beautiful silk" one—but was never turned in to headquarters.[43] It was an achievement of unprecedented glory. In a particularly unchivalrous but personally consistent act of combat euphoria that the wounded Ben probably missed, Gen. Alexander Hays and two aides gathered a clutch of captured Confederate flags and dragged them in the dust along the Third Division line from the backs of their cantering horses. This was observed by at least one Confederate commander as the surviving attackers withdrew.[44]

Ben's other tactical concern was the lack of Federal pursuit of the repulsed rebels. The October narrative was armed with hindsight honed by the abundant newspaper and army palaver about Gen. George G. Meade's cautious pursuit of the retreating Confederates. "Oh, for a thousand or two fresh men to charge upon the discomfited Foe, and push them Home," wrote Ben. He was still willing to consider that the Army of the Potomac was too played out to counterattack. His July 5 observation was fresher and different: "If our Artillery could have helped us but very few would have got away." Indeed, according to one account a fresh battery unlimbered just to the 14th Connecticut's left, in the position earlier vacated by Arnold's Battery, and opened fire on the Confederate clusters just as they began to fall back.[45] Yet both of Ben's portrayals have a common theme: *something* should have been done immediately following the repulse of Longstreet's men.

The next day, July 4, and on the march in pursuit of Lee's army, only nine of the Rockville boys were present for duty in Company D.[46]

Ben's immediate circle of readers back home included Sarah, her mother living with her for a time, his friend Luther Morse and his wife, and a fellow worker named Frink. Sarah also was expected to show his and his brother's letters to anyone else she felt would be interested. The Important

Events narratives were too carefully and laboriously constructed, how-ever, for this limited group alone. His October narrative was published in the local newspaper in 1887, and passages of it appeared later without attribution in the regimental history. Conceivably his role model in this was Capt. Samuel Fiske of the 14th's Company G, whose "Dunn Browne" dispatches were read by Ben and other soldiers of the regiment.[47]

In 1887 he serialized not only his Gettysburg accounts but also his and John's other war narratives for the Rockville *Journal*. (John's letters were liberally doctored by Ben's more flowing pen.) Ben remained as proud of his eloquence as he was ultimately proud of his behavior in battle. In a sense both sources of pride stemmed from a single larger source—his efforts to embody the ideals of manhood that then prevailed in his social class and community.

After Gettysburg he was transferred to the Veterans' Reserve Corps and did not preserve his correspondence. When the war ended, he returned to Rockville and decided to get out of the mills. He opened a dry goods store that featured ladies' millinery, and later he joined the GAR. He remained very active in the Society of the 14th Connecticut and posed proudly among them for group pictures on old battlefields. In later years he moved his business to Springfield, Massachusetts, but retained his close ties with Rockville. He died in 1908 of gangrene and arteriosclerosis; Sarah had by then been committed to the Massachusetts Home for the Insane in Northampton.[48] Ben and Sarah were buried beside John in Rockville. For Ben the Civil War may well have been the high point of his life, and the apex of that high was unquestionably the third day's battle at Gettysburg.

At a generalizing analytical level, one of Reid Mitchell's conclusions is particularly appropriate to this essay: "Combat, military discipline, ide-ology, and leadership have all been evaluated as determinants of soldiers' conduct during the war, but community values were equally important. In fact, they were crucial to the way in which Americans made war from 1861 to 1865. . . . During combat, could men think of their reputations? The answer is probably yes."[49]

Here Mitchell's and other general analytical insights have been applied to a particular individual, in an effort to show how both his behavior in the third day's battle and his construction of it for readers were con-strained by a wider prevailing worldview. Ben's earlier correspondence, his service and pension records, and documentation from others in his unit have helped to illuminate the more specific ideological context within which he acted out his social image. A combination of the two levels of insight brings him into better focus as a person—that is, as a product of his culture.

NOTES

1. The number of published collections of letters and diaries is increasing dramatically. An excellent example of this type is Elisha Hunt Rhodes, *All for the Union*, ed. Robert Hunt Rhodes (New York: Orion, 1991). Postwar memoirs are often more readable than wartime correspondence as constructed reality, but as such they are influenced by the author's retrospective rearrangement. Sam R. Watkins's *"Co. Aytch," Maury Grays, First Tennessee Regiment; or, A Side Show of the Big Show* (1900; reprint, Wilmington, N.C.; Broadfoot, 1987), Carlton McCarthy's *Detailed Minutiae of Soldier Life in the Army of Northern Virginia, 1861–1865* (1882; reprint, Alexandria, Va.: Time-Life Books, 1982), and John Billings's *Hardtack and Coffee* (1887; reprint, Alexandria, Va.: Time-Life Books, 1982) are classics of the memoir genre. Bell Irvin Wiley's *The Life of Billy Yank* (1952; reprint, Baton Rouge: Louisiana State University Press, 1978) and *The Life of Johnny Reb* (1943; reprint, Baton Rouge: Louisiana State University Press, 1978) are the outstanding prototypes of the generalizing approach, masterfully applied more recently in Gerald F. Linderman's *Embattled Courage: The Experience of Combat in the American Civil War* (New York: Free Press, 1987), Reid Mitchell's *Civil War Soldiers* (New York: Viking, 1988), and James I. Robertson, Jr.'s *Soldiers Blue and Gray* (Columbia: University of South Carolina Press, 1988). Randall C. Jimerson's *The Private Civil War: Popular Thought during the Sectional Conflict* (Baton Rouge: Louisiana State University Press, 1988) is a valuable broader analysis of prevailing Civil War worldviews. Michael Barton's *Goodmen: The Character of Civil War Soldiers* (University Park: Pennsylvania State University Press, 1981) is an important study of worldviews based on a quantitative content analysis of letters and diaries.

2. Seventy of Ben's letters and his journal have been preserved, along with another eighty letters from Ben's brother John, by the Alden Skinner Camp, Sons of Union Veterans of the Civil War, in Rockville, Conn. I am grateful to members of the camp for allowing me to transcribe the complete set of letters. In this essay the collection is referred to as the Alden Skinner Camp Collection and hereafter cited as ASCC.

3. John Hirst, Declaration for Original Invalid Pension, November 4, 1881, Pension File WC 666–960, National Archives, Washington, D.C. (hereafter cited as NA); Benjamin Hirst, Certificate of Disability for Discharge, July 10, 1865, Pension File WC 688–730, NA.

4. Burpee was mustered into Federal service along with the rest of the company,

but five days later he resigned to become a major in the 21st Connecticut Infantry. Ben later hinted this was a breach of faith on the captain's part. See B. Hirst to Sarah, February 5, 1863, File No. 31, ASCC. Burpee was mortally wounded while courageously leading the 21st in combat at Cold Harbor on June 9, 1864, and the GAR Post in Rockville was named for him in 1884.

5. During the first half of the war, companies commonly were made up of men from the same town—an extension of the community, as Reid Mitchell describes it in "The Northern Soldier and His Community," in *Toward a Social History of the American Civil War*, ed. Maris A. Vinovskis (New York: Cambridge University Press, 1990), 80. The territorial linkage weakened later as substitutes and conscripts from elsewhere were brought into the units.

6. The first lot was left behind on the march to Antietam and was never recovered (although the logistical efforts to do so are intriguing). The second set was lost in the confusion of Chancellorsville. Light-fingered substitutes later stole knapsacks from individual veterans in the 14th, including John Hirst. Understandably, John as a color-bearer was wearing his latest knapsack during a charge in the Boydton Plank Road battle of October 1864. See J. Hirst to Ben Hirst, October 30, 1864, File No. 131, ASCC.

7. In *Embattled Courage*, 110, 98, Linderman writes of the "heroic vocabulary" in soldiers' letters and declares that "it was an idiom of elevated sentimentality, one less needful of recounting what was observed than of confirming that proper values motivated what was observed."

8. B. Hirst to Sarah, December 20, 1862, File No. 23, ASCC.

9. The three items are File Nos. 68 (written in pencil on a torn-off sheet of lined note paper), 69 (written in pencil on lined paper, with stains obliterating some words), and 70 (abridged), ASCC.

10. This letter was written from "Union town," not Union Mills. B. Hirst to Sarah, June 30, 1863, File No. 67, ASCC.

11. Benjamin Hirst, "War Papers: Gettysburg," Rockville *Journal*, June 9, 1887, p. 5.

12. Linderman argues that courage—"heroic action undertaken without fear" —was the central value for all Civil War soldiers. He draws a distinction between courage and manliness but sees them as closely related in soldiers' "constellations of values": "A failure of courage in war was a failure of manhood" (Linderman, *Embattled Courage*, 17, 8). Reid Mitchell also describes the centrality of courage as a value for soldiers struggling to live up to the expectations of their home folks. See Mitchell, "Northern Soldier," 85.

13. Linderman quotes Gen. Joshua L. Chamberlain's comment that, after passing the test of courage in combat, it was considered "'the highest quality of

manhood'" to care for the wounded. But he further notes that the constraints of courage made such acts risky, as will be seen in Ben Hirst's case. See Linderman, *Embattled Courage*, 27.

14. B. Hirst to Luther Morse, September 20, 1862, File No. 6; B. Hirst Journal Excerpt No. 3; B. Hirst to Sarah, September 21, 1862, File No. 7, all in ASCC.

15. Compare this to Linderman's general observation: "Often the most powerful fear was that one's fear would be revealed—and that meant a prohibition on discussion. . . . Fear was not an anxiety to be shared but a weakness to be stifled" (Linderman, *Embattled Courage*, 23).

16. B. Hirst to Sarah, December 30, 1862, File No. 24, and Journal Excerpt No. 8, ASCC.

17. B. Hirst to Sarah, January 11, 18, 31, 1863, File Nos. 26, 27, 30, ASCC.

18. B. Hirst to Sarah, December 18, 1862, File No. 22, ASCC.

19. B. Hirst to Sarah, January 11, 1863, File No. 26, ASCC.

20. Ibid.

21. Linderman, *Embattled Courage*, 129.

22. B. Hirst to Sarah, May 5, 1863, File No. 52, ASCC.

23. Under the pen name of "Dunn Browne," Fiske wrote a series of dispatches to the Springfield (Mass.) *Republican* between 1862 and 1864. They were later compiled and published as "Dunn Browne" (Samuel Fiske), *Mr. Dunn Browne's Experiences in the Army* (Boston: Nichols and Noyes, 1866). The essays are outstanding. References here are to pp. 54 and 86 of the book.

24. Ben did not mention the dead man's name or rank in either of the Gettysburg narratives reprinted here. Charles D. Page, *History of the Fourteenth Regiment, Connecticut Vol. Infantry* (Meriden, Conn.: Horton, 1906), 143, describes the corporal's death at his post, as does Ben's 1887 "War Paper: Gettysburg" account in the Rockville *Journal*.

25. Page, *History of the Fourteenth Regiment*, 142 (italics added).

26. Men armed with Sharps teamed up, with one firing and the other loading. This afforded a significantly higher rate of defensive fire but also made the rifle barrels very hot. Men used canteen water to cool them periodically. "Accounts seem to agree that the Confederate line broke quicker in the immediate front of the Fourteenth than any where else," wrote Page in *History of the Fourteenth Regiment*, 152–53, 155. If true, the Sharps may have been a major factor. Several times the regimental history praised the effectiveness of the Sharps in later battles.

27. See Elwood W. Christ, *"Over a Wide, Hot, . . . Crimson Plain"—The Struggle for the Bliss Farm at Gettysburg, July 2nd and 3rd, 1863* (Baltimore: Butternut and Blue, 1993).

28. Page, *History of the Fourteenth Regiment*, 149.

29. Ibid., 151; George R. Stewart, *Pickett's Charge: A Microhistory of the Final Attack at Gettysburg, July 3, 1863* (Boston: Houghton Mifflin, 1957), 183, 187.

30. Linderman, *Embattled Courage*, 32.

31. In addition to the two hits he reported to Sarah on July 5, a spent round or shell fragment bruised his heel as he and the other skirmishers were falling back to the main defensive line on Cemetery Ridge. See Hirst, "War Papers: Gettysburg."

32. Linderman notes that many soldiers used these same phrases to describe fear in others. See Linderman, *Embattled Courage*, 23.

33. In *Pickett's Charge*, 134–35, 171, Stewart describes General Hays's enthusiasm in battle as "an almost sexual excitement." After testing McClellan at Antietam, Burnside at Fredericksburg, and Hooker at Chancellorsville, Ben Hirst concluded the "peer of McCllenan [*sic*] is not yet found" (B. Hirst to Sarah, May 9, 1863, File No. 53, ASCC).

34. Linderman, *Embattled Courage*, esp. 103.

35. Mitchell, *Civil War Soldiers*, 88–89.

36. Stewart, *Pickett's Charge*, 201.

37. Throughout *Goodmen*, Michael Barton describes the various manifestations of self-control valued by Victorians.

38. Stewart, *Pickett's Charge*, 186.

39. Mitchell, *Civil War Soldiers*, 26.

40. Linderman observes in *Embattled Courage*, 236, that front-line soldiers "seemed to denounce all parties to the war except the enemy in combat."

41. B. Hirst to Sarah, May 9, 20, 28, 1863, File Nos. 53, 56, 57, ASCC.

42. Page, *History of the Fourteenth Regiment*, 43–44.

43. Mitchell, *Civil War Soldiers*, 34; Page, *History of the Fourteenth Regiment*, 156.

44. Identifying the Confederate as Artillery Maj. W. T. Poague, Stewart places him next to a distressed Gen. George E. Pickett at that moment. See Stewart, *Pickett's Charge*, 224–25.

45. Stewart declares that Arnold's Battery remained in position along the wall and delivered a final volley of double-shotted canister just as the Confederates were about to reach the defensive line. See Stewart, *Pickett's Charge*, 201. The 14th's regimental history, however, insists that Arnold's Battery withdrew immediately after the afternoon barrage, leaving one gun that had rolled forward down the slope. See Page, *History of the Fourteenth Regiment*, 150, 153, 165. At stake in the discrepancy is the role played by the 14th in repulsing the charge. Federal artillery commander Henry J. Hunt's postwar recollection supports the regiment's version. See Henry J. Hunt, "The Third Day at Gettysburg," in *Battles and Leaders of the Civil War*, ed. Robert Underwood Johnson and Clarence C. Buel, 4 vols. (New York: Century, 1887–88), 3:374. Reportedly, no battery replaced Arnold's

until after the assault had been repulsed. The new battery immediately opened with canister and managed to kill one member of the 14th and wound others who by then were dashing down the slope in front of the wall to chase after retreating Confederates. See H. S. Stevens, *Souvenir of the Excursion to Battlefields by the Society of the Fourteenth Connecticut Regiment and Reunion at Antietam September 1891; With History and Reminiscences of Battles and Campaigns of the Regiment on the Fields Revisited* (Washington, D.C.: Gibson Brothers, 1893), 33. The replacement battery's action was not reported in the later and more considered *History of the Fourteenth Regiment*.

46. John Hirst to Sarah, July 6, 1863, File No. 71, ASCC.

47. When Fiske was captured at Chancellorsville, Ben wrote his brother Joe: "That Chap who writes for the papers under the name of Dunne Brown is Little Capt Fisk of ours" (B. Hirst to Joseph Hirst, June 7, 1863, File No. 59, ASCC). Captain Fiske was later mortally wounded in the second day's battle of the Wilderness on May 6, 1864.

48. Much of this information is gleaned from Benjamin Hirst Pension File WC 688–730, NA.

49. Mitchell, "Northern Soldier," 79–80, 85. The last sentence of the quote is somewhat out of context here. Mitchell goes on to say that the soldier under fire was preoccupied with other issues as well.

*Meade's Pursuit of Lee*

# FROM GETTYSBURG TO FALLING WATERS

### A. Wilson Greene

Did Maj. Gen. George Gordon Meade and his Army of the Potomac fumble an opportunity to cripple their enemy and possibly win the Civil War after the battle of Gettysburg? "We think that the question is an open one capable of much discussion and of opposite views," thought a Union veteran in 1867.[1] The historical record of the last 125 years has sustained that assessment. Several better-known debates have emerged from the aftershocks of Gettysburg, but the conduct of the Union army between the afternoon of July 3 and the morning of July 14, 1863, presents as intriguing a controversy as any confronting the student of Civil War military leadership.

Meade's contemporaries disagreed about the nature of his generalship following Pickett's Charge. Brig. Gen. Henry J. Hunt, the respected chief of Union artillery, endorsed virtually every aspect of Meade's campaign in a postwar letter: "He was right in . . . making his battle a purely defensive one[,] . . . right in not attempting a counter-attack at any stage of the battle,—right as to his pursuit of Lee." Other prominent officers in the Army of the Potomac saw the matter differently, but the harshest early criticisms of Meade came from civilian officials. Speaking of Lee's escape into Virginia at a cabinet meeting on July 17, 1863, Abraham Lincoln allowed that Meade "has committed a terrible mistake." Secretary of the Navy Gideon Welles decried Meade's "want of decision and self-reliance in an emergency," while Secretary of War Edwin M. Stanton wrote on July 22 that "since the world began no man ever missed so great an opportunity of serving his country as was lost by his neglecting to strike his adversary." Some soldiers, such as Pvt. Theodore Gerrish of the 20th Maine, thought a vigorous pursuit could have trapped Lee in Maryland and determined the destiny of the rebellion north of the Potomac.

Charles A. Dana of the War Department stated the case against Meade as plainly as anyone in a letter written two weeks after the campaign: "Had Meade finished Lee before he had crossed the Potomac, as he might have done & he should have done . . . we should now be at the end of the war."[2]

Historians have evaluated Meade's performance in similar proportions. Richard M. Bache, an early biographer of Meade, defended the general in concluding that by "harassing the enemy's retreat from the beginning, capturing prisoners, waggons, [*sic*] and other trophies, Meade had apparently accomplished all that was possible." William Swinton stopped just short of condemnation in his 1866 chronicle of the Army of the Potomac, declaring that the Union pursuit "was conducted with an excessive circumspection." Union artillerist Maj. J. Watts De Peyster recognized that Meade's sudden elevation to command placed him in a difficult situation. Still, wrote De Peyster in 1867, "the fact that Lee was not pursued, instantly and effectively, and energetically attacked, harassed and pressed as long as he remained on Northern soil, was one of the greatest errors and misfortunes of the war." Former cavalryman George B. Davis adopted a similar stance when he told the Military Historical Society of Massachusetts in 1900 that "the Army of Northern Virginia was permitted to escape from a situation which should have gone far to compass its defeat, if not its utter discomfiture."[3]

These early critics set the stage for modern historians who found Meade's performance wanting. Edward J. Stackpole titled the pertinent chapter in his monograph on Gettysburg "A Lost Opportunity to End the War" and charged Meade with a pathetic failure to grasp the post-Gettysburg opportunity. More respected writers shared this view. Allan Nevins called Meade's campaign from Gettysburg to Falling Waters "preternaturally slow" and accused Meade of lacking courage and skill. Kenneth P. Williams levied perhaps the harshest indictment. In a chapter he called "A Feeble Effort at Pursuit," Williams concluded that Meade used the ten days after Gettysburg "as ineffectively as McClellan had used the 14th, 15th, and the 16th of the preceding September."[4] Michael C. C. Adams placed Meade's conduct within a broader pattern of Union reluctance in the Eastern Theater to pursue an offensive against Lee and his army. As in previous campaigns, the Army of the Potomac "simply tried to stave Lee off and push him away" at Gettysburg. "This was the tenor of Meade's congratulatory address, delivered after the battle," observed Adams, "in which he said that the enemy had been baffled and must next be driven off Northen soil. There was no mention of destroying him." Lack of fresh troops does not explain Meade's conduct because "his men were certainly as fresh as the rebels, who expected an attack daily." Conditioned to defeat at the hands of Lee and the Army of Northern Virginia, Meade and many others in his command scarcely could conceive of accomplishing more than a repulse of the enemy.[5]

Events subsequent to the failed Confederate assault against Cemetery Ridge on July 3 are much less difficult to narrate than to analyze. While Lee rallied his defeated men west of the Emmitsburg Road and pondered retreat toward Virginia, Meade rode from Ziegler's Grove south to Little Round Top. Arriving late in the afternoon in the company of Gens. Gouverneur K. Warren, George Sykes, and Alfred Pleasonton, Meade issued orders for a skirmish line to locate the enemy and weigh the wisdom of a counterattack. The hour had grown late, however, and the Federals did not test Lee's resilience. Meanwhile, the Sixth U.S. Cavalry fought the 6th and 7th Virginia Cavalry near Fairfield but retired in the face of Confederate pressure, ending any immediate threat to Lee's probable routes of retreat. Darkness then fell on the grisly scene at Gettysburg.[6]

Lee met with some of his officers that night and began preparations for his departure. He shifted Richard S. Ewell's Second Corps from its position opposite the Union right to a line along Oak and Seminary ridges, where Ewell's veterans dug in. Ambrose Powell Hill's troops and James Longstreet's men remained concealed in the woods south and west of Gettysburg. Lee ordered most of his wagons and ambulances to move on July 4 through Cashtown Pass and Greenwood and Greencastle, Pennsylvania, to Williamsport, Maryland, on the Potomac River. Brig. Gen. John D. Imboden would escort this entourage with 2,100 cavalry. After remaining in position all day on July 4, Lee sent his infantry toward the mountains at sunset with Hill in the lead followed by Longstreet and Ewell. Their route along the Fairfield Road toward Hagerstown, Maryland, then south to Williamsport would be the shortest path to Virginia.[7]

A heavy rain on the fourth added to the misery of the weary warriors from both armies. Meade advanced reconnaissance parties from Henry W. Slocum's Twelfth Corps, Oliver O. Howard's Eleventh Corps, and Sykes's Fifth Corps to ascertain Confederate locations and intentions. Slocum quickly discovered the southerners absent from his front, and Howard moved into Gettysburg itself, liberating Union fugitives who had been hiding in the town for three days. A Fifth Corps brigade advanced a mile west of Little Round Top through the Wheatfield and "found that Lee had refused his right flank, but was still holding a strong position toward the centre of the line." Meade spent the rest of the day burying the dead, scouring the battlefield for usable equipment, and collecting supplies from his railhead at Westminster, Maryland. He declined to accept Lee's offer of a prisoner exchange and waited out the storm at a brigade commander's headquarters, being "drowned out" at his own.[8]

Some Union troops did see action on July 4. Cavalry under the control of Maj. Gen. William H. French at Frederick rode up the Potomac and destroyed the pontoon bridge at Falling Waters, Lee's best access into Virginia. That night a small mounted force under Brig. Gen. Judson Kilpatrick ripped into some of Ewell's wagons and mounted guards at Monterey Pass near Fairfield, an affair of small consequence reported to Meade the next afternoon.[9]

In the meantime Meade received reports from signal officers of long gray columns snaking westward toward Cashtown and Fairfield. The

Union commander summoned his senior officers to a conference that evening to determine the army's best response to this information. Meade reminded the assemblage of his overriding instructions to protect Washington and Baltimore and mentioned the possibility that Lee might try to maneuver around the Union left flank and interpose himself between the Army of the Potomac and its capital. He then posed four questions to his corps commanders: "Shall this army remain here?" If so, "Shall we assume the offensive?" Did the officers "deem it expedient to move towards Williamsport, through Emmettsburg [*sic*]?" Finally, "Shall we pursue the enemy if he is retreating on his direct line of retreat?"[10] All of Meade's subordinates except Slocum, cavalry commander Pleasonton, and First Corps chief John Newton voted to remain at Gettysburg. None of the attendees advised going on the offensive; most favored direct pursuit only with cavalry once Lee's retreat was confirmed. Under such circumstances, the infantry should follow east of the mountains and try to intercept Lee before he crossed the Potomac. Meade accepted this judgment and closed the meeting by instructing Warren to use troops from the Sixth Corps at 4:30 the next morning "to find out the position and movements of the enemy."[11]

Maj. Gen. John Sedgwick roused the slumbering soldiers of his Sixth Corps at 3:00 A.M. on July 5 to ready them for their reconnaissance. The Federals found no Confederates when they probed cautiously toward the Emmitsburg Road and Seminary Ridge at early dawn. Union signal stations verified that the Army of Northern Virginia also had vanished from its positions elsewhere along the Union front.[12]

Meade ordered his chief of staff, Maj. Gen. Daniel Butterfield, to prepare orders for pursuit. He divided the army into three wings: the First, Third, and Sixth corps under Sedgwick; the Second and Twelfth under Slocum; and the Fifth and Eleventh under Howard. Each wing would aim toward a July 7 rendezvous at Middletown, Maryland, via separate routes to expedite the movement. Meade then informed General in Chief Henry W. Halleck in Washington that "the enemy retired, under cover of the night and heavy rain, in the direction of Fairfield and Cashtown."[13]

Meade also entertained Brig. Gen. Herman Haupt at his headquarters that morning. Haupt had been superintending the restoration of railroad communications with the army and consequently missed the battle; he was not privy to Meade's plans for pursuit. His interview with the Union commander convinced Haupt that Meade did not intend to improve upon his victory. Frustrated by the reticent and apparently unmotivated Meade,

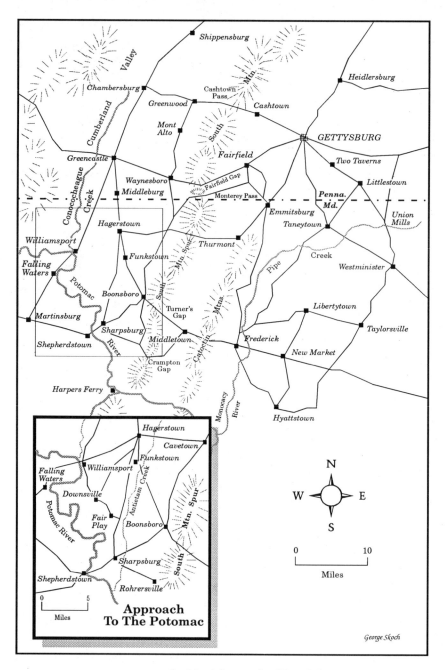

**AREA OF OPERATIONS** for Meade's pursuit of Lee, July 4–14, 1863

Main map labels:

Shippensburg

Valley

Chambersburg

Cashtown Mtn.

Heidlersburg

Greenwood

Cashtown Pass

Cashtown

GETTYSBURG

Cumberland

Mont Alto

South

Fairfield

Two Taverns

Greencastle

Fairfield Gap

Littlestown

Waynesboro

Middleburg

Monterey Pass

**Penna. Md.**

Conococheague Creek

Emmitsburg

Union Mills

Hagerstown

Taneytown

Williamsport

Thurmont

Westminister

Funkstown

Mtn. Spur

Pipe

Creek

Falling Waters

Potomac

Boonsboro

South

Libertytown

Martinsburg

Turner's Gap

Mtns.

Taylorsville

Sharpsburg

Middletown

Frederick

New Market

Shepherdstown

River

Crampton Gap

Catoctin

Harpers Ferry

Monocacy River

Hyattstown

Inset map ("Approach To The Potomac"):

Hagerstown

Cavetown

Funkstown

Falling Waters

Williamsport

Antietam Creek

Mtn. Spur

Downsville

Potomac River

Fair Play

Boonsboro

Sharpsburg

South

Shepherdstown

Rohrersville

0    5
Miles

**Approach To The Potomac**

N
W   E
S

0          10
Miles

George Skoch

Haupt stalked away from Gettysburg and made his way quickly to Washington. His interpretation of the military situation would have important ramifications.[14]

Haupt's departure coincided, ironically, with Meade's decision to authorize the army's southward march. With Meade's concurrence, Warren and Sedgwick decided to employ the entire Sixth Corps in a continuing reconnaissance to the west, in effect turning the operation into a direct pursuit. The rest of the Union army shuffled south on the Emmitsburg and Taneytown roads while the soldiers of Sedgwick and Warren crept west on the Fairfield Road during the afternoon. Troops from Brig. Gen. Thomas H. Neill's brigade, supported by the New Jerseyians of Brig. Gen. Alfred T. A. Torbert, bumped up against the rearguard of Ewell's corps about 5:00 P.M. After absorbing less than a dozen casualties, Sedgwick ordered a halt and sent word to Meade that the gap at Fairfield was strongly defended and would be difficult to force. Meade responded by suspending the progress of the army and informing Sedgwick that he could call on the First, Third, Fifth, and Eleventh corps for help should he need it.[15]

Meade further instructed Sedgwick at 2:00 A.M. on July 6 to press his reconnaissance and ascertain "how far the enemy has retreated, and also the character of the gap and practicability of carrying the same, in case I should determine to advance on that line." Sedgwick obeyed but at 8:30 A.M. reported the gaps beyond Fairfield too strong to assail. He repeated this assessment at noon. Meade accordingly decided to resume the movement toward Middletown, detaching Neill with a rifled battery and a brigade of cavalry to "follow the enemy cautiously as he [the enemy] retires, keeping the commanding general constantly informed."[16] The Army of Northern Virginia made substantial progress toward the Potomac on July 6. Longstreet reached Hagerstown, with Ewell not far behind at Waynesboro and Hill bringing up the rear. Imboden's cavalry had engaged troopers under Brig. Gen. John Buford at Williamsport; Maj. Gen. J. E. B. Stuart's cavalry, supported by infantry and artillery, simultaneously turned back an assault by Kilpatrick at Hagerstown. By contrast, the Union infantry had made but little headway, being scattered between Fairfield, Gettysburg, Emmitsburg, and Littlestown.[17]

Convinced beyond doubt by July 7 that Lee was in retreat, Meade abandoned any consideration of direct pursuit and launched his army on the southward trek he had originally ordered two days earlier. His men's already high spirits escalated as they shook off the mud of the Keystone

State and entered western Maryland. An Ohio soldier described an incident that occurred near Two Taverns, Pennsylvania, illustrative of the attitude evinced by some Adams County residents once the dangers posed by Lee's rebels had dissipated:

> The people were not glad to see us. One dumpy sort of woman, whom we took to be a lineal descendant of some original Hessian, from her dress and curious jargon . . . reminded one of Irving's Aix-la-chapelle people, who spoke bad English, bad French, and what [was] worst of all, good Dutch; she refused to admit us to her kitchen, saying that we were too "ornery." She wanted a dollar a gallon for milk, and a half dollar for a cruet of vinegar. Our cook, however, had spring chickens, etc., for breakfast next morning. We never inquired the price, but ate what was set before us and asked no questions—for conscience sake.[18]

On the other hand, a Pennsylvania volunteer admitted that "in all the Maryland towns on our route of march the residents did their best to supply us with bread, cakes, and other articles of food at reasonable rates, and always had for us words of encouragement and cheer."[19] Such treatment helped buoy an Army of the Potomac already flushed with the glow of victory. "A man who would not fight in a country," gushed one officer, "where, in passing through the towns and villages, the females, young and aged, assemble to greet your arrival with baskets of food, pitchers of water and wine, and shower all kinds of kindnesses upon you, is no man."[20] The army sought to finish the job it had started at Gettysburg. "We hope to wipe Lee's Army out of existence & secure peace to the Union before long," a Michigander wrote his parents. General Butterfield testified after the campaign that the troops "were in splendid spirits, very exultant, and I think would have undergone any privations with a view to pursuit."[21]

The army's actual condition tested Butterfield's hypothesis. Noted artillerist Col. Charles S. Wainwright recorded in his diary that "the men have even a more dirty appearance than usual. As for myself, I never was so dirty before in all my life. . . . I feel horribly nasty." Filth was bad enough, but the troops suffered more material problems. "The men have pressed on since the fight, barefooted, hungry, lousy and faint, animated by the hope of giving Lee his finishing blow," wrote a soldier in the 83rd Pennsylvania. Col. Rufus R. Dawes of the 6th Wisconsin confided in a letter home that "our men have toiled and suffered as never before. Almost half . . . have marched barefooted for a week. . . . I have not slept in a dry blanket or had on dry clothing since crossing the Potomac before the battle." A soldier in the 14th Brooklyn observed that "in many cases the men had not even as much as a sock for protection."[22]

Bad roads exacerbated the army's misery. A Massachusetts man described the highways in Maryland as "one immense hogwallow the entire distance." Another New Englander remembered that the thoroughfare he traveled "was narrow and rough . . . literally a bed of mud resting on a foundation of small sharp stones." Most of the infantry marched beside the highways, reserving the prepared surfaces for vehicles. Plowing through "standing grass, corn and grain . . . was much harder," thought a New Yorker, than marching on the tortuous roads. Even northern horseflesh suffered. "Our cavalry and artillery horses [were] shod with contract nails, which would not hold shoes on rocky ground for two days," complained cannoneer Hunt.[23]

Most important of all, the Gettysburg campaign had diminished considerably the army's strength and command structure. George Davis wrote that the army's "losses in battle, which had been unusually severe, following closely upon a series of long and fatiguing marches, had operated . . . to impair its efficiency for immediate operations, and deprived it . . . of its power to respond to the desires and plans of its leaders." Brig. Gen. Andrew A. Humphreys testified that "a field return of the army on the 5th of July showed that its seven infantry corps had, on an average, the numbers usually found in a division, four of them having about 5,000 enlisted men each, the total of the seven amounting to 47,087 enlisted men armed and equipped."[24] The army's officer cadre on July 7 little resembled the cast that marched into Pennsylvania a week earlier. Corps commanders John F. Reynolds, Winfield S. Hancock, and Daniel E. Sickles lay either dead or severely wounded. Losses at the divisional and brigade level were equally devastating. Meade replaced Reynolds with Newton, Hancock with Brig. Gen. William Hays, and Sickles with French. Although the presence of French weakened Meade's inner circle not at all and the substitution of Humphreys for the wounded Butterfield as chief of staff on July 8 marked a substantial improvement, Meade would miss the experience and aggressive nature of Reynolds and Hancock.[25]

Despite all of these hardships, the Army of the Potomac exhibited a determination and elasticity on July 7 equal to that of any Civil War command. Most of the troops covered fifteen to twenty miles during the drenching day, with the Twelfth Corps marching twenty-nine miles and the supposedly demoralized Eleventh Corps thirty-two. By 11:00 P.M. all of the army except the Second and Twelfth corps had reached the Catoctin Mountains or the Middletown Valley. Meade established his headquarters at the United States Hotel in Frederick, across the street from the B&O Railroad depot, where local citizens enthusiastically serenaded the general after dark.[26]

Meade had achieved in one muddy turn of the earth what he thought would take two or three. But already he began receiving dispatches from Halleck urging him to greater exertion and perhaps implying that the army was not exercising its maximum effort to catch the rebels north of the river. "Push forward, and fight Lee before he can cross the Potomac," Halleck instructed Meade. The general in chief wired that the Confederates suffered from a shortage of artillery ammunition and were thus particularly vulnerable "if vigorously pressed."[27]

The Confederate rearguard arrived in Hagerstown on the morning of the seventh, and Lee began examining the surrounding terrain. Until he could build a bridge to replace the one French had destroyed three days earlier, or until the river receded sufficiently to allow his troops to ford it, Lee maintained contact with the Virginia shore solely by means of two flatboats attached to wire ropes. These craft transported his wounded and sick to the southern bank and brought ammunition and other supplies to Maryland on the return trip. A single transit of the river required seven minutes.[28]

On July 8 Meade concentrated the army in Middletown. Shoes and other essentials reached his bedraggled forces from a new base at Frederick. Some Federal units ascended South Mountain, while one division crossed the range and occupied Boonsboro. Establishing headquarters at Middletown, Meade responded to more of Halleck's misinformed prodding. "Old Brains" revealed to Meade "reliable information" that the enemy was crossing at Williamsport. "The President is urgent and anxious," advised Halleck, "that your army should move against [Lee] by forced marches." Meade replied that Lee remained on the northern bank "between Funkstown and Williamsport." He also vented his resentment of Halleck's thinly veiled criticism of his pursuit: "My army is and has been making forced marches, short of rations and barefooted. . . . I take occasion to repeat that I will use my utmost effort to push forward this army."[29]

Lack of progress on July 9 belied this promise. While Lee consolidated his lines covering the Potomac River crossings, Meade inched his army across South Mountain on a line five miles long from Rohersville to Boonsboro. He moved his headquarters to the Mountain House at Turner's Gap, scene of the Confederate defense of South Mountain the previous September.[30] In fairness to Meade, it should be acknowledged that the army still suffered from exhaustion and inadequate resources. Two corps marched without artillery because their horses had broken down completely. The roads remained quagmires. The ragged veterans of Gettysburg also greeted reinforcements with predictable derision. Noticing the bright buttons, varnished knapsacks, and paper collars of the newcomers, a Massachusetts regiment pelted them with a volley of pork and hard bread. The scarcity of fresh troops and the lack of adequate rations rendered targets and ammuntion for more such encounters prohibitively dear.[31]

Halleck experienced a change of attitude on July 9, backing off his previous position to agree that "the evidence that Lee's army will fight north of the Potomac seems reliable." "Do not be influenced by any dispatch from here against your own judgment," he told Meade. "Regard them as suggestions only. Our information here is not always correct." Halleck scrambled to bring forces to bear on Lee from the north and west while the Federal cavalry maintained contact with Stuart's troopers at a number of places.[32]

For the next three days Meade carefully maneuvered closer to Lee's defenses. Federals crossed Antietam Creek and its tributary, Beaver Creek, and assumed a position from Bakersville north through Funkstown. The army commander reported to Halleck that the Confederates had entrenched a line from the Potomac at Falling Waters northeast to near Hagerstown. Halleck advised Meade to "postpone a general battle till you can concentrate all your forces and get up your reserves and reenforcements." He warned against "partial combats" and promised to send the Army of the Potomac as many fresh troops as possible.[33]

Lee had prepared to receive an attack by describing a defensive perimeter anchored on a hill one mile west of Hagerstown and following high ground for nine miles through Downsville to the Potomac. Marsh Creek fronted a portion of the line occupied by Ewell on the left, Hill in the center, and Longstreet on the right. Ordnance bristled from various key locations, and Confederate horsemen prowled the flanks informing Lee of Meade's gradual approach.[34] The Federal soldiers constructed their own works out of rails and earth, but Meade harbored more aggressive inclinations. "It is my intention to attack . . . to-morrow," he informed Halleck at 4:30 P.M. on July 12, "unless something intervenes to prevent it."[35]

That something proved to be Meade's own subordinates. The general convened a council at his headquarters tent the evening of July 12. Attendees included corps commanders Hays, French, Sykes, Sedgwick, Howard, and Slocum. Newton was ill, so Brig. Gen. James S. Wadsworth represented the First Corps. Pleasonton, Warren, and Humphreys also sat in as nonvoting participants. "I do not think I ever saw the principal corps commanders so unanimous in favor of not fighting as on that occasion," remembered Warren. Only Howard and Wadsworth endorsed Meade's offensive notions, although Pleasonton and Warren also agreed with their chief.[36]

In view of this reluctance to risk an attack and a realization of his own imperfect knowledge of Lee's position and strength, Meade postponed the assault, ordering instead a reconnaissance for the next day. Fog and rain hindered Federal efforts to gather intelligence on the thirteenth. General Howard contributed his talents by scanning the countryside from the steeple of the Funkstown Lutheran Church in the company of Senator Henry Wilson and Vice-President Hannibal Hamlin. The weather limited Meade's personal observations. He nevertheless returned to his headquarters during the day and announced to a staff officer, "We shall have a great battle to-morrow." [37]

Meade issued orders at 9:00 P.M. that reflected less than absolute commitment to a decisive assault. A force of at least four divisions would advance simultaneously at 7:00 A.M. on July 14 to unmask the Confederate position. Corps commanders were to evaluate the terrain and the enemy's preparations, assessing the advisability of defensive as well as offensive operations. Meade clearly anticipated that this large-scale reconnaissance might lead to a general engagement, however, and instructed his subordinates to hold their troops under arms for a potential attack.[38]

Unknown to the Federals, Lee had decided to abandon his lines. The Confederates had completed a makeshift bridge at Falling Waters, and the Potomac had dropped enough to enable Ewell's infantry to wade across at Williamsport. Longstreet's corps quietly left its entrenchments after dark and led the escape across the bridge. The Second Corps forded the swirling waters during a night Ewell considered awash with sheer confusion. In spite of rain, darkness, and nearly impassable roads, Lee managed to cross most of his men by early morning, including the lead division of Hill's corps at Falling Waters.[39]

The other two divisions of the Third Corps were preparing to escape when Union cavalry under Kilpatrick and Buford attacked their rearguard.

Brig. Gen. J. Johnston Pettigrew fell mortally wounded and, contrary to the claims of Maj. Gen. Henry Heth and Lee himself that the Yankees snagged only a few stragglers, as many as 1,000 other Confederates became casualties. The remaining southerners tramped across their rickety span, then severed it from the right bank and watched it float uselessly downstream.[40]

"Lee's retreat was admirably managed and evinced great forecast," wrote Brig. Gen. Horatio G. Wright. "My own pickets—not 200 yards from his main line did not discover the retreat till day light."[41] Other witnesses reported Lee's departure on the morning of the fourteenth, including a loyal black man from Williamsport. Meade then ordered his entire army to "advance in the pursuit of the enemy, and come up with him, if possible, before he succeeds in crossing." Except for the affair at Falling Waters, however, Lee retreated without molestation. The previous night's rain swelled the Potomac beyond fording stage again, thus concluding another chapter of the Gettysburg campaign.[42]

Meade telegraphed the news to Halleck at 11:00 A.M. on July 14. The general in chief replied that "the escape of Lee's army without another battle has created great dissatisfaction in the mind of the President, and it will require an active and energetic pursuit on your part to remove the impression that it has not been sufficiently active heretofore."[43] Stung by these words, Meade turned to his quartermaster, Brig. Gen. Rufus Ingalls, and sarcastically asked, "Ingalls don't you want to take command of this army?" "No I thank you," replied Ingalls, "It's too big an elephant for me." "Well it's too big for me, too," answered Meade. The angry commander promptly telegraphed Washington with a request to step down: "Having performed my duty conscientiously and to the best of my ability, the censure of the President conveyed in your dispatch of 1 P.M. this day, is, in my judgment, so undeserved that I feel compelled most respectfully to ask to be immediately relieved from the command of this army."[44]

Halleck declined to accept a resignation, and Meade would lead the Army of the Potomac for the remainder of the war. But the displeasure voiced by Lincoln through Halleck on July 14, 1863, resonated through many subsequent accounts of the Gettysburg campaign. It would be useful, therefore, to assess the various criticisms of Meade's post-Gettysburg generalship. Should he have pursued Lee more vigorously? Did he miss an opportunity to inflict a decisive defeat on the Army of Northern Virginia? Or was his conduct reasonable in light of the difficulties he confronted in the two weeks following the battle?

**MAJ. GEN. HENRY
WAGER HALLECK**
Francis Trevelyan Miller, ed.,
*The Photographic History of the
Civil War*, 10 vols. (New York:
Review of Reviews, 1911),
2:321

Many analysts believe that Meade lost his best chance to crush the Army of Northern Virginia on July 3. Maj. Gen. Abner Doubleday, who commanded the First Corps after the wounding of John Reynolds, wrote that a counterattack across the Emmitsburg Road "would have saved two years of war with its immense loss of life and countless evils." Maj. Gen. Carl Schurz of the Eleventh Corps lowered the stakes only slightly in asserting that "had our success at Gettysburg been so followed up as to destroy Lee's army, or at least to render it unable to keep the field, the war would have probably been a year shorter." From a Confederate perspective, Col. Edward Porter Alexander, the brilliant Georgia artillerist, thought that "the enemy here lost the greatest opportunity they ever had of routing Lee's army by a prompt offensive."[45]

Union officers such as Warren, Hancock, Wadsworth, Pleasonton, and Sixth Corps division commander Brig. Gen. Albion P. Howe all affirmed that Meade erred in not advancing after the Pickett-Pettigrew-Trimble fiasco. Hancock and Pleasonton also claimed they advised Meade to seize the offensive on the afternoon of July 3. Three hours of daylight remained; the Fifth and especially the Sixth corps had seen relatively light action and awaited word to go forward. Lee's army, reduced to "a disorderly and demoralized mob," probably had run short of ammunition. Moreover, the Army of the Potomac had suffered only moderate casualties during the day, was well-rested as a result of its stationary defensive fighting, and evinced the greatest eagerness to deliver a blow.[46]

Meade ignored these favorable circumstances, however. He limited Pleasonton to a reconnaissance to determine if the Confederates were retiring, while the infantry gently probed the far Confederate right and failed to exploit a wide gap between those troops and Pickett's survivors. "Any determined advance on Meade's part would only have added to the confusion now being caused in the Confederate ranks by the flight of the troops lately composing Pickett's column," wrote a later student of the campaign. "It is more than likely that this confusion would have extended to the remaining six brigades of Hill's corps. . . . Thus it would seem that Meade missed the opportunity of splitting Lee's line." Why did the army commander neglect so grand an invitation for triumph? "I think that General Meade did not . . . appreciate fully the completeness of his victory," speculated Wadsworth.[47]

The situation did not improve on July 4. Critics insist Meade did little to discover the enemy's activities and nothing to harness the desire of his soldiers to attack. "On the morning of the 4th General Meade ordered demonstrations in front of our line, but they were very feebly made," complained Warren. As a result, the conference that evening opted to remain in place until more could be ascertained about Lee's intentions. But Meade's signal stations had reported Lee's withdrawal by that time, information the commander failed to forward to Halleck. Furthermore, Lee's morning request for a prisoner exchange and descriptions by liberated Union prisoners of Confederate preparations for retreat should have revealed the opposition's plans.[48]

Did Meade immediately unleash his exhilarated and well-rested divisions in direct pursuit when he confirmed Lee's departure on the morning of July 5? According to Meade's own report, the fifth and sixth of July "were employed in succoring the wounded and burying the dead." Only a portion of the Sixth Corps trailed Lee's retreat, and Sedgwick reflected Meade's supposedly conservative desires by failing to interfere in any meaningful way with the Confederate flight. "The enemy made good use of all this precious time in pushing on toward Williamsport as rapidly as possible," said a letter to the *New York Herald* signed only HISTORI-CUS. "They were burdened with heavy trains filled with plunder, without ammunition, and wofully [*sic*] demoralized. Had the half of our army, flushed with success, fallen on them in flank or rear . . . General Lee might have got across the Potomac, but his army never."[49]

"When [Meade] did move, whither did he direct his victorious army, all of it but a portion of one corps," asked J. Watts De Peyster. "Upon the enemy? No. Examine the map for the direction of his march, and that of Lee. The latter took the direct road to Williamsport. The left of his lines at Williamsport was less than 30 miles, the right not over 35. Meade's route to his right was over 50 miles, to his left about 55." William Swinton agreed that Meade miscalculated by not following Lee directly. In Swinton's view the Confederates could not have held the mountain passes against a concerted effort, leaving the Federals free to nip at Lee's heels all the way to the river.[50]

Most historians admit that once the army moved, it concentrated at Middletown with commendable speed. But between July 9 and 12 the Federals made little geographic progress. "Meade advanced cautiously, perhaps too much so, for fear of being surprised into a premature engagement which could have unfortunate results," wrote Edwin B. Coddington. Kenneth P. Williams ascribed Meade's excessive timidity to the report of a Confederate deserter who on July 9 warranted that Lee eagerly awaited a fight and had little desire to cross the river. Both Meade and Halleck credited this intelligence, which, according to Williams, explains why the general in chief temporarily modified his impatient and bellicose posture.[51]

By July 12, as noted above, Meade determined to make his assault pending the counsel of his corps commanders. According to Meade's detractors, he committed the worst blunder of the campaign by heeding the advice of his subordinates that evening. "It is perfectly absurd to suppose that the enemy would choose a position on the bank of a deep river for the purpose of fighting us," Doubleday told a congressional panel. Pleasonton, Hancock, and De Peyster all agreed that Meade should have attacked. "It will doubtless be the verdict of history, that the hesitancy of General Meade at this time was his great mistake," averred Dr. George T. Stevens of the 77th New York.[52]

Would Union assaults at Williamsport have succeeded? "It is my opinion," said Howe, "that, with a comparatively small fight, the rebels would have been thrown into utter disorder, and could not have got across the river." Maj. Gen. David B. Birney agreed that an offensive on July 13 would have resulted in "the utter defeat of the rebel army." Swinton and De Peyster further suggested that Lee's vulnerable left afforded Meade the option of not relying entirely on a frontal attack to overwhelm the Confederate position.[53]

The evidence also demonstrates that the Federal rank and file sought a confrontation north of the Potomac. "You do not know with what confidence this jaded-out army goes forth to the harvest of death," wrote a Massachusetts soldier. A reporter remembered that "the troops were in superb spirits, and their confidence that they could whip the rebels was stronger than I have ever yet seen it." Surgeon Stevens recalled that "much as the veterans, who knew too well the risks of battle, usually dreaded a general engagement, this time there seemed a universal desire, on the part of the men . . . to strike a blow which should destroy their adversaries before they should be able to cross the river again."[54] Eager to initiate a battle that portended decisive results, some Federals believed Lee's army deficient in ammunition, morale, and strong fortifications. One soldier described the Confederate works as "built of wheat sheaves covered with earth, so slightly covered that when [I] jumped upon them they let [me] through." Allan Nevins characterized Lee's engineering at Williamsport as "merely heaped earth covering a continuous line of piled rails." Confederate deserters and prisoners from the cavalry skirmishes also wove tales of war weariness in the southern ranks, and many of Meade's critics contend that Lee's cannoneers superintended empty caissons.[55]

Why then did Meade and his underlings fail to test the mettle of their troops? Pleasonton believed that the corps commanders were more willing to attack than Meade realized—never did they insist that their cautious advice necessarily should scuttle Meade's plans. "It does not make any difference what our opinions are," explained General French after the July 12 council. "If you give the order to attack, we will fight just as well under it as if our opinions were not against it." Warren believed that Meade accepted the judgment of his subordinates so readily because the general felt "if the enemy fell back across the river, he could follow them into their own country and give them battle under . . . as favorable circumstances as were there presented to him; that is, he thought if he lost that opportunity he could have another one."[56]

Meade's critics also have decried the ease with which Lee actually executed his withdrawal. How, they ask, could the Army of Northern Virginia disengage from the Union front without the Federals realizing it? Even worse, why did Meade allow the retreat to continue on the morning of July 14 with only the cavalry action at Falling Waters interfering with Lee's river crossing? "How can any Union general, who had the slightest choice or option to move, excuse that paralysis, which neither heard, saw, nor acted on the morning . . . of the 14th," asked the relentless De Peyster. "Except in the case of McClellan after Antietam, is there a parallel?"[57] "Thus escaped Lee and the Army of Northern Virginia, and with it the best opportunity that we . . . had until Appomattox's fateful day, to destroy . . . their main army, and shorten up the Rebellion," lamented a New Englander. "It was a sad morning on the 15th, when we went over the slight knoll and through the weak rifle pits—which the enemy had hastily dug—and realized that they had gone—vanished—and our faces were again directed toward Virginia." The Washington correspondent for the Sacramento *Union* overheard two northern soldiers whose succinct evaluation summarized the consequences of Meade's presumptively faulty leadership during the Federal pursuit: "Well, here goes for two years more."[58]

The reaction to Lee's escape elsewhere in the North ranged from bitter disappointment to unmitigated outrage. Lt. Col. David Hunter Strother observed from Washington on July 15, "The particulars of Lee's escape are confirmed. . . . This is about the meanest and most humiliating incident of the war. Hooker would have done better and no one could have done worse. Meade is proved—a plain soldier fit to lead a corps but without power or ambition and utterly incompetent at the head of a hundred thousand men." Secretary of War Stanton considered Meade's failure to destroy Lee "the greatest mortification of the war," and the more he thought of it, the worse it seemed. Vice-President Hamlin (a man, according to Meade's son, who "does not look like as if he had two ideas in his old beastly head") raised his hands at the news of Lee's crossing "and turned away his face with a gesture of despair." Secretary of the Navy Gideon Welles cynically ascribed the situation to a desire on the part of Meade's generals to maintain the war and thus protect their exalted positions.[59]

No one regretted Meade's failure to strike at Lee more than Abraham Lincoln. When the bad news reached a cabinet meeting on July 14, Welles noted that "the President's countenance indicated trouble and distress." Lincoln canceled the session and walked across the White House lawn with the navy secretary. "Meade has been pressed and urged, but only one of his generals was for an immediate attack. . . . The rest held back," said the discouraged chief executive. "What does it mean, Mr. Welles? Great God! What does it mean?"[60]

Lincoln believed from the very outset of Lee's campaign into Pennsylvania that the Confederates had placed themselves in mortal danger. The victory at Gettysburg reinforced this conviction. But a number of events persuaded the president that Meade would allow the Confederates to slip through his hands.[61] Meade had congratulated his army on July 4 in General Orders No. 68, the third paragraph of which mentioned that more work remained in order to "drive from our soil every vestige of the presence of the invader."[62] Lincoln understandably interpreted this as evidence that "the old idea of driving the Rebels out of Pennsylvania and Maryland, instead of capturing them, was still prevalent among the officers." Herman Haupt nurtured this feeling in a letter to Halleck on the night of July 4 wherein he related his "fear that while Meade rests to refresh his men and collect supplies, Lee will be off so far that he cannot intercept him." Haupt carried this message to Washington on July 6, meeting successively with Halleck, Stanton, and Lincoln.[63]

The press fueled a public impression that Lee's army teetered on the brink of annihilation. The *New York Tribune* ran a story on July 6 under the banner, "The Great Victory. The Rebel Army Totally Defeated. Its Remains Driven Into the Mountains. It is There Surrounded and Hemmed In. Its Retreat Across the Potomac Cut Off." Reporters circulated wild rumors that Longstreet had been killed, Meade had captured 20,000 prisoners, and Lee was trapped in the mountains.[64]

General readers in the North and official Washington knew about the additional troops that, in concert with Meade, descended on the supposedly vulnerable Confederates. Units from the west under Brig. Gen. Benjamin F. Kelley and brigades moving south under Brig. Gen. William F. Smith and Maj. Gen. Darius N. Couch coordinated with the Army of the Potomac's advance from the east. With the rebels trapped in Maryland by the raging Potomac, the specter of inescapable constriction loomed large in the public psyche.[65]

Within this context, Lincoln's sharp reaction to Lee's escape seems understandable. "We had them within our grasp," lamented the president. "We had only to stretch forth our hands and they were ours. And nothing I could say or do could make the army move."[66] The distraught president

**ABRAHAM LINCOLN**
Benson J. Lossing, *A History of the Civil War, 1861–65* (New York: War Memorial Assoc., 1912), p. 3

drafted a letter to Meade that summarized his perception of the military situation and anticipated the indictments leveled against the Union commander by many students of the campaign:

> I have been oppressed nearly ever since the battles at Gettysburg, by what appeared to be evidences that yourself, and Gen. Couch, and Gen. Smith, were not seeking a collision with the enemy, but were trying to get him across the river without another battle. . . . The case . . . is this. You fought and beat the enemy at Gettysburg; and, of course, to say the least, his loss was as great as yours. He retreated; and you did not, as it seemed to me, pressingly pursue him; but a flood in the river detained him, till, by slow degrees, you were again upon him. You had at least twenty thousand veteran troops directly with you, and as many more raw ones within supporting distance, all in addition to those who fought with you at Gettysburg; while it is not possible that he had received a single recruit; and yet you stood and let the flood run down, bridges be built, and the enemy move away at his leisure, without attacking him. . . . I do not believe you appreciate the magnitude of the misfortune involved in Lee's escape.

**A. WILSON GREENE**

He was within your easy grasp, and to have closed upon him would, in connection with our other late successes, have ended the war.[67]

Lincoln thought better of sending this missive, but its apparent logic is more responsible than any other evidence for the conventional interpretation of Meade's generalship in the ten days following the battle of Gettysburg. Implicit in Lincoln's condemnation is the assumption that Meade had no intention of finishing the job started at Gettysburg. General Orders No. 68, Herman Haupt, and an exaggerated impression of Lee's vincibility prejudiced the president's perception of Meade's pursuit. After meeting with Haupt, Lincoln wired Halleck from his refuge at the Soldiers' Home that Meade's generalship "appear[s] to me to be connected with a purpose to cover Baltimore and Washington, and to get the enemy across the river again without a further collision, and . . . not . . . with a purpose to prevent his crossing and to destroy him." Years after the war, E. Porter Alexander viewed the situation similarly. "The enemy had pursued us as a mule goes on the chase of a grizzly bear—as if catching up with us was the last thing he wanted to do."[68]

Distinguished historians such as T. Harry Williams and Bruce Catton perpetuated this verdict in widely read treatments of the campaign. "Like McClellan at Antietam," Williams wrote in 1952, Meade "was satisfied to see the enemy withdraw intact from his front. He felt that he had done something great by holding his ground and forcing Lee out of Pennsylvania." In a colorful passage, Catton summarized the Union commander's attitude as being, "if the Rebels wanted to go back to Virginia, it seemed like a good idea to wish them Godspeed and let them go." Lincoln himself later told Meade that the general's demeanor toward Lee during the week after Gettysburg reminded him of "an old woman trying to shoo her geese across the creek."[69] Williams agreed with this assessment in his landmark study of Union military leadership, but he hypothesized that Meade may not have realized his own true intentions. "Meade was trying to get the Confederates over the Potomac without risking a battle," wrote Williams. "He did not say so in his communications to the government, and he probably did not admit even to himself that he was avoiding a showdown. But . . . his defensive victory at Gettysburg ruined him as an offensive general."[70]

Williams's theory that Meade deluded himself into thinking he actually wanted to bring Lee to bay seems too speculative to accept at face value.

It raises the possibility, in fact, that Lincoln's evaluation, perpetuated by historians of the 1950s, may be flawed. The best way to determine Meade's intentions and assess his generalship is to examine the Pennsylvanian's own words and then match them to his actions.

As early as July 4, Meade expressed his desire to pursue Lee once he knew the Confederates had withdrawn from their fortified positions at Gettysburg. "As soon as it can be definitely ascertained that Lee is retiring into the Valley, I shall move rapidly in a southerly direction," he informed Couch at 1:30 P.M. Meade pressed Sedgwick on July 5 to discover Lee's whereabouts and intentions. "Time is of great importance," he told his subordinate, "as I cannot give order[s] for a movement without explicit information from you." Meanwhile, the general urged Halleck to forward fresh troops to Frederick without delay to join the Army of the Potomac in its pursuit.[71]

Meade clearly stated his goal in a wire to Halleck on July 6: "As soon as possible I will cross South Mountain, and proceed in search of the enemy." "If I can get the Army of the Potomac in hand in the Valley," stated Meade, "and the enemy have not crossed the river, I shall give him battle, trusting, should misfortune overtake me, that a sufficient number of my force . . . would reach [Washington] so as to render it secure." He repeated these sentiments to Couch, warning that if the Army of the Potomac's attack failed, the latter should be prepared to defend against a renewed Confederate offensive.[72]

Once the army began to concentrate in Middletown, Meade reaffirmed his commitment to fight. "I most earnestly desire to try the fortunes of war with the enemy on this side of the river," he telegraphed the general in chief. "I think we shall have another battle before Lee can cross the river," he confided to his wife the same day, "though from all accounts he is making great efforts to do so. For my part, as I have to follow and fight him, I would rather do it at once and in Maryland than to follow into Virginia." Again on July 9 Meade predicted to Halleck that "the decisive battle of the war will be fought in a few days"; the next day he penned a similar sentiment to his wife: "I expect in a few days, if not sooner, again to hazard the fortune of war."[73] Professor Williams's conjecture that these dispatches and private letters represented no more than whistling past the graveyard may have been correct; however, it seems more likely, as Edwin B. Coddington concluded, that "Meade set out after Lee for the express purpose of battling him again, the sooner the better."[74]

The incontrovertible reality remains, however, that no such engagement occurred. If Meade's private and public words reflected his true sentiments, were there valid reasons why the general failed to bring about the combat he desired? There certainly were on the afternoon of July 3, notwithstanding General Hancock's comment that "I think that our lines should have advanced immediately, and I believe we should have won a great victory." Meade shared Hancock's offensive inclinations following Pickett's defeat. "As soon as the assault was repulsed, I went immediately to the extreme left of my line, with the determination of advancing the left and making an assault," Meade informed the Joint Committee on the Conduct of the War. But after ordering skirmishers forward to locate the enemy and arranging his available units for an attack, he discovered that "the great length of the line, and the time required to carry these orders out to the front and left, caused it to be so late in the evening as to induce me to abandon the assault which I had contemplated."[75]

A successful Union counterattack on July 3 would have required three elements: a vulnerable opponent, an organized and powerful force available for the offensive, and a commander willing to undertake reasonable risk. Meade was game, but the Army of Northern Virginia recovered from its failure on Cemetery Ridge with exemplary speed. "On our right Hood and McLaws; in the center, Anderson; and on the left, the whole corps of Ewell stood as steady and unmoved as if they had witnessed the mimic evolutions of a holiday review," intoned a proud Confederate after the war. Not only was the southern army "undismayed, but [it was] eager to welcome their antagonists 'with bloody hands to hospitable graves.'" Conceding a generous allowance for hyperbole, this judgment rings essentially true. There can be no greater tribute to the discipline and morale of Lee's soldiers than their steadfastness following the army's most infamous tactical defeat. James Longstreet spoke for many others in the Army of Northern Virginia when he expressed no doubt that his troops would "have given those who tried [to attack us] as bad a reception as Pickett got."[76]

Only a Federal attack launched on the literal heels of Pickett's retreat would have enjoyed a legitimate opportunity to deliver a knockout blow. But the Army of the Potomac could not do this. "We were in no condition to renew immediate hostilities," said surgeon Stevens. "The men were exhausted by their tedious marches and hard fighting, while our ammunition was well nigh spent." Meade had quite correctly deployed his divisions defensively, and it took time, as the general admitted, to realign them for an attack. Moreover, the Sixth Corps, which all of Meade's critics cite as the eminently available shock troops chafing for the offensive, lay widely dispersed along various portions of the line. Five of its eight brigades occupied positions distant from the Round Tops, where Meade intended to begin his attack.[77]

These factors prompted Henry Hunt to change his mind about the feasibility of a counteroffensive on July 3: "I did not see a disposable force sufficiently large, immediately on the ground, to attack the enemy in position . . . where I knew, from my experience of that day, that they had more than one hundred guns in position, a much larger force of artillery than we could bring to bear against them." The man who would have led the Sixth Corps into action, John Sedgwick, stated simply, "I do not think it would have been expedient to have attacked. . . . I think that was pretty much the opinion of most of the general officers present there." Finally, the Army of the Potomac's losses on July 3, when added to the heavy casualties among officers and men in the ranks during the previous two days, significantly compromised its offensive potential.[78]

Meade clearly recognized the desirability of exploiting the enemy's afternoon defeat. But the quick Confederate recovery, diminished Federal strength, the need to reorganize for an assault, and the absence of a powerful force poised for the kill prevented him from executing his preferred course of action. Simply stated, circumstances dictated and justified Meade's generalship on July 3.

Those same circumstances prevailed on July 4. The Army of Northern Virginia crouched defiantly behind a good line. "It was plainly to be seen that on the face of every Confederate as they stood behind Alexander's grim guns was a look of determination . . . that at once renewed faith in the morale and discipline of those grand old veterans and a blind confidence in our God-like leader, Robert E. Lee, and that all would be well with us in the end. Whipped? No!," boasted a Tennessean. Although written long after the battle, these defiant words likely reflected the predominant attitude among Lee's soldiers on July 4.[79]

The Army of the Potomac refused to test its enemy's determination. "We . . . learned that [Lee] expected, during the whole day, that we would attack him, hoping to get his revenge," stated a Third Corps brigade commander. "But General Meade, content with his victory, would not take the risk of compromising it by leaving his position before Lee had abandoned his, in which he acted wisely, whatever may have been said to the contrary." Colonel Wainwright agreed that "the Saxon bulldog blood in [the Confederates] would have made the rebels fight harder than ever to pay off the scores . . . while I could plainly see that our men thought they had had fight enough for once. . . . Taking the composition of the two armies into consideration, I feel sure that Meade was right in not [attacking]." Meade confirmed in a letter home that he sized up the situation in precisely these terms: "They awaited . . . expecting that, flushed with success, I would attack them when they would play their old game of shooting us from behind breastworks." [80]

Reasons beyond the disposition and morale of his opponents helped persuade Meade to remain in place. As defined in the orders naming him to army command, his primary mission remained essentially defensive— to "maneuver and fight in such a manner as to cover the capital and also Baltimore." The army's position at Gettysburg accomplished this purpose. The men needed supplies, ammunition, and rest, all of which could be acquired while Lee remained on the scene. Drenching rains rendered offensive movement difficult if not impossible. To assume a new position farther south, closer to both Washington and Lee's possible routes of retreat, would have abandoned the battlefield to Lee and diluted the moral impact of the Union victory. Equally relevant, four of Meade's seven corps commanders were new, including three acting as replacements for recent battle casualties. This helps explain the cautious judgments at the council on the evening of July 4, which to a significant extent guided Meade's generalship the following day. [81]

Meade possessed at least three options after discovering Lee's departure early on the morning of July 5. He could remain at Gettysburg and refit his exhausted army; he could march south, cross the mountains in Maryland, and hope to catch the Confederates before they reached the Potomac; or he could follow directly on Lee's path. He chose a combination of elements from all three alternatives.

While most of the army recuperated, Meade learned on July 4 and perhaps earlier that the Confederates easily could defend the passes in South Mountain west of Fairfield and Cashtown. He accordingly contemplated a move east of the mountains to Frederick and then westward into the Cumberland Valley. This strategy not only would allow him to crest the ridges unimpeded, but it also would cover Baltimore and Washington, a necessity of which Halleck reminded him on July 5. Moreover, Frederick offered excellent rail communications and thus the secure, efficient supply line necessary for his battered forces to maintain active operations. [82]

But Meade did not rule out entirely a direct pursuit. Sedgwick's armed reconnaissance toward Fairfield might have sparked a significant engagement, or at least so the Sixth Corps commander informed Meade on July 6. Meade reacted to this possibility by placing four additional corps in position to assist Sedgwick should a struggle for the mountain gaps ensue. Sedgwick made no aggressive move toward the passes and eventually informed Meade that a very small force could hold him in check for a considerable time.[83] What might have transpired if an officer bolder than Sedgwick oversaw the reconnaissance on July 5 and 6? The terrain west of Fairfield was rugged, and Lee's army remained a formidable force. Even if the Federals had pressed their momentum and succeeded in capturing the gaps, Lee still could have reached Hagerstown and prepared a strong defense with only minimum lead time secured by a delaying action in the mountains. Speculation aside, it is important to note that Meade, although preferring to pursue via Frederick for the sensible reasons previously cited, did provide Sedgwick the means and discretion to commit most of the army to an attack beyond Fairfield should the commander of the Sixth Corps believe the military situation favorable. Based on the advice of this senior officer, however, Meade detached only a small force to shadow Lee and sent the rest of his army on the southerly route.[84]

General French, whose troopers had performed the inestimable service of wrecking Lee's bridge across the Potomac at Falling Waters, kept Meade and Halleck informed of the river's condition. The Union high command realized, therefore, that Lee could not cross the Potomac until its waters receded or he replaced the bridge, but they knew less about how Lee planned to react to this reality. "I have to grope my way in the dark," Meade complained in a letter to his daughter.[85]

While Meade groped, Lee's soldiers dug. The Confederate commander had dispatched engineers on July 4 to select a line in rear of Hagerstown should the Army of Northern Virginia be compelled (or opt voluntarily) to remain in Maryland. Meade had been informed of the naturally strong defensive terrain around Williamsport, and Lee took every advantage of that ground beginning on July 7 and continuing through the twelfth.[86] His defenses stretched from Conococheague Creek a mile west of Hagerstown to Downsville near the Potomac. The Confederates also erected an inner line covering the river crossings at Falling Waters and Williamsport. Lee's three corps spanned nearly nine miles, but roads running in the Confederate rear accommodated rapid reinforcement anywhere along the line. Longstreet reported that after the first day's construction his troops were "comfortably intrenched." Ewell said his men were "well protected," and Stuart stated that once the infantry had built its works, "it was no longer desirable to defer the enemy's attack."[87]

The Federals watched the Confederate engineering progress, including the establishment of abatis, double lines of entrenchments, and strong artillery emplacements. Humphreys affirmed that "the position was naturally strong, and was strongly intrenched; it presented no vulnerable points [and] much of it was concealed from view. . . . Its flanks were secure and could not be turned." Much of the Confederate position fronted a cleared field of fire more than a mile wide behind Marsh Creek. Charles Wainwright saw the works after Lee's departure and declared them to be "by far the strongest I have seen yet; evidently laid out by engineers and built as if they meant to stand a month's siege. The parapet was a good six feet wide on top, and the guns, which were very thick, were all placed so as to get a perfect cross fire and to sweep their whole front." No doubt some places on the long Confederate line were less formidable than the segments Wainwright described, but the Confederates had prepared a materially powerful reception for any attacking force.[88]

They also possessed the necessary spiritual fortitude to defend their ground. Lee told President Davis on July 8 and again four days later that the army was in "good condition" and that "its confidence is unimpaired." Cavalryman Harry Gilmor wrote that "all the silly stuff we read in the Northern accounts of 'flying rebels' and 'shattered army' are pure fictions prepared for the Northern market." Moreover, the Confederates wanted nothing more than a chance to avenge Gettysburg by smashing a Union assault. "We hope soon to get up another fight," wrote a staff officer on July 7, and a brigade commander reported that his men "were exceedingly anxious to meet the enemy."[89]

References made so often by Meade's critics to a presumed Confederate shortage of ammunition lack a basis in fact. "We have a good supply of ammunition," Lee wrote Davis on July 10. Nor did most of the Union high command assume a crisis of Confederate ordnance. "I did not hear any one say that the enemy did not have ammunition enough," stated Warren to the joint committee. "All the information which I obtained," agreed Meade, "led to the belief that his army had been supplied with ammunition from Winchester."[90]

Except for French's troops and a few scattered regiments that joined the Army of the Potomac from Washington, the Union reinforcements on which Lincoln counted so heavily proved utterly useless. Kelley's command never approached Lee's line closely enough to cause the Confederates a moment's worry. Smith described his militia as "an incoherent mass" whose main occupation seemed to be ravaging civilian livestock and crops. Some troops arrived from Baltimore and North Carolina but remained at Harpers Ferry and Maryland Heights, duty commensurate with their experience and ability. Coddington estimates that Meade added only about 8,000 effectives to the Army of the Potomac after Gettysburg, despite the illusion of legions descending on the cornered Confederates. "Really and practically," admitted Meade, "I was in front of the enemy at Williamsport with very much the same army that I moved from Gettysburg."[91]

Meade still believed that the Army of the Potomac outnumbered the Confederates, but not every Federal officer shared his confidence. "We are in no condition in point of strength to attack [Lee] in position," wrote division commander Wright. "In an equal fight I have no doubt we could whip him not withstanding his superior numbers; but give him the advantage of position . . . and the chances are largely against us." Wright estimated that the Army of Northern Virginia numbered as many as 80,000 after Gettysburg, compared with fewer than 50,000 Union infantry: "Surely . . . it would not have been prudent to attack a force considerably stronger than our own," he concluded. Sedgwick shared Wright's perspective, and perhaps other participants in the July 12 council did as well. In fact, the Army of the Potomac enjoyed a 5 to 3 numerical advantage at Williamsport, sufficiently short odds to justify some caution even had Lee's actual strength been universally understood.[92]

Meade made it clear that he intended to attack under either one of two scenarios. Had his corps commanders endorsed the concept on the night of the twelfth, he would have risked the full-scale battle his powerful armed reconnaissance might have precipitated. Absent the recommendation of his subordinates, Meade sought more intelligence about Lee's position to avoid "blindly attacking the enemy" without "some reasonable degree of probability that the attack would be successful."[93]

Because Lee retreated before Meade could inaugurate an attack, modern students must rely on contemporary opinions about the likely result. The overwhelming majority of that testimony agrees with General Humphreys that "an assault upon [Lee's position] would have resulted disastrously to us." Sedgwick, Slocum, Sykes, and Hays all thought so.[94] Even Warren and Howard, who favored attack on July 12, reversed their views after seeing the Confederate works. "Had I attacked Lee the day I proposed to do so, and in the ignorance that then existed of his position," wrote Meade himself on July 31, "I have every reason to believe the attack would have been unsuccessful, and would have resulted disastrously." Confederates saw it similarly. "I am sure that if Meade had attacked [at Williamsport] a bloody repulse awaited him, because Lee's army was again in its usual fighting trim and ready in spirit to measure lances with the foe," stated Tennessee captain June Kimble.[95]

What then could Meade have done? Sedgwick suggested moving the Sixth and Eleventh corps through Hagerstown during the night of the twelfth to gain a position on the Confederate left flank and rear, an idea the council rejected. Rain and fog, together with Confederate mobility and vigilance, would have made that effort problematical. Identifying potential weaknesses in the Confederate line seemed the best prelude to an offensive—the course Meade pursued. If the Federal commander could locate vulnerable targets, organize his divisions on narrow fronts to concentrate their striking power, and prepare coordinated advances, he stood a chance of driving Lee into the Potomac or, a more likely scenario, upstream toward crossings near Hancock.[96]

A letter printed in a New York newspaper a month after the campaign summarized well the dilemma Meade faced on July 13: "The question was, should he order a blind attack when ignorant of all essential matters, having therefore no clear view that success was probable against a splendidly-posted, desparate and powerful enemy, when his five corps commanders advised against it, and when to be defeated was to lose all the benefit of the past victory, and to place the North and Washington again at the command of Lee and his army?" Not surprisingly, the letter's author concluded that "General Meade acted as a prudent man would have done." Historian Glenn Tucker, writing nearly a century later, agreed in no uncertain terms: "It seems unlikely Meade could have done much better than Burnside did at Fredericksburg."[97]

Meade's explanation for his failure to advance on July 13 elicited an oft-quoted reaction from Halleck. "You are strong enough to attack and defeat the enemy before he can effect a crossing," the general in chief wrote with more importunity than accuracy. "Act upon your own judgment and make your generals execute your orders. Call no council of war. It is proverbial that councils of war never fight."[98]

Meade needed no prodding to commit his army to the offensive on July 14. His orders called for the reconnaissance-in-force "to commence punctually at 7 A.M." and to consist of at least a division each from the Twelfth, Second, Fifth, and Sixth corps. Why Meade scheduled the movement to begin two hours after daylight is puzzling. Coddington suggests that he did so to ensure concert of action. No doubt part of the reason may be found in Meade's belief that Lee had no intention to retreat, thus making the earliest advance unnecessary. In any event, each minute Meade delayed allowed additional Confederates to reach Virginia in safety.[99] General Howard reported abandoned Confederate works in his front on the Union right at 6:35 A.M. and moved forward immediately. Ewell's corps finished wading the Potomac about an hour later, however, giving Howard no chance to interfere with its crossing. Meade delayed until 8:30 A.M. before committing his entire army to the pursuit. The action at Falling Waters occurred late in the morning, and, according to Lee, all of Hill's troops had reached safety on the Virginia side of the river by 1:00 P.M.[100]

The noise from Lee's creaking wagons and artillery carriages carried into Federal lines east of Falling Waters. Union officers and men guessed the origin of the sound, but Meade failed to act until he received confirmed reports of Lee's withdrawal. Because the Confederates had broken camp after dark on the thirteenth, most of their units enjoyed an insurmountable lead despite the dreadful weather conditions. Still, it seems reasonable to expect that Meade should have commenced his reconnaissance at early dawn and pushed his troops harder once he knew his quarry was on the run. De Peyster states that "the inactivity of those few hours, on that eventful morning, present more of the incomprehensible than any other period of the war." That overstates the case, and even if acting more expeditiously, Meade might not have inflicted more damage to Lee's two trailing divisions. But here more than anywhere else during his pursuit Meade's caution is difficult to defend.[101]

With Lee's army on the Virginia shore, Meade issued orders to march downstream toward pontoon crossings at Harpers Ferry and Berlin. "I start tomorrow to run another race with Lee," Meade told his wife in an unofficial epitaph for his unsuccessful chase. More than 1,000 Union soldiers became casualties in the twenty encounters between Fairfield and Falling Waters, including 121 killed. Despite their sacrifice and the best effort of their commander, the Army of Northern Virginia escaped and prosecuted the war for twenty-one additional months.[102]

This outcome caused the disappointment and dissatisfaction described earlier and also unleashed radical elements in Congress to seek Meade's removal from command. Abetted by testimony from Howe, Doubleday, Birney, Pleasonton, and especially Sickles, some members of the Joint

Committee on the Conduct of the War accused Meade of criminal vacillation in his failure to arrest Lee's retreat. The radicals sought to replace Meade with Hooker, whose political views coincided more closely with their own.[103] These machinations failed largely because Meade had friends in the army and in Congress who defended his post-Gettysburg generalship.

Meade's political survival and the evidence presented here suggest neither a flawless Union pursuit nor an inevitable escape to Virginia for the Confederates. Both Meade's physical condition and his self-confidence suffered during the campaign, factors that contributed to a pattern of decision making that always erred on the side of prudence. On July 8 the general wrote his wife that "from the time I took command till today, now over ten days, I have not changed my clothes, have not had a regular night's rest, and many nights not a wink of sleep, and for several days did not even wash my face and hands, no regular food, and all the time in a great state of mental anxiety. Indeed, I think I have lived as much in this time as in the last thirty years." A postwar account claims that Meade admitted to being "so exhausted of mental power that he could not think" after the battle of Gettysburg. "Being conscious of this [he] did not dare to take the responsibility of immediately conducting another battle." Although Meade probably never confessed to such incapacity, the strain of directing a campaign of such magnitude only days after assuming army command almost certainly tested his nerves.[104]

Meade did admit that his newness in command led to a greater than ordinary reliance on the advice of his corps commanders. He denied that the meetings he convened were councils of war, calling them instead consultations. "They were probably more numerous and more constant in my case," he stated, "from the fact that I had just assumed command of the army, and felt that it was due to myself to have the opinions of high officers before I took action on matters which involved such momentous issues." This is an understandable point of view and is consistent with a man whose demeanor, wrote Regis De Trobriand, was "more reserved than audacious, more modest than presumptuous, on which account he treated his corps commanders rather as friends than as inferiors." Such an outlook, however, did not engender the risk-taking courage that great captains like Lee, Grant, and Sherman displayed to accomplish heroic deeds.[105]

Had Meade possessed such personal attributes, what might he have done differently? As the course of the pursuit unfolded, Meade failed to exploit three feasible opportunities to bring about Lee's defeat. First, he might have sent a combined force of infantry, cavalry, and artillery around Lee's right flank to Fairfield on July 4. If the Federals could have held the mountain gaps west of that village, Lee would have been forced to do one of two things. He might have attacked Meade, raising the possibility of being assailed in the rear by the rest of the Union army before he could cut his way through. Lee also could have moved north and crossed the mountains at Cashtown Gap. But the latter course would have lengthened considerably his march to Williamsport and delayed his arrival at the river. The Army of the Potomac was exhausted on July 4, the weather was horrible, and Meade was uncertain about Lee's intentions or how badly the battle had punished the Confederates. Still, a move toward Fairfield would have placed Lee in a dilemma and forced him to fight at a disadvantage or sacrifice his inside track to the Potomac.[106]

Second, Meade could have trusted his instincts and authorized his reconnaissance-in-force on July 13. Objections by subordinates, uncertainty about Confederate locations and strength, and the potential for a morale-shattering tactical defeat posed substantial obstacles. As Humphreys explained, however, had the Federals been defeated on the thirteenth, "we had pretty good ground to which to [withdraw] and [withstand] a return attack on their part. . . . I do not think, if they had attacked us in turn, that we could not have driven them back." E. P. Alexander believed that "the rare chance of ruining us which success would have given" should have encouraged Meade to try "it for all he was worth." De Trobriand pointed out that "if we succeeded, the road to Richmond was opened before us; if we failed, the road to Washington was still closed to them." Henry Hunt denied that the fate of Lee's army rested in the balance: "As to bagging Lee—bah! How many instances of bagging can you find in history?" Nevertheless, the same circumstances that prompted Meade to advance on July 14 existed on July 13, and he should have exploited them.[107]

Finally, Meade erred by not moving more quickly on the morning of July 14. The chance to engage the entire Army of Northern Virginia unquestionably vanished with the previous sunset, but earlier probes followed by immediate pursuit once the Confederate absence became known might have resulted in a greater disaster to A. P. Hill's corps at Falling Waters. The cavalry did well, although compromised by some tactical mistakes. Who can say how much more might have been accomplished had Union infantry joined Buford and Kilpatrick?[108]

Meade attributed Lee's river crossing to Federal efforts to bridge the Potomac at Harpers Ferry and move cavalry upstream on the right bank. In fact, Union engineers completed such a bridge on the afternoon of the fourteenth. Meade intended to advance his troopers to a position from which they could interdict the makeshift Confederate supply line in Virginia and impede any enemy withdrawal across the Potomac. Herman Haupt argued for such an operation earlier in the pursuit, and Henry Hunt testified before the joint committee that "a comparatively small force, which might have consisted mostly of cavalry, with some infantry, could, if thrown across the river, whether from that army, or pushed up from Frederick or from Washington, have prevented their crossing, and have shut them up on the north side of the river, where they would have been compelled to stand an attack from us." [109]

Hunt's idea had merit only if bridges could be built quickly and an adequate force advanced to thwart Lee's operations on the Virginia side of the river. The engineers encountered the usual problems of obtaining and transporting materials for the bridge at Harpers Ferry, so they may not have been able to span the river much more quickly. Had Meade divided his army, he might have invited a Confederate attack on one of his two wings, neither of which could have been easily reinforced. Could a force of cavalry really have obstructed a river crossing by Lee's army? Could troops from the Washington garrison have arrived in time and in sufficient condition to oppose the Confederates in the absence of Meade's own corps? These questions at least raise doubts about the efficacy of a downstream crossing. [110]

George Meade's performance from July 3 through July 14 was cautious, competent, and committed to combat. Handicapped by his recent elevation to command and an army reduced at all levels by the exigencies of a brutal battle, Meade sought to avoid defeat as well as to culminate victory. Contemporary criticisms of his pursuit sprang from an imperfect understanding of the military situation generated by the press and unreliable witnesses. Later detractors found their motivation in political or personal agendas, all of which have been repeated with distressing frequency and imbalance by modern historians. Had Meade acted more boldly, his accomplishments might have increased, and the opportunity offered by the combined events at Vicksburg, in Middle Tennessee, and at Gettysburg makes the gamble seem worthwhile. But it would have taken an extraordinary general, aided by generous doses of good fortune, to have brought the incomparable Army of Northern Virginia to grief in Adams or Washington counties. Meade was no more a failure in his post-Gettysburg leadership than he was extraordinary.

ACKNOWLEDGMENTS

The author wishes to acknowledge Steven Wright of the Civil War Library and Museum in Philadelphia, Kathy G. Harrison and Robert Prosperi of the Gettysburg National Military Park, Dr. Richard J. Sommers and Louise Arnold-Friend of the United States Army Military History Institute, Carlisle Barracks, Pennsylvania, and William A. Blair of Pennsylvania State University for research assistance during the preparation of this essay.

NOTES

1. J. Watts De Peyster, "After Gettysburg and at Williamsport," *Army and Navy Journal* 4 (July 27, 1867): 775. De Peyster authored this article under the pseudonym "Anchor."

2. Henry J. Hunt to Alexander S. Webb, January 19, 1888, in *Papers of the Military Historical Society of Massachusetts*, 14 vols. and index (1895–1918; reprint, Wilmington, N.C.: Broadfoot, 1989–90), 3:239 (hereafter cited as *PMHSM*); Gideon Welles, *The Diary of Gideon Welles*, ed. Howard K. Beale, 3 vols. (1911; reprint with corrections, New York: W. W. Norton, 1960), 1:374–75; Stanton and Dana quoted in Benjamin P. Thomas and Harold M. Hyman, *Stanton: The Life and Times of Lincoln's Secretary of War* (New York: Alfred A. Knopf, 1962), 275; John W. Schildt, *Roads from Gettysburg* (Parsons, W.V.: McClain, 1979), 61.

3. Richard Meade Bache, *Life of General George Gordon Meade* (Philadelphia: Henry T. Coates, 1897), 359; William Swinton, *Campaigns of the Army of the Potomac* (1866; reprint, Secaucus, N.J.: Blue & Grey Press, 1988), 367; J. Watts De Peyster, *Gettysburg and After* (1867; reprint, Gaithersburg, Md.: Olde Soldier Books, 1987), 72; George B. Davis, "From Gettysburg to Williamsport," in *PMHSM*, 3:469.

4. Edward J. Stackpole, *They Met at Gettysburg* (Harrisburg, Pa.: Stackpole, 1959), 306–10; Allan Nevins, *The War for the Union*, 4 vols. (New York: Charles Scribner's Sons, 1959–71), 3:113, 115; Kenneth P. Williams, *Lincoln Finds a General*, 5 vols. (New York: Macmillan, 1949–59), 2:730.

5. Michael C. C. Adams, *Our Masters the Rebels: A Speculation on Union Military Failure in the East, 1861–1865* (Cambridge, Mass.: Harvard University Press, 1978), 147.

6. Edwin B. Coddington, *The Gettysburg Campaign: A Study in Command* (New York: Charles Scribner's Sons, 1968), 532, 537, 805–6 n. 204, 810 n. 20.

7. Ibid., 537–38.

8. George G. Meade, ed., *The Life and Letters of George Gordon Meade*, 2 vols. (New York: Charles Scribner's Sons, 1913), 2:113–14; William H. Powell, *The Fifth Army Corps (Army of the Potomac): A Record of Operations During the Civil War in the United States of America, 1861–1865* (1896; reprint, Dayton, Ohio.: Morningside, 1984), 562–63; Coddington, *Gettysburg Campaign*, 540–41; Kenneth P. Williams, *Lincoln Finds a General*, 2:731–32; Daniel Butterfield in U.S. Congress, *Report of the Joint Committee on the Conduct of the War at the Second Session, Thirty-Eighth Congress*, 2 vols. (Washington, D.C.: GPO, 1865–66), 1:426 (hereafter cited as *JCCW*).

9. Coddington, *Gettysburg Campaign*, 542, 548.

10. U.S. War Department, *The War of the Rebellion: A Compilation of the Official Records of the Union and Confederate Armies*, 127 vols., index, and atlas (Washington, D.C.: GPO, 1880–1901), 27(3):516 (hereafter cited as *OR*; all references are to series 1); David B. Birney in *JCCW*, 1:367–69; Butterfield in *JCCW*, 1:426–27; George G. Meade in *JCCW*, 1:350–51; Harry W. Pfanz, "The Gettysburg Campaign after Pickett's Charge," *Gettysburg Magazine* 1 (July 1989): 120; Coddington, *Gettysburg Campaign*, 544.

11. *OR* 27(3):517.

12. Meade, *Life and Letters*, 2:119; Schildt, *Roads from Gettysburg*, 50–51.

13. *OR* 27(3):532–33; Coddington, *Gettysburg Campaign*, 545; *OR* 27(1):79.

14. Herman Haupt, *Reminiscences of Herman Haupt* (Milwaukee: Wright and Joys, 1901), 223–24.

15. Coddington, *Gettysburg Campaign*, 548; George T. Stevens, *Three Years in the Sixth Corps* (1866; reprint, Alexandria, Va.: Time-Life Books, 1984), 255; Meade, *Life and Letters*, 2:124; *OR* 27(1):669–70, (3):537.

16. *OR* 27(3):554–55, 561; Schildt, *Roads from Gettysburg*, 66.

17. Meade, *Life and Letters*, 2:130–31; Coddington, *Gettysburg Campaign*, 552–54.

18. *OR* 27(3):554; Frank Sawyer of the 8th Ohio quoted in Schildt, *Roads from Gettysburg*, 68–69.

19. Robert L. Stewart of the 140th Pennsylvania quoted in Schildt, *Roads from Gettysburg*, 69.

20. "An officer in the field" quoted in De Peyster, *Gettysburg and After*, 104.

21. John B. Kay, Co. D, 6th Michigan Cavalry to his parents, July 9, 1863, typescript in the collections of Gettysburg National Military Park Library, Gettysburg, Pa.; Butterfield in *JCCW*, 1:431.

22. Charles W. Wainwright, *A Diary of Battle: The Personal Journals of Colonel Charles S. Wainwright, 1861–1865*, ed. Allan Nevins (New York: Harcourt, Brace & World, 1962), 256; Oliver Norton quoted in Schildt, *Roads from Gettysburg*, 148; Rufus R. Dawes, *Service with the Sixth Wisconsin Volunteers* (1890; reprint, Dayton, Ohio: Morningside, 1984), 185; C. V. Tevis and D. R. Marquis, *The History of the Fighting Fourteenth* (New York: Brooklyn Eagle Press, 1911), 105.

23. Robert Goldthwaite Carter, *Four Brothers in Blue* (1913; reprint, Austin: University of Texas Press, 1978), 329; Schildt, *Roads from Gettysburg*, 70, 88; Henry Hunt to Eunice, July 28, 1863, typescript in U.S. Army Military History Institute Collection, Carlisle Barracks, Pa. (hereafter cited as USAMHI).

24. Davis, "Gettysburg to Williamsport," 452–53; Andrew A. Humphreys, *From Gettysburg to the Rapidan* (1883; reprint, Baltimore: Butternut and Blue, n.d.), 1.

25. Freeman Cleaves, *Meade of Gettysburg* (Norman: University of Oklahoma Press, 1960), 173; Coddington, *Gettysburg Campaign*, 558–59. William Hays had been a brigade commander in the Second Corps at Chancellorsville, where he was captured on May 3. He was exchanged in mid-May.

26. Schildt, *Roads from Gettysburg*, 84, 88–89; *OR* 27(1):761. On July 7 the First Corps marched from Emmitsburg to Hamburg; the Second Corps from Two Taverns to Taneytown; the Third Corps from Gettysburg to Mechanics-town (Thurmont); the Fifth Corps from Moritz's Cross Roads to Utica; the Sixth Corps from Emmitsburg to near Hamburg; the Eleventh Corps from Emmits-burg to Middletown; and the Twelfth Corps from Littlestown to Walkersville. See *OR* 27(1):145–47, for the army's complete itinerary during the pursuit.

27. Coddington, *Gettysburg Campaign*, 555; *OR* 27(1):82–83.

28. Coddington, *Gettysburg Campaign*, 566, 818 n. 140.

29. *OR* 27(1):85, (3):605–6.

30. Coddington, *Gettysburg Campaign*, 556; *OR* 27(3):601; Schildt, *Roads from Gettysburg*, 98.

31. Schildt, *Roads from Gettysburg*, 98; Carter, *Four Brothers*, 330.

32. *OR* 27(1):88; Schildt, *Roads from Gettysburg*, 97.

33. *OR* 27(3):616–17, (1):89–90.

34. Pfanz, "After Pickett's Charge," 122.

35. Humphreys, *Gettysburg to Rapidan*, 6; *OR* 27(1):91.

36. Coddington, *Gettysburg Campaign*, 567; Schildt, *Roads from Gettysburg*, 118–19; Gouverneur K. Warren in *JCCW*, 1:381.

37. Isaac R. Pennypacker, *General Meade* (New York: D. Appleton, 1901), 211; Oliver Otis Howard, *Autobiography of Oliver Otis Howard*, 2 vols. (New York: Baker & Taylor, 1908), 1:446; *OR* 27(3):671; Schildt, *Roads from Gettysburg*, 124;

Charles Carleton Coffin, *The Boys of '61 or Four Years of Fighting* (Boston: Estes and Lauriat, 1896), 323. According to Coffin, Meade addressed Seth Williams, his assistant adjutant general.

38. *OR* 27(3):675.

39. *OR* 27(2):361, 448–49.

40. Schildt, *Roads from Gettysburg*, 132–35; *OR* 27(2):303–4, 609, 642, (1):991. Robert E. L. Krick of Richmond National Battlefield Park has made an extensive study of Confederate casualties at Falling Waters and concludes that the Federals captured "roughly 1000 men" (Robert E. L. Krick, undated letter to author ca. April 1992). See also Meade, *Life and Letters*, 2:138.

41. Horatio G. Wright to wife, July 18, 1863, typescript in USAMHI.

42. Lorenzo L. Crounse, "The Escape of Lee's Army," in *The Rebellion Record*, ed. Frank Moore, 12 vols. (New York: G. P. Putnam, 1861–63; D. Van Nostrand, 1864–68), 7:347; *OR* 27(3):687, (1):667.

43. *OR* 27(1):92.

44. Evelyn Page, ed., "Frederick Law Olmstead on the Escape of Lee," *Pennsylvania Magazine of History and Biography* 75 (October 1951): 440–41; *OR* 27(1):93.

45. Abner Doubleday, *Chancellorsville and Gettysburg* (New York: Charles Scribner's Sons, 1882), 207; Carl Schurz, *The Autobiography of Carl Schurz*, abridged in one volume by Wayne Andrews (New York: Charles Scribner's Sons, 1961), 283; Alexander quoted in Doubleday, *Chancellorsville and Gettysburg*, 206.

46. Warren in *JCCW*, 1:387; Winfield S. Hancock in *JCCW*, 1:408–9; James S. Wadsworth in *JCCW*, 1:414–15; Alfred Pleasonton in *JCCW*, 1:360; Albion P. Howe in *JCCW*, 1:314–15; Schurz, *Autobiography*, 281–82; De Peyster, *Gettysburg and After*, 117.

47. Pleasonton in *JCCW*, 1:360; Lt. Col. R. M. Blatchford, "The Third Day of Gettysburg and Retreat of the Confederate Army Across the Potomac at Williamsport, Virginia," Army War College Session 1911–12, p. 35, in USAMHI; Wadsworth in *JCCW*, 1:415.

48. Warren in *JCCW*, 1:379; *OR* 27(3):516; Kenneth P. Williams, *Lincoln Finds a General*, 2:731–34; Butterfield in *JCCW*, 1:434.

49. *OR* 27(1):117, 134. Although Freeman Cleaves in *Meade of Gettysburg*, 229–30, identifies HISTORICUS as John B. Bachelder, historians remain uncertain of HISTORICUS's real identity. See Richard A. Sauers, *A Caspian Sea of Ink: The Meade-Sickles Controversy* (Baltimore: Butternut and Blue, 1989), 50.

50. De Peyster, *Gettysburg and After*, 92; Swinton, *Army of the Potomac*, 368.

51. Coddington, *Gettysburg Campaign*, 564–65; Kenneth P. Williams, *Lincoln Finds a General*, 2:746–47.

52. Doubleday in *JCCW*, 1:312; Pleasonton in *JCCW*, 1:361; Hancock in

*JCCW*, 1:412; De Peyster, *Gettysburg and After*, 100–101; Stevens, *Sixth Corps*, 265.

53. Howe in *JCCW*, 1:316; Birney in *JCCW*, 1:369; Swinton, *Army of the Potomac*, 370–72; De Peyster, *Gettysburg and After*, 100–101.

54. Carter, *Four Brothers*, 330; Crounse, "Escape of Lee's Army," 347; Stevens, *Sixth Corps*, 264.

55. "A remarkably intelligent soldier of the Sixth corps" quoted in De Peyster, *Gettysburg and After*, 96; Nevins, *War for the Union*, 3:114; Pleasonton in *JCCW*, 1:361; Stevens, *Sixth Corps*, 264.

56. French quoted by Pleasonton in *JCCW*, 1:361; Warren quoted in De Peyster, *Gettysburg and After*, 150.

57. *OR* 27(1):134; De Peyster, *Gettysburg and After*, 131.

58. Carter, *Four Brothers*, 335; Noah Brooks, *Washington in Lincoln's Time* (New York: Century, 1895), 94.

59. David Hunter Strother, *A Virginia Yankee in the Civil War: The Diaries of David Hunter Strother*, ed. Cecil D. Eby, Jr. (Chapel Hill: University of North Carolina Press, 1961), 192–93; Brooks, *Washington in Lincoln's Time*, 95; Meade's son quoted in Cleaves, *Meade of Gettysburg*, 184; Welles, *Diary*, 1:368, 371.

60. Welles, *Diary*, 1:370.

61. Coddington, *Gettysburg Campaign*, 546.

62. *OR* 27(3):519. Coddington, *Gettysburg Campaign*, 547, defends Meade's phrasing as "a good rhetorical device."

63. Welles, *Diary*, 1:363; Haupt, *Reminiscences*, 221, 227–28.

64. *New York Tribune* quoted in Richard Elliott Winslow III, *General John Sedgwick: The Story of a Union Corps Commander* (Novato, Calif.: Presidio Press, 1982), 108; J. Cutler Andrews, *The North Reports the Civil War* (Pittsburgh: University of Pittsburgh Press, 1955), 431.

65. As head of the Department of West Virginia, Kelley led some 6,000 troops toward Lee. Couch commanded the Department of the Susquehanna and on June 28 received orders from Halleck to cooperate with Meade under Meade's direction. See *OR* 27(3):385. Smith served under Couch in command of all the troops on the southern side of the Susquehanna in the vicinity of Harrisburg. See *OR* 27(3):330.

66. John Hay diary quoted in Coddington, *Gettysburg Campaign*, 572.

67. Abraham Lincoln, *The Collected Works of Abraham Lincoln*, ed. Roy P. Basler, 8 vols. and index (New Brunswick, N.J.: Rutgers University Press, 1953–55), 6:327–28.

68. *OR* 27(3):567; Edward Porter Alexander, *Fighting for the Confederacy: The*

*Personal Recollections of General Edward Porter Alexander*, ed. Gary W. Gallagher (Chapel Hill: University of North Carolina Press, 1989), 270–71.

69. T. Harry Williams, *Lincoln and His Generals* (1952; reprint, New York: Dorset Press, 1989), 265; Bruce Catton, *Bruce Catton's Civil War*, 3 vols. (New York: Fairfax Press, 1984), 2:416. This material originally appeared in *Glory Road* (Garden City, N.Y.: Doubleday, 1952), the second volume in Catton's trilogy on the Army of the Potomac. Lincoln quoted in Schildt, *Roads from Gettysburg*, 85.

70. T. Harry Williams, *Lincoln and His Generals*, 266–67.

71. *OR* 27(3):515, 535, (1):79.

72. *OR* 27(1):80, (3):578.

73. *OR* 27(1):84, 86; Meade, *Life and Letters*, 2:132–33.

74. Coddington, *Gettysburg Campaign*, 547.

75. Hancock quoted in Samuel P. Bates, *The Battle of Gettysburg* (1875; reprint, Gaithersburg, Md.: Ron R. Van Sickle, 1987), 175; Meade in *JCCW*, 1:333.

76. Maj. John W. Daniel quoted in Pennypacker, *General Meade*, 204; Longstreet quoted in Nevins, *War for the Union*, 3:112.

77. Stevens, *Sixth Corps*, 253; Coddington, *Gettysburg Campaign*, 533, 806 n. 211. Four Sixth Corps brigades supported the First or Second Corps and another served on Culp's Hill.

78. Henry J. Hunt in *JCCW*, 1:454; John Sedgwick in *JCCW*, 1:460; Coddington, *Gettysburg Campaign*, 532–33; *OR* 27(1):75.

79. Alexander, *Fighting for the Confederacy*, 267; June Kimble, "Tennesseeans at Gettysburg," *Confederate Veteran* 18 (October 1910): 461.

80. Regis De Trobriand, *Four Years with the Army of the Potomac* (1889; reprint, Gaithersburg, Md.: Ron R. Van Sickle, 1988), 515; Wainwright, *Diary of Battle*, 253; Meade quoted in Schildt, *Roads from Gettysburg*, 53.

81. *OR* 27(1):61, 78; Pennypacker, *General Meade*, 204–5, cites Warren's testimony that the quality of Meade's new corps commanders—John Newton, William Hays, David Birney, and George Sykes—limited the army's ability to take the offensive on July 4. For a summary of the reasons Meade did not attack on July 3 or 4, see Cleaves, *Meade of Gettysburg*, 174, Coddington, *Gettysburg Campaign*, 539, and Pfanz, "After Pickett's Charge," 120.

82. *OR* 27(3):515, (1):80; Bache, *Life of Meade*, 358; Pfanz, "After Pickett's Charge," 120–21; Coddington, *Gettysburg Campaign*, 556.

83. *OR* 27(3):555; Meade in *JCCW*, 1:334.

84. Humphreys, *Gettysburg to Rapidan*, 7–8. Coddington, *Gettysburg Campaign*, 551–52, and Cleaves, *Meade of Gettysburg*, 175, are critical of Sedgwick's timidity in confronting the Confederates at Fairfield Pass.

85. *OR* 27(3):564; Meade quoted in Cleaves, *Meade of Gettysburg*, 179.

86. Douglas Southall Freeman, *R. E. Lee: A Biography*, 4 vols. (New York: Charles Scribner's Sons, 1934–35), 3:135–36; *OR* 27(3):588; Alexander, *Fighting for the Confederacy*, 269–70.

87. Coddington, *Gettysburg Campaign*, 565–66; *OR* 27(2): 361, 448, 705.

88. Samuel W. Crawford in *JCCW*, 1:473; Pennypacker, *General Meade*, 202–3, 213; Humphreys, *Gettysburg to Rapidan*, 6; Wainwright, *Diary of Battle*, 261–62.

89. *OR* 27(2):299, 301; Gilmor quoted in Schildt, *Roads from Gettysburg*, 41; Walter Taylor quoted in Freeman, *R. E. Lee*, 3:138; Bradley Johnson quoted in Schildt, *Roads from Gettysburg*, 115. See also Coddington, *Gettysburg Campaign*, 536.

90. *OR* 27(2):300; Warren in *JCCW*, 1:380; Sedgwick in *JCCW*, 1:462–63; Meade in *JCCW*, 1:337. See also Schildt, *Roads from Gettysburg*, 80–81.

91. Coddington, *Gettysburg Campaign*, 560–63, 572; *OR* 27(3):611; Stevens, *Sixth Corps*, 258, 261; Meade in *JCCW*, 1:338.

92. Wadsworth in *JCCW*, 1:415; Horatio Wright to his wife, July 18, 1863, typescript in USAMHI; John Sedgwick, *Correspondence of John Sedgwick*, 2 vols. (New York: De Vinne Press, 1902–3), 2:134–35; Page, "Olmstead on Escape of Lee," 438. Coddington, *Gettysburg Campaign*, 569, estimates that the Army of the Potomac and the Army of Northern Virginia numbered 80,000 and 50,000, respectively, on July 10. In *Regimental Strengths and Losses at Gettysburg* (Hightstown, N.J.: Longstreet House, 1986), John W. Busey and David G. Martin place Meade's postbattle strength at roughly 71,000 men and Lee's at just less than 48,000.

93. Meade in *JCCW*, 1:336; *OR* 27(1):106.

94. Humphreys, *Gettysburg to Rapidan*, 7.

95. Coddington, *Gettysburg Campaign*, 568; *OR* 27(1):700, 109; Kimble, "Tennesseeans at Gettysburg," 461. Although recorded long after the war, Kimble's views mirrored those of many Confederates who penned their observations while the Army of Northern Virginia remained in its defensive position at Williamsport. See the first essay in this book for a sampling of comments from the second week of July 1863.

96. Cleaves, *Meade of Gettysburg*, 181; Winslow, *Sedgwick*, 111; Davis, "Gettysburg to Williamsport," 463.

97. *New York Evening Post*, "General Meade and the Escape of Lee," August 11, 1863; Glenn Tucker, *High Tide at Gettysburg: The Campaign in Pennsylvania* (Indianapolis: Bobbs-Merrill, 1958), 387.

98. *OR* 27(1):92.

99. *OR* 27(3):675; Coddington, *Gettysburg Campaign*, 570; John G. Nicolay

and John Hay, *Abraham Lincoln: A History*, 10 vols. (New York: Century, 1890), 7:277.

100. *OR* 27(3):683, 686, (2):323, 310.

101. Schildt, *Roads from Gettysburg*, 139; De Peyster, "After Gettysburg," 775.

102. *OR* 27(3):695; Meade, *Life and Letters*, 2:134; *OR* 27(1):193.

103. J. G. Randall, *Lincoln the President*, 4 vols. (New York: Dodd, Mead, 1945–55), 2:289; T. Harry Williams, *Lincoln and the Radicals* (Madison: University of Wisconsin Press, 1941), 303; Sauers, *Caspian Sea of Ink*, 43, 45–46.

104. Meade quoted in Schildt, *Roads from Gettysburg*, 92; Albert H. Walker, "General Meade at Gettysburg. Did Not Pursue Lee's Army Because of Mental Exhaustion," *New York Times*, July 4, 1913. See also *OR* 27(3):581.

105. Meade in *JCCW*, 1:350–51; De Trobriand, *Four Years*, 518–19.

106. Coddington explores this possible course of action in *Gettysburg Campaign*, 539–40.

107. Andrew A. Humphreys in *JCCW*, 1:398; Alexander, *Fighting for the Confederacy*, 271; De Trobriand, *Four Years*, 520; Henry Hunt to Eunice, July 28, 1863, typescript in USAMHI.

108. For brief summaries of the fighting at Falling Waters and Kilpatrick's "faulty" generalship, see Coddington, *Gettysburg Campaign*, 570–72, and Stephen Z. Starr, *The Union Cavalry in the Civil War*, 3 vols. (Baton Rouge: Louisiana State University Press, 1979–85), 1:458–60.

109. Sedgwick in *JCCW*, 1:463; *OR* 27(1):118; Meade in *JCCW*, 1:337; Haupt, *Reminiscences*, 224–29; Hunt in *JCCW*, 1:456.

110. *OR* 27(3):691; Cleaves, *Meade of Gettysburg*, 176.

# BIBLIOGRAPHIC ESSAY

The notes direct readers to sources on which the authors based their essays. For anyone seeking an overview of the third day at Gettysburg and the other subjects addressed in this volume, the following titles should serve as a satisfactory starting point. Richard A. Sauers, Jr., comp., canvassed the literature in *The Gettysburg Campaign, June 3–August 1, 1863: A Comprehensive, Selectively Annotated Bibliography* (Westport, Conn.: Greenwood Press, 1982). Readers should be aware that in the last dozen years many new titles have joined the nearly 2,000 sources Sauers listed. A mass of basic documents relating to July 3, 1863, at Gettysburg and to movements of the armies following the battle are collected in U.S. War Department, *The War of the Rebellion: A Compilation of the Official Records of the Union and Confederate Armies*, 127 vols., index, and atlas (Washington, D.C.: GPO, 1880–1901). Series 1, vol. 27, pts. 1–3 of the *Official Records* (more popularly known as the *OR*) include almost 3,500 pages of correspondence, orders, and official reports pertinent to Gettysburg. Valuable postwar testimony abounds in the *Papers of the Military Historical Society of Massachusetts*, 14 vols. (1895–1918; reprinted in 15 vols. with a general index, Wilmington, N.C.: Broadfoot, 1989–90); *The Gettysburg Papers*, ed. Ken Bandy and Florence Freeland, 2 vols. (Dayton, Ohio: Morningside, 1978), which reprints important items from the preceding title as well as from the volumes published by the state commanderies of the Military Order of the Loyal Legion of the United States in the late nineteenth and early twentieth centuries; and *Gettysburg Sources*, ed. James L. McLean, Jr., and Judy W. McLean, 3 vols. (Baltimore, Md.: Butternut and Blue, 1986–90). *Gettysburg: Historical Articles of Lasting Interest* (Dayton, Ohio, 1989– ), a biannual scholarly magazine, contains a number of articles on the battle's third day and aftermath.

There are no monographs devoted to the third day as a whole, but several studies address specific elements of the fighting. George R. Stewart's *Pickett's Charge: A Microhistory of the Final Attack at Gettysburg, July 3, 1863* (Cambridge, Mass.: Houghton Mifflin, 1959) remains the best treatment of Longstreet's final assault, while *Nothing but Glory: Pickett's Division at Gettysburg*, by Kathleen R. Georg and John W. Busey (Hightstown, N.J.: Longstreet House, 1987), provides great detail on the most famous command in the attack. Harry Pfanz's *Gettysburg:*

*Cemetery Hill and Culp's Hill* (Chapel Hill: University of North Carolina Press, 1993), a worthy companion to the author's superb earlier discussion of fighting on the southern end of the field on July 2, satisfies a long-standing need for a serious work on the third day's action at Culp's Hill. Among books on the entire battle, Edwin B. Coddington's *The Gettysburg Campaign: A Study in Command* (New York: Charles Scribner's Sons, 1968) presents a good introduction to the third day; Clifford Dowdey's *Death of a Nation: The Story of Lee and His Men at Gettysburg* (New York: Alfred A. Knopf, 1958) follows an interpretive trail blazed by Lost Cause writers; and Glenn Tucker's *High Tide at Gettysburg: The Campaign in Pennsylvania* (Indianapolis: Bobbs-Merrill, 1958) sometimes sacrifices accuracy for the sake of literary drama.

Michael Shaara's novel *The Killer Angels* (New York: David McKay, 1974), among the most popular books ever written on the battle, explores the roles of R. E. Lee, James Longstreet, and Lewis Armistead on July 3 in fascinating and sometimes controversial portraits. *Gettysburg: A Journey in Time* (New York: Charles Scribner's Sons, 1975), by William A. Frassanito, permits students to compare modern photographs of the field with those taken in the nineteenth century, and Jack McLaughlin's *Gettysburg: The Long Encampment* (New York: Appleton-Century, 1963) allocates several dozen pages and numerous photographs to the history of the battlefield after 1863.

A handful of personal accounts, diaries, and printed letters stands out in the voluminous literature by participants. On the Confederate side, James Longstreet defends his conduct at Gettysburg in *From Manassas to Appomattox: Memoirs of the Civil War in America* (Philadelphia: J. B. Lippincott, 1896); *The Wartime Papers of R. E. Lee* (Boston: Little, Brown, 1961), ed. Clifford Dowdey and Louis H. Manarin, conveniently gathers Lee's crucial letters from June and July 1863; and Edward Porter Alexander's *Fighting for the Confederacy: The Personal Recollections of General Edward Porter Alexander*, ed. Gary W. Gallagher (Chapel Hill: University of North Carolina Press, 1989), and *Military Memoirs of a Confederate: A Critical Narrative* (New York: Charles Scribner's Sons, 1907) set an analytical standard unmatched by any other soldier in either army. Necessary Union titles include George Meade [the general's son], *Life and Letters of George Gordon Meade*, 2 vols. (New York: Charles Scribner's Sons, 1913), a superior source on the Federal commander, and Frank Haskell's classic *The Battle of Gettysburg* (Madison: Wisconsin History Commission, 1908). The third volume of Robert Underwood Johnson and Clarence Clough Buel, eds., *Battles and Leaders of the Civil War*, 4 vols. (New York: Century, 1887), offers articles on the third day and the Confederate retreat by Union artillery chief Henry J. Hunt, Confederate cavalryman John D. Imboden, and other key officers.

A pair of superb accounts by foreign observers are FitzGerald Ross, *Cities and Camps of the Confederate States*, ed. Richard Barksdale Harwell (1865; reprint, Urbana: University of Illinois Press, 1958), and A. J. L. Fremantle, *Three Months in the Southern States: April–June, 1863* (1864; reprint, Lincoln: University of Nebraska Press, 1991). Officers in the Austrian and British armies, respectively, Ross and Fremantle accompanied Longstreet's headquarters as keen observers whose descriptive and analytical passages possess enduring value for historians.

The debates among Virginians and other southerners regarding Pickett's Charge may be traced in the pages of the *Southern Historical Society Papers*, ed. J. William Jones and others, 52 vols. (1877–1959; reprint, with 3-vol. index, Wilmington, N.C.: Broadfoot, 1990–92) (commonly known as the *SHSP*); *Histories of the Several Regiments and Battalions from North Carolina in the Great War 1861–'65*, ed. Walter Clark, 5 vols. (1901; reprint, Wilmington, N.C.: Broadfoot, 1991–92); *The Southern Bivouac* (1882–87; reprint, 5 vols., Wilmington, N.C.: Broadfoot, 1992–93); and *Confederate Veteran*, 40 vols. (1894–1932; reprint, with 3-vol. index, Wilmington, N.C.: Broadfoot, 1990). The *SHSP* presents the Virginian case, while *North Carolina Regiments*, the *Bivouac*, and the *Veteran* give ample airing to the views of non-Virginians. Indispensable on the role of Gettysburg in the development of Lost Cause explanations for Confederate defeat are Thomas L. Connelly's strident *The Marble Man: Robert E. Lee and His Image in American Society* (New York: Alfred A. Knopf, 1977); Connelly and Barbara L. Bellows's *God and General Longstreet: The Lost Cause and the Southern Mind* (Baton Rouge: Louisiana State University Press, 1982); and Gaines M. Foster's *Ghosts of the Confederacy: Defeat, the Lost Cause, and the Emergence of the New South* (New York: Oxford University Press, 1987).

Among essential biographical studies are Douglas Southall Freeman's *R. E. Lee: A Biography*, 4 vols. (New York: Charles Scribner's Sons, 1934–35), which renders harsh judgments about Longstreet on July 3, 1863, and *Lee's Lieutenants: A Study in Command*, 3 vols. (New York: Charles Scribner's Sons, 1942–44), a more even-handed treatment of Lee and Longstreet on the third day. Alan T. Nolan's *Lee Considered: General Robert E. Lee and Civil War History* (Chapel Hill: University of North Carolina Press, 1991) criticizes Lee's decision to press the tactical offensive for a third day at Gettysburg. Freeman Cleaves's generally laudatory *Meade of Gettysburg* (Norman: University of Oklahoma Press, 1960) is the best biography of the Federal chief; William Garrett Piston's *Lee's Tarnished Lieutenant: James Longstreet and His Place in Southern History* (Athens: University of Georgia Press, 1987), which focuses on the postwar years, and Jeffry D. Wert's *General James Longstreet* (New York: Simon and Schuster, 1993), with its wartime emphasis, provide careful and largely favorable assessments of their subject. George E. Pickett has yet to receive the attention of a serious biographer, and the unwary should be warned that all of LaSalle Corbell Pickett's writings—and especially *The Heart of a Soldier as Revealed in the Intimate Letters of Genl. George E. Pickett, C.S.A.* (New York: Seth Moyle, 1913), which purports to print part of the general's wartime correspondence—should be used with great care.

Any listing of books on the third day at Gettysburg must mention three landmark multivolume works. Kenneth P. Williams's *Lincoln Finds a General*, 5 vols. (New York: Macmillan, 1949–59), boasts a number of valuable insights regarding Federal leadership. Bruce Catton's *Glory Road* (Garden City, N.Y.: Doubleday, 1952), the middle installment of his three volumes on the Army of the Potomac, and Shelby Foote's *The Civil War: A Narrative*, 3 vols. (New York: Random House, 1958–74), display the impressive narrative gifts of their talented authors.

# CONTRIBUTORS

**ROBERT L. BEE** is professor of anthropology at the University of Connecticut. He has edited, with interpretive commentary, the Civil War letters of Ben and John Hirst under the title "The Boys from Rockville: Civil War Narratives of Ben and John Hirst, Company D, 14th Connecticut Volunteers."

**GARY W. GALLAGHER** is head of the Department of History at Pennsylvania State University. He has published widely on the Civil War, including *Stephen Dodson Ramseur: Lee's Gallant General* and *Fighting for the Confederacy: The Personal Recollections of General Edward Porter Alexander*, and presently is at work on a biography of Jubal A. Early.

**A. WILSON GREENE**, president of the Association for the Preservation of Civil War Sites, holds degrees in American history from Florida State University and Louisiana State University. He is the author of *Whatever You Resolve to Be: Essays on Stonewall Jackson* and *J. Horace Lacy: The Most Dangerous Rebel of the County*, and co-

author of *National Geographic Guide to the Civil War National Battlefield Parks*.

**ROBERT K. KRICK** grew up in California but has lived and worked on the Virginia battlefields for more than twenty years. He has written dozens of articles and ten books, the most recent being *Stonewall Jackson at Cedar Mountain* and *Stonewall Jackson at Cross Keys and Port Republic*.

**WILLIAM GARRETT PISTON** is a member of the Department of History at Southwest Missouri State University. The author or editor of a number of publications on the Civil War, including *Lee's Tarnished Lieutenant: James Longstreet and His Place in Southern History*, he is working on a study of the campaign of Wilson's Creek.

**CAROL REARDON** is the military historian at Pennsylvania State University and author of *Soldiers & Scholars: The U.S. Army and the Uses of Military History, 1865–1920*. Among her current projects is a book-length examination of the image of Pickett's Charge in American history.

# INDEX

Adams, Michael C. C., 163
Aiken, David Wyatt, 11
Alabama units: 4th Infantry, 81; 5th
  Infantry Battalion, 80; 5th Infantry,
  3; 13th Infantry, 80
Albertson, Jonathan, 62–64
Alexander, Edward Porter, 12–13,
  40–44, 47, 174, 181, 184, 192
Alexander, Peter W., 63
Alexander, William, 5
Anderson, J. R., 99
Anderson, Richard H., 98, 183
Andrews, George, 103
Antietam. *See* Sharpsburg, Md.
Antietam Creek, 171
Appomattox, Va., 56, 65, 73, 78–79,
  178
Archer, James J., 57, 73, 79
Arizona unit: 3rd Cavalry, 112
Arkansas River: Garnett posted on,
  105
Armistead, Cecilia Lee Love, 104–5
Armistead, Elizabeth Stanley, 94
Armistead, George, 94, 123
Armistead, Lewis Addison, viii–ix, 57,
  61–62, 69, 79–81, 84, 93, 132;
  premilitary life, 94–95; at West
  Point, 97–100; in Old Army, 101–
  13; CSA career of, 115–19; death
  of, 120–23
Armistead, Walker Keith (Lewis
  Armistead's father), 94–95
Armistead, Walker Keith (Lewis
  Armistead's son), 104
Army of Northern Virginia, ix, 2, 48,
  57–58, 63, 66, 118, 163, 165, 167,

173–74, 178, 183, 186, 188, 190,
  192, 194; morale of, 3–22, 183–
  84, 187
Army of the Potomac, ix, 5, 10, 16–
  20, 31, 35, 143, 154, 161–63, 165,
  168–69, 171, 175, 179, 182–84,
  187–88, 192
Army of the Valley, 48
Ashe, Samuel A., 77
Atkinson, Henry, 103
Aylett, William R., 69

Bache, Richard M., 162
Bachelder, John, 81
Baird, E. R., 75
Baker, W. J., 65
Bakersville, Md., 171
Balaclava: British assault at compared
  to Pickett's Charge, 61
Baltimore, Md., 5, 59, 82, 123, 142,
  165, 181, 185, 188
Baltimore & Ohio Railroad, 170
Baltimore Pike, 139
Barksdale, William, 40, 93
Barrier, William L., 14
Beauregard, P. G. T., 98
Beaver Creek, 71
Benicia, Calif., 107–8, 111, 113
Benning, Henry L., 10
Bent's Fort, Colo., 105–6
Berkeley, Norborne, 122
Berlin, Md., 190
Bethel, Va., 78–79
Bingham, Henry H., 120–21
Bird, Edgeworth, 10–11, 15
Birney, David B., 177, 190

Blackford, Charles Minor, 10, 15
Blackford, Eugene, 3
Blackford, William M., 25 (n. 12)
Blanton, Leigh, 61
Bliss Farm, 140, 148
Bloody Lane, 143
*Blue & Gray Magazine*, 84
Bomford, J. V., 103
Bond, William R., 72–73, 77
Boonsboro, Md., 170–71
Bragg, Braxton, 1–3, 7, 98
Branch, Lawrence O'Bryan, 93
Brewer, Richard Henry, 112
Bright, Robert Anderson, 75, 81, 122
Brockenbrough, Eleanor, 95
Brockenbrough, J. M., 57, 73
Brooke, George Mercer, 95, 97, 102
Brooke, John Mercer, 95
Brown, Joseph E., 7
Buckner, Simon B., 98, 102
Buell, Don C., 98
Buford, John, 167, 172, 192
Bunker Hill, W.Va., 8, 15
Burnside, Ambrose E., 189
Burpee, Thomas, 133
Butterfield, Daniel, 165, 168

Cady, Albemarle, 103
Calder, William, 59
Calhoun, John C., 6
Camp Bateman, Kans., 105
Camp Fitzgerald, Calif., 112
Camp Lee, Va., 115
Camp Prentiss, Calif., 109
Canadian River: Garnett posted on, 105
Cannae: battle of Gettysburg compared to, 60
Carrollton, Miss., 80
Cashtown, Pa., 164–65, 185, 192
Catoctin Mountains, 170
Catton, Bruce, 181
*Cavalry Journal*, 82
Cedar Creek, 48
Cedar Mountain, Va., 114

Cemetery Hill/Cemetery Ridge, viii, 31–32, 35, 38, 40–47, 67, 69, 76, 80, 84, 106, 120–21, 132, 139, 146, 148, 163, 183
*Century Magazine*, 39, 72
Chamberlain, Dr., 123
Chambersburg, Pa., 122
Chancellor House, 145
Chancellorsville, Va., 112, 119,143, 145
Chapultepec, Mexico, 102–3
Charleston, S.C., 1, 6, 15, 63
Charleston *Daily Courier*, 5
Charleston *Mercury*, 5, 19–20
Cherokee Indians, 103
Chester, Pa., 133, 149
Cheyenne Indians, 105
Chickamauga, Ga., 78–79
Churubusco, Mexico, 102
Cimarron River: Garnett posted on, 105
Clark, Walter, 77, 79
Clarke, Newman, 103
Clemson, Floride, 6
Cobb, Thomas R. R., 93, 113–14
Cochise, 113
Cocke, William F., 67
Cocke, William Henry, 58
Coddington, Edwin B., 32, 38, 46, 176, 182, 188, 190
Coghill, J. F., 24 (n. 6)
Colorado River, 94, 108–11
*Confederate Veteran*, 79–80
Connecticut unit: 14th Infantry, ix, 132–56
Connelly, Thomas L., 47
Conococheague Creek, 186
Contreras, Mexico, 102
Cooke, John Esten, 70
Cooke, Philip St. George, 105
Cooper, Samuel, 33, 104
*Cosmopolitan*, 82
Couch, Darius N., 179–80, 182
Crazy Horse, 104
Crocker, James, 81

Garnett, Robert Selden, 95–96, 98, 101

Garnett, William (Richard Garnett's father), 95, 97

Garnett, William (Richard Garnett's son), 104

Garnett, William Henry (Richard Garnett's brother), 95

Geiger, George H., 67

Georgia units: Cobb's Legion, 113; 3rd Infantry, 116; 12th Infantry, 14; 21st Infantry, 16; 24th Infantry, 15; 26th Infantry, 16

Gerrish, Theodore, 161

Gibbon, John, 141, 151

Gilmor, Harry, 187

Goodell, William, 136–37

Gorgas, Josiah, 2, 16, 98

Graham, Joseph, 23 (n. 6)

Grammer, John, 119

Grant, Ulysses S., 2–3, 6, 8, 99, 104, 191

Grattan Massacre, 104

Greencastle, Pa., 164

Greene, John, 103

Greenwood, Pa., 164

Gregg, Maxcy, 93

Hagerstown, Md., 13–15, 17, 164, 167, 170–71, 186, 189

Halleck, Henry W., 165, 170–71, 173–76, 179, 181–82, 185–86, 189

Hamlin, Hannibal, 172, 178

Hampton, Wade, 3

Hancock, Almira, 112

Hancock, Winfield Scott, 84, 99, 102–3, 106, 112, 120–21, 132, 169, 174–76, 183

Hancock, Md., 189

Hanover, Pa., 142

Harney, William S., 106

Harpers Ferry, W.Va., 188, 190, 193

Harrisburg, Pa., 2

Harrison, Walter, 66

Haupt, Herman, 165, 167, 179, 181, 193

Hays, Alexander, 98–99, 142, 151, 154

Hays, Harry T., 13

Hays, William, 169, 172, 188

Hazlewood, Martin, 75

Hendrick, Henry C., 121

Heth, Henry, 18–19, 35, 38, 57, 59, 71, 73, 83, 103, 106, 173

Hill, A. P., 11, 32, 34, 57, 60–61, 72, 83, 164, 167, 171, 175, 190, 192

Hill, D. H., 117

Hilton, Joseph, 16

Hirst, Benjamin, ix, 132, 134–35, 143–56; prewar life, 133; letters by, 136–42

Hirst, Bill, 133

Hirst, Joe, 133, 135, 144

Hirst, John, 133, 135–38, 144, 149–50, 153, 155

Hirst, Sarah Quinn, 133–36, 138, 143–46, 149, 151, 153–54

Hodges, James Gregory, 82

Hoffman, William, 103

Holden, William Woods, 4

Hollywood Cemetery (Richmond), 67, 123

Holmes, Emma, 5–6

Hood, John Bell, 31, 34–36, 39, 45–46, 50–51, 115, 183

Hooker, Joseph, 17, 98, 178, 191

Hotchkiss, Jedediah, 58

Howard, Oliver O., 164–65, 172, 188, 190

Howe, Albion P., 174, 176, 190

Huger, Benjamin, 115, 117

Humphreys, Andrew A., 169, 172, 187–88, 192

Humphreys, Benjamin G., 40

Hunt, Henry J., 123, 161, 169, 184, 192–93

Hyde, Elbert, 135

Imboden, John D., 164, 167
Ingalls, Rufus, 173

Jackson, Andrew, 97
Jackson, Thomas J. "Stonewall," 44, 48, 82, 95, 114
Jackson, Miss., 7
Jenkins, Micah, 93
Johnson, Edward, 98
Johnston, Albert Sidney, 107, 112–13
Johnston, Joseph E., 106
Joint Committee on the Conduct of the War, 183, 187, 190–91, 193
Jones, John B., 2
Jones, John M., 93, 98
Jones, John T., 64
Julian, John, 136–37

Kean, Robert G. H., 2–3
Kelley, Benjamin F., 179, 187
Kelly, William Aiken, 9–10
Kemper, James L., 57, 61–62, 67, 71
Kernstown, Va., 114
Kershaw, Joseph B., 3
Key, Francis Scott, 94
Kilpatrick, Judson, 164, 167, 172, 192
Kimble, June, 189
Kingsbury, T. B., 71
Kirkpatrick, James J., 58–59

Lacy House, 144
Landers, Eli Pinson, 8
*Land We Love, The*, 70
Lane, James, 57, 73, 83
Lang, David, 57, 63
Langhorne, James Henry, 125 (n. 5)
Laramie River: Armistead posted on, 106
Lawton, Alexander R., 98
Lecompton, Kans., 105–6
Lee, Fitzhugh, 67, 73
Lee, Francis, 103
Lee, Henry "Light-Horse Harry," 70
Lee, Mary, 17–19

Lee, Richard Henry, 104
Lee, Robert E., viii–ix, 1–2, 4–6, 11–13, 15–16, 22, 31, 57–58, 63, 67–68, 72, 76, 83, 118, 154; criticized, 3, 21; praised, 7–9, 14, 65–66, 122, 184; analysis of own campaign, 16–22; versus Longstreet, 31–51; retreat from Gettysburg, 161–94
Lee, Stephen Dill, 81
Liberty, Md., 138
Lincoln, Abraham, ix, 22 (n. 1), 76, 161, 170, 173, 178–82, 187
Linderman, Gerald, 145, 148–49, 151
Little Round Top. *See* Round Tops
Littlestown, Pa., 167
Long, Armistead L., 47, 50–51, 67
Longstreet, James, viii–ix, 9, 31, 56–57, 61, 63, 67–68, 72, 75–76, 83–84, 98, 102, 117, 119, 152–54, 164, 167, 171–72, 179, 183, 186; versus Lee, 31–51; criticized, 67
Looking Woman, 104
Loomis, Gustavus, 103
Los Angeles, Calif., 112–13
"Lost Cause" tradition, viii, 22 (n. 1), 47, 49–50, 56, 67–68
Louisiana units: Washington Artillery, 41–42; 9th Infantry, 8
Luvaas, Jay, 44
Lynchburg *Virginian*, 4–5

McCabe, W. Gordon, 71
McClellan, George, 69, 163, 178, 181
McLaws, Lafayette, 9, 15, 31, 34–36, 39, 44–46, 50–51, 98, 183
McNeil, Alexander, 3
McPherson, James M., 2
Magruder, John B., 117
Mahone, William, 115
Maine unit: 20th Infantry, 161
Mallory, Francis, 112
Malvern Hill, Va., 23 (n. 6), 117, 119

Fluvanna Artillery, 9; Richmond Howitzers, 69; 6th Cavalry, 163–64; 7th Cavalry, 164; 1st Infantry, 61; 4th Infantry, 125 (n. 5); 8th Infantry, 24 (n. 8), 114–15; 9th Infantry, 58, 81, 116; 11th Infantry, 61, 74; 12th Infantry, 14; 14th Infantry, 82, 115, 120; 18th Infantry, 68, 114; 19th Infantry, 67, 114, 122; 28th Infantry, 114; 38th Infantry, 116; 53rd Infantry, 69, 115–16, 119; 55th Infantry, 112; 56th Infantry, 114; 57th Infantry, 115

Wadsworth, James S., 172, 174–75
Wainwright, Charles S., 168, 184, 186
Walla Walla, Wash., 107–8
Walton, James B., 40
Warren, Gouverneur K., 163, 165, 167, 172, 174–75, 177, 187–88
Washington, D.C., 9, 14, 20, 48, 165, 167, 173, 178, 181–82, 185, 187, 189, 192–93
Washington and Lee University, 47, 49
Watkins, Sam, 133
Waynesboro, Pa., 167
Webster, Daniel, 104
Welch, Spencer G., 15
Welles, Gideon, 161, 178–79

Wert, Jeffry, 48
Westminster, Md., 164
Wheatfield, 53 (n. 29), 164
Wheatland, Wyo., 104
Whiting, David, 135–37
Wilcox, Cadmus M., 57, 74–76, 80, 83
Wilderness, the, 120
Williams, Kenneth P., 163, 176
Williams, T. Harry, 181–82
Williamson, Thomas H., 95
Williamsport, Md., 17, 164–65, 167, 170, 172–73, 176–77, 186, 188–89, 192
Wilmington, Del., 142
Wilmington, N.C., 71
Wilson, Henry, 172
Winchester, Va., 60, 95, 187; third battle of, 48
Winterhaven, Calif., 109
Wisconsin unit: 6th Infantry, 168
Wise, Henry A., 97
Wise, John S., 74
Wofford, William T., 8, 16
Wright, Ambrose R., 13–15
Wright, Horatio G., 98, 173, 188

Young, Louis G., 65
Yuma, Ariz., 109, 112

Ziegler's Grove, 80, 163